NATIVE HARVESTS
American Indian Wild Foods and Recipes

E. Barrie Kavasch

Illustrations by the Author

DOVER PUBLICATIONS, INC.
Mineola, New York

Bibliographical Note

This Dover edition, first published in 2005, is an augmented republication of the revised and expanded second edition of the work published by Birdstone Publishers, The Institute for American Indian Studies, Washington, Connecticut, in 1998. The first edition, *Native Harvests: Recipes and Botanicals of the American Indian* by Barrie Kavasch, was published by Random House, New York, in 1979. The author has written a new preface, a new list of acknowledgments, and a few other additions, and has supplied about a dozen new plant illustrations specially for the Dover edition.

Acknowledgments

Grateful acknowledgment is made to the following for permission to reprint previously published material:

Ballantine Books, A Division of Random House, Inc.: Excerpt from *Eating from the Wild* by Dr. Anne Marie Stewart. Copyright © 1975 by Dr. Anne Marie Stewart and Leon Kronoff.

Doubleday and Co., Inc. and McIntosh and Otis, Inc.: Excerpt from *The Art of American Indian Cooking* by Yeffe Kimball and Jean Anderson. Copyright © 1965 by Yeffe Kimball and Jean Anderson. Reprinted by permission of Doubleday and Co., Inc. and McIntosh and Otis, Inc.

National Geographic Society: Excerpt from "Mexico's Window on the Past," *National Geographic Magazine*, October 1968.

Stackpole Books: Excerpt from *Feasting Free on Wild Edibles* by Bradford Angier. Copyright © 1966 by Stackpole Books.

Walker and Company: Excerpt from *A Cooking Legacy* by Virginia T. Elverson and Mary Ann McLanahan. Copyright © 1975 by Virginia Elverson and Mary Ann McLanahan. Used with permission of the publisher, Walker and Company.

Library of Congress Cataloging-in-Publication Data

Kavasch, E. Barrie.
   Native harvests : American Indian wild foods and recipes / E. Barrie Kavasch ; illustrations by the author.
      p. cm.
   Originally published: Native harvests : recipes and botanicals of the American Indian. New York : Random House, 1979.
   Includes index.
   ISBN-13: 978-0-486-44063-7
   ISBN-10: 0-486-44063-X
      1. Indians of North America—Food. 2. Ethnobotany—North America. 3. Indian cookery. 4. Indians of North America—Ethnobotany. I. Title.

E98.F7K37 2005
641.5997—dc22

2004061765

Manufactured in the United States by Courier Corporation
44063X06
www.doverpublications.com

To the American Indians
their history
and
their future

SONGS OF HUEXOTZINGO
(Aztec Poetic Lament)

Will I leave only this:
Like the flowers that wither?
Will nothing last in my name —
Nothing of my fame here on earth?

At least flowers!
At least song!

PERSONAL
ACKNOWLEDGMENTS

This enlarged and expanded edition of NATIVE HARVESTS further amplifies our respect for the fields of American Indian ethnobotany and ethnomycology. New chapters and numerous updates and additions and illustrations serve to weave a larger circle. Closer ties with the sacred and spiritual aspects of the food quest and healing bless this book on many levels.

A number of our native botanicals and fungi are common across North America as well as worldwide. Long before the twentieth century, many organisms (like the birds) were globe-trotters. The primary emphasis of NATIVE HARVESTS is on the wealth of native species, yet it also encompasses numerous introduced species with significant uses by American Indians. A primary aim of my work is to indicate the exchange and sharing between cultures, both Old World and New World. Many different cultures of our American Indian ancestors, along with many different cultures of our European, Asian, and African ancestors, contributed to our contemporary knowledge.

Native People from many tribal backgrounds, and folks of multiethnic ancestry have contributed their diverse wisdom to this book. I am most grateful for valuable time spent with so many noted Elders, storytellers, historians, artists, craftspeople, leaders, healers, herbalists, and medicine people. I am sincerely grateful to my friend Margaret "Peggy" Cooper for years of supportive ideas, inspirations, and sound advice.

My grandparents, aunts and uncles, parents, and all of my diverse ancestors have instilled in me the essential love of nature and respect for all life forms. They also helped me to realize that there is nothing we cannot do if we really want to achieve it. These gifts I have passed on to my own children and grandchildren, and wish for the generations yet to come. Our bright future is in their hands. Gratitude and love to my son Chris and wife Fran, my four wonderful grandchildren Derek, Sarah, Jeffrey, and Brooke, and to daughter Kim, and especially my Mom.

Great praise to the libraries and librarians who have nurtured me and whose support enriched this book. Numerous botanical gardens and environmental centers have supported this work for so long, especially the Institute of Ecosystem Studies in Millbrook, NY and the New York Botanical Garden and Brooklyn Botanical Garden.

Many museums have supported and enriched this work. My gratitude to the American Museum of Natural History, the National Museum of American Indians, and especially The Institute for American Indian Studies in Washington, Connecticut – have my gratitude and respect.

Countless, wonderful people and institutions contributed to this information and work, yet ultimately, I am responsible for any errors or omissions – for which I apologize (in advance). I welcome comments and corrections.

E. Barrie Kavasch, Bridgewater, CT

CONTENTS

"We're deeply involved in the spirits of all forms of life, not just human life." –
Slow Turtle (John Peters),
     Wampanoag Supreme Medicine Man, Massachusetts

Chiefly Feasts

Much has changed since my early work in this field back in the 1960s. I learned a great deal from many fine Native Americans, who graciously shared their wisdom with me. My respect grows as I look for ways to commemorate them through my work. *Native Harvests* continues to support amazing aspects of Native American cuisines through its well-used pages. Yet "wild edibles" no longer has the same luster it once did because, as conservationists, we must be much more sensitive to the environment and also be very careful not to collect from polluted areas. Roadside and railroad track margins, and areas where aerial spraying and soil treatments have occurred, can produce tainted or poisonous plants and mushrooms. You must really know the areas that you collect within, and seek permission to collect in regions beyond your own property. We know that plants and mushrooms take up poisons in their roots and cellular fibers and can be systemically poisoned. Scientists are using many different plants, like sunflowers and cattails, to help clean up toxic lands. Today many wildfoods enthusiasts who can, bring favorite wild plants into protected wild meadows and other "safe areas" for dependable harvests.

Wild edibles continue to inspire and create new areas in the food industries. From Native American "cactus cuisine" to the growing gourmet markets for ranched or farmed buffalo, alligator, antelope, and rabbit, along with jicama, prickly pear cactus, and spirulina, American Indian foodways inspire our lives to be healthier and ever more delicious. As a culinary historian I am fascinated by this rich regional diversity. Native harvest and native ingenuities influence many unique food categories.

> *Native people knew the importance of making prayers and offerings to key plants before any of them could be harvested. Collecting plants in a sacred manner activates their therapeutic qualities to the highest levels. This wisdom applies to everything this book stands for.*

Powwow Foods reflect the easy favorites, American Indian fast foods that are encountered across the country at various powwows and rodeos. Fry bread and Navajo tacos (page 123) are fairly universal, and likely to be found from coast to coast served with soda pop, coffee, or fruit smoothies, teas, and lemonades. Chili-stuffed baked potatoes, fried alligator, grilled bluefish and salmon, quahog fritters (page 109), boiled corn or roasted ears of corn, buffalo burgers and venison burgers, soups and stews, clambakes, and crawfish jambalayas are tasty regional additions that visitors may enjoy. These are easily mass produced for thousands of hungry visitors over long weekends.

Soul Foods are the treasured childhood stuff of memories, elders' gatherings, and family get-togethers; these can include the back-home regional specialties of soffkee (a distinctive corn soup or beverage), grape dumplings, grits (pages 120–121), red bean and corn dumplings, fish fries, and fried potatoes. "Wild green onion" dinners still bring families together at church functions and neighborhood reunions across the south from the Virginias to Oklahoma. Regional specialties might include roast stuffed possum, muskrat stew, baked prairie turnips, wild spinach, roasted beavertail cactus pads (nopalitas), and jicama salads. Soul foods are the regional spicy chilis and homemade specialties found at backwater BBQ shacks, oyster huts, catfish parlors (page 116), chili parlors, and crawdad dens where black-eyed peas (in hoppin' Johns), fried frogs' legs, and biscuits with red-eye gravy fill generous plates.

Festival Foods feed large gatherings of tribal folks for special events like puberty rites, sun dances, chantway ceremonies, and Pueblo feast days. Hospitalities often extend out to invited guests and visitors who also share these gatherings, so huge amounts of foods are prepared to feed everyone, like red and green roasted chili stews, mutton stew, green corn, diverse corn and bean dishes, pumpkin fry breads, strawberry breads (page 127), squash breads, corn breads, and sweet berry desserts, or fry bread with honey. The old "wild foods" dishes are usually reserved for late in the festival to feed the elders and special guests, as many of the wild foods are increasingly harder to find and harvest, and no one wants to see them wasted.

Foods of Indian Socials nurture the periodic "potluck dinners" where families and friends come together to celebrate seasonal events, honor sobriety gatherings, or affirm native traditions, and each family brings its favorite dish. These special gatherings are important times to strengthen tribal, clan, and family bonds, honor those in the armed services and tribal athletes, and to gather around the drum and sing. Fry breads, cornbreads (pages 122–123), tacos, squash breads, fruitbreads, and bannocks (page 122) often accompany favorite corn, bean, and squash soups, meat stews (page 91), baked beans, baked or steamed fish, and barbecued chicken, pork, buffalo, or beef. Various salads and desserts and beverages swell the seasonal tables, satisfying everyone.

Cactus Cuisine personifies the diversity of foods made from cacti, many of which have striking health benefits. We cultivate the large treelike deerhorn cactus, or night-blooming cereus, for its big fragrant white flowers, yet American Indians in the Southwest dug the large wild roots to boil as a starchy vegetable. (See page 61.) The prickly pear or beavertail cactus is a much more widespread bristly, shrublike cactus growing all across North America, and its young pads and ripe red fruits are also delicious. These foods and their anti-inflammatory, mucilaginous juices are often mixed in cornmeal dishes to help clear skin conditions, stabilize blood sugar problems, and treat diabetes. Many health benefits are experienced from drinking the aloe vera juice. These "exotic" foods are found today only in health-food and specialty markets, where discerning shoppers depend upon them.

Nutriceuticals are healing foods and herbal supplements "that have nourishing effects on the body, mind, spirit, and even one's rhythms and balance," as I have written about them in *The Medicine Wheel Garden* book. These can range from energy-enhancing supplements of spirulina, and pumpkin seeds, to steamed nettles (page 48) and hen-of-the-woods mushroom (page 83). Many everyday foods can be spiced up with a modest addition of bee balm (page 132) and other fresh or dried mint leaves, crumbled, dried bayberry leaves, ginger root, or chili peppers. Some of the classic wild teas and seasonings become "kitchen medicinals" when formulated to help improve memory, increase circulation, and detoxify the liver, which can lead to clearer skin.

Cosmeceuticals are soothing treatments and remedies for minor skin conditions easily made in the kitchen from wild harvests—herbal footbaths and facial steams along with relaxing herbal teas (chapters IX, XI, and XII). Various therapeutic qualities are alive in each plant, and it depends upon our honoring the plant's spirit in order to engage maximum benefits. Native people knew the importance of making prayers and offerings to key plants before any of their kin could be harvested. Collecting plants in a sacred manner activates their therapeutic qualities to the highest level of benefits. This wisdom applies to everything this book stands for.

Cancer and Diabetes Remedies from Native American Wisdom continue to strengthen several notable formulas in the mainstream health-food markets today. Native plants like slippery elm bark and sheep sorrel figure prominently in an old Ojibwa anticancer and antitumor treatment, containing additional herbs, known as Essiac (pages 29 and 154). Additional healing herbs were added to make this lymphatic cleanser work to further detoxify the human system in a commercial product called Flor*Essence. The Hoxsey cancer treatment emerged in the late 1880s to treat cancerous tumors in horses and other animals, and has also been used to help countless humans battle this disease. Pokeroot, bloodroot, prickly ash, barberry, and Oregon holly grape root are a part of this formula. From teas and tinctures to extracts and formulas, native healing herbs provide quite the harvests for general wellness and preventive medicines.

Herbal Traditions: Medicinal Plants in American Indian Life is included within the pages of this edition bringing together the best of the illustrations and information from the award-winning SITES (Smithsonian Institutes Traveling Exhibition Service) booklet. This accompanied the SITES Native Harvests Exhibition that toured the United States and Canada for four years during the mid 1980s.

After the success of *Native Harvests*, I wrote *Enduring Harvests: Native American Foods and Festivals for Every Season*, exploring the broad range of exciting seasonal celebrations all across North America and the native foodways encountered at each one. I have always been intrigued by the healing properties in some foods and particular plants—seemingly well known by many native people. These interests led me to later write and illustrate *American Indian Healing Arts: Herbs, Rituals, and Remedies for Every Season of Life*, and then *The Medicine Wheel Garden: Creating Sacred Space for Healing, Celebration, and Tranquility*. I think perhaps I have come full circle now.

I extend very special appreciation to Drs. Lee Taylor and Jane Taylor, Department of Horticulture at Michigan State University in East Lansing, Michigan, who were early readers of this book back in 1977 and have remained in touch and become good friends. I am grateful for comments and input from many different folks along the way. I take full responsibility for any perceived problems.

My appreciation and respect to John Riess and the fine team at Dover Publications, Inc., for making this edition possible, and for consummate vision in keeping selected older books alive and readily available. I congratulate you all for thoughtfulness. I know that *Native Harvests: American Indian Wild Foods & Recipes* joins a fine pantheon of classic books. The future is ever brighter!

Acknowledgements & Appreciations

Each of these people has enriched my life with knowledge, and I am most grateful for the sharings of time, traditions, insights, and trust. I apologize for any omissions.

Roberta Banketewa (and family), Zuni traditional baker and cook
Meredith Begay (and family), Mescalero Apache medicine woman

Salli Benedict, Akwesasne Mohawk basketmaker and educator

Ellyn Bigrope, Mescalero Apache teacher and museum educator

Roy Black Bear (and family), Oneida silversmith and educator

Greg Borland, Lakota spiritual leader

Marge Bruchac, Abenaki storyteller and educator

Joseph Bruchac (and family), Abenaki storyteller and writer

Sharon Burch, Navajo musician, singer, and songwriter

Desiree Mays Calavaza (and family), Zuni silversmith and
businesswoman

Dale Carson, Abenaki artist and educator

Nathanial "Stan" Chee (and family), Mescalero Apache
medicine man

Rita and Andrea Chrisjohn (and family), Oneida artists and
educators

Katsi Cook (and family), Mohawk midwife, herbalist, and educator

Linda Coombs, Wampanoag educator and dancer

Barry Dana, Penobscot chief, educator, artist, and survivalist

Joel Dancing Fire, Cherokee artist, poet, and educator

Wendell Deer With Horns, Lakota Pipe Carrier and educator

Big Eagle, Paugussett chief and beadwork artist

Rita Edaakie (and family), Zuni museum educator

Eva Geronimo (and family), Mescalero Apache eldercare worker

Robert Geronimo (and family), Mescalero Apache elder and
rodeo cowboy

Melanio Gonzales (and family), Taino artist and educator

Aaron Moses and Toni Gooday, Apache photographer and
educators

Rayna Green, Cherokee folklorist and educator

June Hamilton (and family), Pawnee educator and dancer

Jeff and Judy Kalin (and family), Cherokee/Seneca artists and
educators

Geri Keams, Navajo storyteller and writer, drummer

Mikka Barkman Kelly (and family), Cree artist, educator, and
model

Myron and Elizabeth Klute, Akwesasne Mohawk healers

Kenneth Little Hawk (and family), Micmac Mohawk storyteller
and musician

Oren Lyons, Onondaga peace chief and artist

David Bunn Martine (and family), Shinnecock artist, poet, and museum director

Jo Beth and Ken Mays (and family), Zuni counsel woman and silversmith

Erin Lamb Meeches (and family), Schaghticoke storyteller

Loretta Micco (and family), Florida Seminole food specialist

Brian and Louise Miles (and family), Mohegan, Navajo traditionalists, educators

Stan Neptune (and family), Penobscot/Passamaquoddy traditional artist and teacher

Kay Olan, Mohawk storyteller and teacher

Max Osceola, Jr., Florida Seminole tribal leader

Ramona Peters, Nosapocket, Wampanoag educator and artist

Tom Porter (and family), Mohawk leader and educator

Mitzi Rawls (and family), Choctaw artist, storyteller, and educator

David Richmond (and family), Snipe Clan Mohawk, educator and historian

Trudie Lamb Richmond (and family), Schaghticoke elder, historian, and storyteller

Ed Sarabia, Tlingit elder and Indian affairs coordinator

Ella Thomas Sekatau, Narragansett Medicine Woman, historian and educator

Alex and Edwin Seowtewa (and family), Zuni church artists

Lizzie Silversmith (and family), Seneca herbalist

Josephine Smith (and family), Shinnecock dancer, educator

Marguerite Smith (and family), Shinnecock tribal counsel

Myra and Geronimo Starr (and family), Creek Nation

Michael Storm, Seminole alligator wrestler and educator

Jake and Judy Swamp, Akwesasne Mohawk Tree of Peace Society

Tall Oak (and family), Mashantucket Pequot, Narragansett medicine man

Gladys Tantaquidgeon (and family), Mohegan medicine woman

Melissa Fawcett Tantaquidgeon (and family), Mohegan historian, writer

Joan Avant Tavares (and family), Wampanoag chef and educator

Monetta Trepp, Creek Nation businesswoman

Tsonakwa, Abenaki storyteller and silversmith
Janis Us, Shinnecock Mohawk beadwork artist and educator
Roberto Velez, Taino educator and storyteller
Richard Velky, Schaghticoke chief
Ron and Cherrie Welburn (and family), Conoy/Cherokee poet,
  educators
Larry White Feather, Cherokee healer and anesthesiologist
Gladys Widdiss, Gay Head Wampanoag chief and potter
Wunneanatsu, Schaghticoke educator and storyteller

In Remembrance and Gratitude
So many gifted elders/teachers have walked the Spirit Path . . .

Helen Attaquin, Wampanoag historian and educator
Hannah Avarett, Mashpee Wampanoag historian and educator
Wendell Chino, Mescalero Apache chief and educator
Richard and Terry Chrisjohn, Oneida craftsmen and educators
Courtland Fowler, Mohegan leader, historian and educator
Keewaydinoquay, Anishinabe' herbalist, ethnobotanist and
  medicine woman
Claude Medford, Jr., Choctaw-Apache basketmaker, storyteller,
  and educator
Nanepashamet, Wampanoag educator, storyteller, and artist
Sara Ransom, Snipe clan Mohawk basketmaker/beadworker,
  storyteller
Tom Ransom, Akwesasne basketmaker, storyteller, and
  farmer/woodsman
Irene Richmond, Snipe Clan Mohawk basketmaker, educator,
  and historian
Stilson "Chink" Sands, Mohegan storyteller, folklorist, and mason
Slow Turtle, Supreme Medicine Man of the Wampanoags and
  folklorist
Harold Tantaquidgeon, Mohegan museum historian and educator
Red Thunder Cloud, Catawba herbalist, storyteller, photographer,
  and educator

PREFACE

My passions for writing, illustrating, harvesting wild foods, and cooking and presenting them beautifully all came together in the 1970s. The more I blended my passions, the more fascinating and delicious they became. Evermore adventurous encounters with native American fare kept pulling me into serendipitous creations with shellfish, coastal edible plants, woodland game dishes with a range of choice wild fungi, and nutritious vegetarian medleys of wild plants. My notebooks and sketch pads grew full as I continually researched these "earth foods" in order to enjoy their fullest potentials. And my family and friends never seemed to tire of my experiments and truly "wild dinner parties."

American Indians wild and cultivated foods - could there possibly be an interest and a market for this? I believed so! There were few books in this field. Native foods at their seasonal best provide a glorious study. Food embraces everything from one's practical survival to the sacred and divine. Native American foods nourished the body, mind, spirit, and emotions, and created the nurturing links with Mother Earth. This essential "earth wisdom" needs to be regained and honored on a much broader scale. These gifts continually embellished my everyday life, and I needed to share them in more ways.

More than 30 years ago, I could see the need to create a usable guide and cookbook about American Indian tribes' wild and cultivated foods. Over 500 different American Indian tribes used their wild foods in strikingly different, fascinating ways. Regional and seasonal game, exotic wild fungi, and diverse wild foods have always peaked my fancy. My first cookbook, written and illustrated in 1977 and published by the American Indian Archaeological Institute (now IAIS), confirmed that the interest and demand was considerable. This certainly continues to grow.

Expanded and published by Random House/Vintage Books in 1979, Native Harvests: Recipes and Botanicals of the American Indians won favorable acclaim. "The most intelligent and brilliantly researched book on the food of the American Indian," said Craig Claiborne in "The New York Times." The book served as an easy guide and reference book as well as a most useful cookery book for those folks eager to know and explore their edible wild environments.

My book also became a teaching text in high schools and on college campuses as well as around campfires and in modern kitchens. Many American Indian teachers enjoyed using it. *Native Harvests* traveled far beyond my wildest dreams and carved a valuable niche in its unique field. It straddles the boundaries of field guide and cookery book, ethnobotany resource, and herbal medicine guide, woven with American Indian uses and wisdoms.

Sharing the Gifts

This Aztec poetic lament and spirited resistance cry opened the 1979 edition of *Native Harvests*.

Will I leave only this:
Like the flowers that wither?
Will nothing last in my name –
Nothing of my fame here on earth?

At least flowers!
At least song!

And, of course, I add foods! The *"Songs of Huexotzingo"* sound an enduring note of ultimate survival in a prayer offering strength to our Mother Earth. This continues to echo four centuries later as we honor the many contributions of flowers, song, and food from many regions of the tribal Americas. Edible blossoms and wild roots and greens fill our hedgerows, meadows, and woods. Some of these, like American Ginseng, Canadian Ginger, Evening Primrose, Slippery Elm, Yarrow, Yellow Dock, and Purslane have become well-recognized as vital healthcare products and restoratives that help our bodies forestall the effects of aging, and deal with stress.

Chocolate, vanilla, pineapple, papaya, strawberry, avocado, and allspice have revolutionized the multi-ethnic worlds of foods and flavorings. These ancient Mayan and Aztec foods originated in the distinctive tropical regions of Central America, Mexico, and the Caribbean Islands. Here, too, were found early origins of corn, cotton, squash, beans, peppers, sunflowers, and the early domestication of turkeys and mallard ducks. As these valuable foods dispersed around the world, they inspired a delicious revolution in ethnic cuisines – which has probably always been occurring on many levels. Food exchanges and trade in foods are one of the oldest human occupations.

Earth Foods for Health & Wellness

Wild edibles and medicinals are a life-long devotion. My early childhood in Ohio and summers spent in Tennessee and Alabama opened me to a broad earth-based wisdom. Grandparents and other family members shaped my interests and taught me so much about the land as farmers and caretakers. My parents grounded me in earth knowledge – how to harvest wild and cultivated foods and medicinal plants. From the home gardens to the meadows and woodlands, respect for the earth was my earliest memory. Fragrances and tastes of the earth were intoxicating. I was privileged to study with people who could expand my particular interests, like my parents (and all previous generations) had done.

I focused my research and writing upon my year-round adventures of growing, harvesting, cooking, and serving these diverse selections. Expanding interests in wild mushrooms and herbs for foods, spiritual needs, and healing continued to grow. I was a young idealist and naturalist thirty years ago, married and living in the country, birthing and raising my son and daughter. It was an era of "back to nature" and I was all for it. Yet all that kept drawing me more deeply, urgently was "Native foods and Native Peoples."

As an artist/illustrator, I was continually drawn to wild plants and mushrooms - to draw them, cook them, and feed them to my family and friends. Among the many versatile wild resources, I especially enjoyed the delicious virtues of wild violets, leeks, cress, chickweed, green onions, and wild mints which were explored fully each spring; burdock, wild plums, sorrel, rose petals, nasturtiums, and Saskatoon berries were eagerly enjoyed in summer; burdock roots, rose hips, black walnuts, hickory nut, acorns, and many wild mushrooms were enthusiastically devoured in autumn; and many more ripe seeds, roots, evergreens, and select wild mushrooms were appreciated during the long winter months.

We are surrounded and nurtured by many unique foods from around the world. How we prepare and eat them is evermore vital to our general health and wellness. We have become absorbed and fascinated by fads, eating patterns, diets, specialty cuisines, and culinary experiences. Where does it all lead? Food and health wisdom is easily over-riden by the temptation of sensory pleasures of foods which are rarely good for us.

"Sensible diets" can scarcely compete in the hedonistic food world of today. Native American Indian foods have been compromised and dismissed. Yet many of our Native American foods have provided the delectable basis of countless fine foods and some high-energy pemmicans and "junk foods" today. And, further studies reveal that many of these foods could benefit our health and possibly save lives.

Cultures & Cuisines

Cuisine, the characteristic manner and style of preparing food, varied from one tribal group to another, even centuries ago, all around North America. Distinctive culture groups treated their seasonal foods quite differently. Numerous foods were boiled into thick soups and stews, and large pieces of game were roasted over campfires and slit and jerked and dried for preservation and long-term future needs. Yet, well beyond the basics, various regional distinctions evolved.

Southeastern tribes hunted, fished, farmed, and grilled their venison, rabbit, and other game meats over hickory and applewood fires. Northeastern tribes hunted, gathered, and some farmed for their seasonal diversities of foods seasoned with cranberries, wild grapes, bearberries, and blueberries, and blended in various chowders, soups, stews, and slow-baked shellfish and beans using deep pit "earth ovens." Fish and small game was baked in clay or wrapped in large generous grape or coltsfoot leaves and baked or boiled.

Algonquian tribes of the Great Lakes regions hunted and fished for seasonal game meats which they cooked with wild rice, blueberries, hazelnuts, and diverse wild mushrooms. Many of the same foods were available, or traded for, from one region to another long before European contact began in the Americas. Tribes of the dynamic tipi and horse culture hunted across the Great Plains sustained by their buffalo-hunting and gathering a seasonal array of wild plants and fungi.

Tribes of the Desert Southwest also hunted, fished, and farmed their arid lands for the sacred triad, the "Three Sisters" of corn, squash, and beans, along with sunflowers, amaranths, and peppers. Seasonal wild harvests of wild beans, seeds, and cactus fruits and roots enriched tribal diets. Now, we understand why those early earthy foods were superior for maintaining health and vigor, rather than the "tin can" diets of the twentieth century.

Tribes of the West Coast regions and Northwest Coastal areas hunted and fished through lush environments sustained by one of the greatest diversities of wild foods. Salmon and halibut were king here, smoked and prepared with great artistry. Native American ingenuity provided the framework for what has become American cuisine today. Countless Native American foods and flavorings have gone round the world to augment other ethnic cuisines and alter the ways other cultures farm, harvest, and cook their modern foods.

My own mixed heritage of Scotch-Irish, German, Cherokee-Creek, and early Powhatan gives me unique balance and perspective on cultures and cuisines. All of these good tribes have contributed their genetic wisdom to my contemporary being. Perhaps, this brings me full circle - appreciating the vast shared foods that nourish us all today. My EuroAmerIndian ancestry serves me well!

As I prepare the twentieth anniversary, expanded edition of *Native Harvests* for publication, I acknowledge the amazing diversity of people who have made this work possible. American Indian and non-Indian specialists in many fields have enriched this work through countless generations of shared wisdom. Two decades of *Native Harvests* readers have honored me with their good comments and support. Many more Native American food, farming, and ranching businesses provide delicious resources. Many more entreprenures are ranching everything from alligator, armadillo, and antelope, to buffalo, rattlesnake, rabbit, oysters and clams.

Unlimited food potentials are available in varied small farming operations of wild and cultivated greens, ginseng, echinacea, and diverse wild mushrooms. Today's foods are also our body's complimentary medicines helping to assure our healthy tomorrows. From gathering wild rice to collecting wild mushrooms, we prosper when we honor the earth and care directly for her fertility. For each harvest, we give an offering of tobacco, or prayer, or a song. Everything in nature is reciprocal, and we learn to give something back for what we take away. *Native Harvests* has served as a certain "bible" in its lush unique fields, and it hopes to educate a new generation to the eclectic wonders of natural American Indian foods.

[Parts of this Preface appeared as an article in the ICR/International Cookbook Revue, Volume III (11), Spring 1998, pages 64-66; S.P.A., Lagasca 27, 1.-E, 28001 Madrid, Spain.]

INTRODUCTION

Food was woven more intimately into the fabric of daily life in ancient times than it is today. It directly fueled physical accomplishments, and almost all work of aboriginal peoples was done by their own power. Long before the native Americans established seasonal settlements, planted and harvested crops, and domesticated animals, they had accumulated an extensive knowledge of plant usage and food preparation. Through observation of their natural environment and experimentation they knew the botanicals to use for foods, medicines, and cosmetics, and which botanicals satisfied the other necessities of clothing, shelter, cordage, and tools. After settling into early horticultural bands, groups, and societies, the Indians continued to use and learn more about the multitudes of wild plants.

A stable culture depends upon a stable food supply. The dawn of farming evolved with the needs of the aboriginal cultures — thousands of years ago. Many of our common cultigens — or cultivated plants — were developed from wild plants by three great Indian nations of South and Meso-America: the Incas of Peru, who irrigated and terraced their South American fields; the Mayas of Central America, who farmed in the fertile wet jungles; and the Aztecs of Mexico, who cleared and burned their arid fields. Numerous North American tribes also cultivated, to some extent, the various wild botanicals that best proliferated in their floral environment.

With experimental ingenuity, these sophisticated early cultures domesticated and hybridized over 150 botanicals, including 6 varieties of corn (over 150 types and colors); 5 main species of beans (with countless colored varieties); squash, gourds, and pumpkins; tomatoes; peppers; peanuts; strawberries; blueberries; Jerusalem artichokes; potatoes, both white and sweet; chocolate; vanilla; sunflowers; and many others.

Squash, gourds, and pumpkins are believed to be the first plants cultivated by these early peoples, over ten thousand years ago, while corn was first cultivated (probably from a wild highland grass) over seven thousand years ago, and beans over four thousand years ago.

Aside from Indian horticultural achievements, there were freshwater and saltwater foods, game, and thousands of varieties of edible wild plants, seasonally available, to be enjoyed raw or cooked. The most important and widely used foods we know today are of native American origin. Almost 75 percent of our present food plants were new to Europeans five hundred years ago. Captain John Smith, writing in 1607, noted that the settlers of Jamestown, Virginia, would have starved if the Indians of that region had not brought corn, squash, and beans to them. This famous Indian triad, the "three sisters," soon became the most important foods in pioneer America. Their planting, harvesting, and preparation reflected the myriad native American usages and customs.

Colonial American pioneers left diaries and journals telling tragic stories of the deaths of nine out of every ten early settlers. "Starving time" it was called. The forests teemed with game, large and small; the waters swarmed with fish; fruits and vegetables were plentiful. Unfortunately many of these early Colonials were city-bred and unfamiliar with country living; even those from rural backgrounds were unprepared for wilderness existence. They failed to bring the necessary tools and equipment and knowledge to cope with their new way of life, so their spiritual diet became one of fear and desperation.

Adaptation was the key to survival. The American Indian became both teacher and savior, instructing the settlers in hunting, food preparation and preservation. Cookbooks from home would have been of little use to the often illiterate housewife, who found herself obliged to prepare ingredients unknown to her in England or Holland, such as corn, pumpkin, and squash.*

*Virginia T. Elverson and Mary Ann McLanahan, *A Cooking Legacy* (New York: Walker & Co., 1975), p. 1.

The Eastern Woodlands Indians were creative and accomplished cooks. Before extensive horticulture, their varied diets were gleaned from the land, lakes, marshes, and coastal regions, and the earth was both their storage cellar and their oven. Early colonial writings describe settlers finding "aboriginal barnes" (underground storage pits lined and covered with tree bark) from Cape Cod north and south through the Virginias. These "windfalls" reflected the prosperity of a gathering and harvesting people, who had put by their surpluses against the winter.

Native American cuisine is a continental cooking entirely our own. The basis of what has become most classic is uniquely American Indian: barbeques and clambakes, steamed lobsters and stuffed oysters, clam and corn chowders and gumbos, multitudes of cranberry creations, Boston baked beans, Brunswick stew, mincemeat pie and spoonbread, plus the infinite variety of cornbreads and puddings and dumplings — dishes as unusual as they are delicious, reflecting as they do the various styles of so many Indian cultures. The cultural differences, linked to distinct geographical locations and regional growing seasons, determined how these various peoples lived, what they ate, and how they cooked.

> American Indians never were a unit. They were scattered in hundreds of tribes with hundreds of cultures and customs. It is these tribal variations that have given color and character to the American past, and a wondrously wide variety of dishes to the American diet.*

Native Harvests reflects the native usage of wild and cultivated botanicals, both indigenous and introduced species. In keeping with the style of food preparation five hundred to one thousand years ago in North America, the recipes collected here should be used merely as springboards, guides to tastier, more creative cooking. As a body of recipes they are salt-free, principally because salt was not a widely used or natural food substance in the early American diet, except for its occasional use during coastal festivities and in a few inland areas.

According to personal taste preference, you may add salt and pepper and your favorite seasonings, or you may remain with the natural "earth seasonings." In those recipes that call for a particularly unusual ingredient I have suggested substitutions whenever possible. In general, flours may usually be substituted for one another. Because corn contains only a

*Will Rogers, Jr., Foreword to *The Art of American Indian Cooking,* by Yeffe Kimball and Jean Anderson (Garden City, N.Y.: Doubleday & Co., Inc., 1965).

small amount of gluten, it may be blended with other flours, especially wheat or rye, in order to lighten breadlike preparations. However, keep in mind that most Indian breads were relatively heavy, sturdy creations. Also, unprocessed peanut butter — the kind available at health food stores and at some commercial supermarkets — may be substituted for the various nut butters many of the recipes call for. Similarly, it is possible in these recipes to substitute one berry for another if necessary, or to use raisins or currants when berries are out of season.

Although a good deal of botanical information is included in this book, *Native Harvests* is intended to serve more as a cookbook than a botanical guide. I have profiled or illustrated most of the plants used in the recipes, but plants familiar to everybody — garden-variety potatoes, tomatoes, corn, and beans, for example—have not received the same treatment. To make the best and the safest use of *Native Harvests*, all foraging and gathering of "the edible wild" should be done in conjunction with dependable trail or identification guides. Consult the reference guide at the back of this book, your library, or a local bookshop for suggestions.

Taste the native harvests. Eat sparingly until you cultivate your new taste experiences. Identify carefully; avoid mistakes. Only a very small proportion of the plant kingdom is poisonous: Less than 1 percent of the known 500,000 plant species are truly deadly (see chapter 15), "Poisonous Wild Plants," for more information). Know your food sources, and take only the plant parts you need. Most important, never overharvest a limited area. Enjoy the integration of wild and cultivated foods for better nutrition. There are so many variables in nature. You have to exercise your own unique "earth sense" in developing seasonings, as well as recipes, to suit your own tastes.

NATIVE HARVESTS

I

NATURE'S
SEASONINGS

"The stones are Earth's bones. They are not dead at all, and anything that has life still retains that life when you use it."

... *Tsonakwa, Abenaki, 1980*

Wild seasonings are as fascinating and limitless as the great outdoors. A knowledge of the safe versus the toxic is vital and easy to acquire. The early Americans evolved an extensive usage of seasonal, indigenous North American flavorings, which is impressive and beneficial to us today.

Use herbs and spices sparingly to enhance, not dominate, the natural flavors of foods. As a rule, a recipe to serve 6 people can use $\frac{1}{2}$ teaspoon (or less) of any coarsely chopped dried herb or spice. Dried herbs are used in less quantity because of their more concentrated form and stronger flavors. Add most herbs during the last 5 to 10 minutes of cooking time, or they will become bitter and lose their nutritive value. The best aroma and flavor of herbs, spices, seeds, and nuts is contained in their aromatic oils, which dissipate with time, some lasting much longer than others. Leaf herbs have the most aromatic oil and the best flavor when fresh.

Early Americans also knew the special properties of *ashes* mixed with their foods, or in water, for various preparations. Ashes of distinctive woods such as cedar, juniper, hickory, and so on, were definite flavorings, as well as cleansing and digestive agents. Ashes also bleach and soften some foods and add trace minerals, subtly influencing taste and consistency. Ashes in water create lye, which will harden and chemically change the substances to which it is added.

Spoon fresh ashes out of a fireplace, woodburning stove, or campfire for use in the recipes. (In some cases substitutions are indicated.) Be sure not to scrape the ashes out of the fireplace, or you will pick up unwanted and harmful tars and residues.

Nuts and Seeds

Conventional salt, sea salt, pepper, sugar, cornsyrup, honey and fruit sugars, cream and butter may be added to some of these recipes as you adapt them to your own personal tastes, but please try to experience these very different tastes on their own merits first. Salt and sugar are certainly flavor enhancers and preservatives, so use them to suit your own tastes as you develop these recipes to their fullest appreciation.

Nut and seed butters and oils were a primary nutritive seasoning among most native Americans. They provided the greatest flavor accents and were a widely used staple in native diets.

Botanically speaking, nuts are any hard-shelled fruit with a large food store, whereas seeds are smaller and have more limited food reserves; both will keep more or less indefinitely.

Nuts were used extensively by many American Indian tribes who taught the early colonists how to gather and prepare them for flour, pastes, oil, butter, pottages and dyes. Part of the Indian's annual cycle of activities included the autumn harvest of the black walnuts, acorns, hickory nuts and chestnuts. Nuts were an important item in the Indian's diet and as winter progressed and the food supply became low, they depended more and more upon them for nourishment. They deemed nuts so important that several tribes named their moons or times of the year after them. For example, the Natchez Indians called their twelfth moon (around the latter part of January) that of the Chestnut and the thirteenth moon (February) that of the nuts.*

BEECHNUTS (*Fagus grandifolia*) are one of the most flavorful products of our northern forests. They are best gathered in late October or November after heavy frosts have dropped them to the ground. Delicious raw or cooked, beechnuts are best gathered before dawn, when possible, to beat the squirrels. Roasted beechnuts, when ground, can be

*Dr. Anne Marie Stewart and Leon Kronoff, *Eating from the Wild* (New York: Ballantine Books, 1975), p. 239.

used as fine caffeine-free coffee. Approximately one sixth of the nut's weight is oil, which is easily extracted by mashing and pressing the small nuts into a paste or by boiling and skimming the oil off the surface of the cooled broth. The flavor of this oil improves with time and keeps well. Beechnuts can also be made into a nutritious *flavor* by simply mashing or grinding the nuts and allowing the paste to dry out completely; then grind further, depending on the fineness desired.

Beech trees were an important part of the Iroquois diet. The inner bark (like that of the pine) was dried, ground, and used to make bread. The young beech leaves were also cooked as greens in the spring.

North American oaks (about 60 native spp.) are divided into two groups: WHITE OAKS *(Quercus alba) and* RED OAKS *(Quercus rubra)*. White oaks generally have rounded lobed leaves and sweet acorns that mature in one season. Red oaks generally have pointed bristle-tipped lobed leaves and bitter acorns that usually require two years to mature.

Oaks of all species produce acorns, which were probably the most important and plentiful nut foot for most tribes. All acorns are edible, nutritious food, but some require careful preparation to make them palatable and safe. White oak acorns may be eaten raw, but before eating

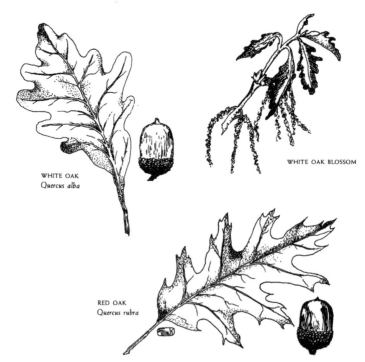

WHITE OAK
Quercus alba

WHITE OAK BLOSSOM

RED OAK
Quercus rubra

red oak acorns it is first essential to leach out the bitter, constipating tannin that makes them toxic. The shelled acorns are soaked in several water baths, sometimes mixed with wood ashes, until the nutmeats sweeten or become less bitter.

Most nutmeats, including sweet white oak acorns, were eaten raw by a number of tribes, especially the Algonquins. Nuts were pounded into meal to be used in breads, soups, and for seasonings; they were also ground in a mortar with water to make a flavorful *nut "milk"* to add to various dishes. *Nut oils* were rendered by boiling the nutmeats and meal, then skimming off the oil. This nutritious staple was used to prepare and to season vegetables, potherbs, and meats, and to spread on breads. The breads were usually "cakes" made by mixing cornmeal with what was left in the bottom of the pot after nut oils were rendered, and then frying this batter in hot fat or roasting it in hot coals.

OIL OF OAK was prepared and used by many Eastern Woodlands tribes. The acorns were pounded into flour and boiled in water containing maple-wood ashes, whereupon the oil was skimmed off. The flour was retained and used in breads and cereals.

HICKORY MILK, (*Carya ovata and C. tomentosa*) a staple ingredient in Eastern Algonquian, Cherokee, and Creek Indian cooking, was prepared by pounding the shelled dried hickory nuts, then boiling this meal in water and straining and reserving the oily part of the liquid, which was rich, like fresh cream. This was especially well used in their various corn preparations.

HAZELNUTS (*Corylus americana* and *C. cornuta*) are excellent nut meats enjoyed raw when they ripen in late summer and early fall. They are also easily ground into a nutritious flour. The dense hazelnut bush flourishes throughout the northeastern United States, bordering fields, hedgerows, and woods.

BLACK WALNUTS (*Juglans nigra*) and BUTTERNUTS (*Juglans cinerea*) are tall hardwood trees much prized for their wood. They are becoming somewhat scarce in many regions. Both produce delicious nuts, tough to crack but worth the effort. The nut butter can be prepared by smashing the husked nuts and boiling in water until the nutmeats and oils rise to the surface and can be skimmed off, while the shell pieces settle to the bottom of the pot. The oil can then be separated from the meats, which can, in turn, be dried and used as a tasty flour.

AMERICAN CHESTNUT (*Castanea dentata*). The only noted Indian remedy for whooping cough records that the chestnut leaves are steeped, with the resulting tea used as a warm astringent drink. The autumn nuts were a highly valued food crop among northeastern Indians and settlers. Once widespread, the American chestnut has been attacked and almost eradicated from our forests by an Oriental fungus blight, which struck our continent in 1904. Experimental forestry is working to inhibit the deadly fungus, and a few American chestnuts are able to resist the blight with the help of a hypovirulent fungus that seems to be able to combat the initial infection.

The delectable chestnut is one of the most popular nuts to roast. Approximately 11 percent protein and 7 percent fat, it is a nutritious and versatile food source with numerous culinary uses.

SUNFLOWER SEEDS (*Helianthus* spp.) from the native North American annual were used extensively by many tribes. The seeds are an excellent protein source raw or roasted. *Sunflower seed oil* is extracted by bruising and boiling the seeds, then skimming the oily residue off the broth. The ground paste, retaining its natural oil, makes a fine *butter*. The roasted seeds and shells make an interesting coffee drink.

SUNFLOWER SEED CAKES (15 cakes)

3 cups shelled sunflower seeds, fresh or dried	6 tablespoons fine cornmeal
	2 teaspoons maple syrup
3 cups water	½ cup oil

Simmer the seeds in the water in a heavy saucepan, covered, for 1 hour. Grind.

Mix the cornmeal and syrup into the ground seeds, 1 tablespoonful at a time, to make a stiff dough. Shape into firm, flat cakes 3 inches in diameter.

Brown the cakes in hot oil in a heavy skillet on both sides. Drain on brown paper and serve hot.

TOASTED PUMPKIN OR SQUASH SEEDS

Spread clean seeds on foil-covered baking sheets. Sprinkle lightly with oil. May be flavored with such herbs as oregano, mint, coltsfoot, and so on. Roast at 325° F until crisp and brown – about 20 minutes. Serve immediately, or cool and store in airtight containers.

NUT BUTTERS AND SEED BUTTERS

Grind 1 cup or more shelled dried nuts or seeds into a paste, using stones, a mortar and pestle, blender, or food processor. Many nut butters (paste) are sweet enough plain. However, others may require a teaspoon or two of honey or maple syrup mixed in to taste.

This excellent, nutritious topping is great on homemade breads and cakes, or served with fresh fruit, or on fresh, crisp vegetables. Nut and seed butters are very rich and should be used sparingly. Keep refrigerated to retard flavor loss and spoilage.

FLAVORED BUTTERS

SPICE (HERB) BUTTER. To ½ cup nut or seed butter, add 2 tablespoons chopped fresh dillweed (or your favorite herb). Add 1 teaspoon honey and 10 crushed allspice or juniper berries, fresh or dried. Blend together thoroughly and seal in a jar or crock. Keep refrigerated.

MUSTARD BUTTER (for fish and game). To 1 cup sunflower seed butter add 2 tablespoons wild mustard seeds, soaked and crushed in 2 tablespoons corn oil and 1 tablespoon bee pollen. Blend thoroughly and store in a covered jar in the refrigerator.

BEECHNUT-CLOVER BUTTER To 1 cup beechnut butter, add 3 tablespoons dried white clover blossoms and their seeds and 1 tablespoon bee pollen. Blend thoroughly and store. Beechnut butter has the greatest keeping quality of all nut butters. Store in a covered jar in the refrigerator.

MINT BUTTER To ½ cup acorn butter, cream in 2 tablespoons ground fresh mint leaves and 1 teaspoon honey. Store in a covered jar in the refrigerator.

SWEET GOLDENROD
Solidago odora

GOLDENROD
Solidago graminifolia

HICKORY NUT-CORN PUDDING (serves 6)

1 ½ cups cooked corn
½ cup shelled dried hickory nuts,
    chopped
2 tablespoons nut butter (see page 9)
1 cup boiling water

2 eggs, beaten
2 tablespoons honey
2 tablespoons fine cornmeal
¼ cup sweet goldenrod blossoms*

Combine all ingredients thoroughly and pour into a well-greased casserole. Sprinkle the top with additional hickory nut meats and bake in a preheated 350° F oven for 1 hour. Serve hot.

*Seeds, raisins, or any other edible blossom may be substituted for goldenrod blossoms.

BLACK WALNUT-MAPLE
COOKIES (yields 3 to 4 dozen large, soft cookies)

1 cup nut butter (see page 9)
2 cups maple sugar
2 large eggs
1 cup shelled dried black walnuts,
    chopped

2 cups cattail flour (see page 66)
2 ½ cups potato flour (see page 66)
1 teaspoon wood ashes (see page 4)
1 cup hot water

In a large bowl gradually cream together all ingredients. Drop the batter by teaspoonfuls onto greased cookie sheets. Sprinkle the tops with additional nuts if desired. Bake in a preheated 350° F oven for 20 minutes.

BEECHNUT PIE (serves 8)

1 uncooked 9-inch pie shell or 2 cups
    blended cornmeal and nutmeal
3 eggs, whipped until frothy
1 cup beechnut butter (see page 9),
    softened

1 cup light corn syrup
½ cup maple sugar
1 cup dried beechnut meats

Prepare a 9-inch pie shell of your favorite pastry recipe, or press blended corn meal and nutmeal evenly into a well-greased pie plate.

Cream together the whipped eggs and beechnut butter, gradually adding the corn syrup and maple sugar. Turn into the prepared pie shell and bake in a preheated 325° F oven for 35 minutes. Remove the pie from the oven and cover the top evenly with the beechnut meats. Return the pie to the oven and bake for another 20 minutes.

This pie recipe can be adapted easily to different nuts. (For Black Walnut Pie, substitute 1 cup dark corn syrup.)

CRANBERRY-WALNUT CAKES (serves 6 to 8)

1 cup cranberries, chopped
¾ cup shelled dried black walnuts,
    chopped
1 egg, beaten with 1 teaspoon water

½ cup honey
2 cups fine cornmeal
1 cup cattail flour (see page 66)

Gradually add each ingredient to the cornmeal and flour, blending thoroughly into a smooth batter. Lighten with additional warm water if the batter seems too heavy or thick. Pour into a well-greased loaf pan (9" x 5") and bake in a preheated 350° F oven for 1 hour. Or spoon into 10 to 12 greased muffin cups and bake until golden on top—about 25 minutes.

BEECHNUT-CURRANT CAKES (yields 12)

1 tablespoon wood ashes (see page 4)
2 cups boiling water
1 cup dried currants
1 cup dried beechnut meats, broken
3 cups fine cornmeal

1 cup beechnut flour (see page 66)
1 cup maple sugar
2 eggs, beaten
3 tablespoons nut butter (see page 9)

Stir the wood ashes into the boiling water and pour this over the currants. Let stand for 15 minutes to cool. Mix together the remaining ingredients; blend in the currants and water. Spread the batter evenly in a greased pan (9" x 9" x 5") and bake for 45 minutes in a preheated 350° F oven. Cool slightly and cut into 12 squares.

MEATLESS PEMMICAN (serves 12)

1/2 cup raisins
1/2 cup peanuts
1/2 cup hickory nuts
1/2 cup dried apples

1/2 cup dried pumpkin or squash
1/2 cup acorn or cornmeal
1/3 cup honey or maple syrup

In order to make sure that the acorn or cornmeal is bone-dry, spread it in a thin layer on a cookie sheet and place it in a warm oven for 15 to 30 minutes, checking frequently. The oven should be at the lowest possible setting. Then combine the dry ingredients and either chop them with a knife or grind them coarsely through a food grinder. Add the honey or maple syrup and blend thoroughly. Divide the mixture into 1/4-cup portions, press into cakes, and store in the refrigerator for use as a high-energy trail snack.

Indians traditionally made these small pressed cakes out of shredded bear, buffalo, or deer meat combined with suet, nuts, and dried fruits or berries.

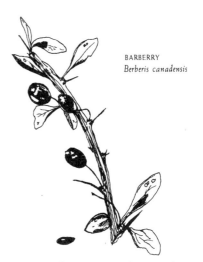

BARBERRY
Berberis canadensis

Berries and Fruits

Native Americans utilized over 250 species of berries and fruits, which they ate raw, used in cooking their foods, mashed for various fruit drinks, and dried for winter additives to their breads, soups, puddings, and pemmicans (dried foods).

The chief nutritive value of berries lies in the minerals and carbohydrates they contain. They are also a rich source of vitamins A and C. To obtain the maximum vitamin benefit, berries should be eaten raw and can be enjoyed fresh in cereals and as complements to other dishes.

Certain wild berries, however, are best cooked to render them less toxic, or sweetened to improve their taste. Cooking also helps to separate certain berries from their large seeds.

AMERICAN CRANBERRY *(Vaccinium macrocarpon)* is a slender, creeping, oval-leaved botanical found growing in northeastern swamps and open bogs. The ripe, shiny berries are tasty raw and have excellent keeping qualities. Traditionally, the cranberry flavored many autumn and winter native foods.

BARBERRY *(Berberis vulgaris, B. canadensis)* bark, leaves, twigs, and fruit are enjoyed by deer, rabbits, and game birds. Fragrant masses of yellow flowers in the spring, amid glossy green leaves through summer, turn to gold and scarlet in late autumn beside the orange-crimson berries, which have one to three shiny brown seeds inside. Both Indians and settlers dried the berries (though they are delicious and tangy raw) for many winter uses and flavor additives. A delightful drink is made by stewing these berries. From them many tarts, preserves, jellies, and pies are derived. The berries are high in pectin and are useful to add to sweeter, blander fruits (such as apples and peaches) to pique their taste. The bitter roots are boiled and used as a healthful, tonic laxative and blood purifier (1 teaspoon powdered root bark in 1 cup water). They are used externally as a lotion to treat various skin diseases. The Indians also made a tea from the leaves and drank it for relief from rheumatism. In addition, they chewed the roots.

BAYBERRY or Candleberry (*Myrica pensylvanica* and 7 native spp.). This is a coastal shrub indigenous to the U.S. The shiny, evergreen aromatic leaves of *Myrica* were used in tanning leather and were dried to keep as a spice (the flavoring is subtle and superb). It has gray bark on radiating branches; the flowers appear in spring clusters before the leaves. Numerous game birds, wild duck, and foxes feed on the berries. Bayberry leaves were a condiment and spice readily available to native Americans. Gather 1 quart fresh leaves, wash them, and spread them to dry, away from the sun or covered. When thoroughly dry and crisp, store in airtight jars. Before using, crumble them into small pieces and blend into cooking sauces, chowders, and stews.

BEARBERRY, Kinnikinnick, Mealberry, Upland Cranberry (*Arctostaphylos uva-ursi*). A widely distributed member of the heath family, bearberry is a trailing, perennial shrub with green, odorless, leathery foliage. Pink, inconspicuous, bell-like blossoms in terminal clusters ripen in autumn to dull red-orange berries. Bearberry is especially sought by the northern black bears in spring. The blandly dry, red berries are good survival food raw, but improve in taste with cooking, especially when mixed with other fruits. The dried and pulverized leaves have been an interest-

BEARBERRY
Arctostaphylos uva-ursi

BEACH PLUM
Prunus maritima

ing frontier tobacco for centuries, both alone and in "herbal tobacco" smoking remedies, as learned from the Indians. The dried leaves are also used for an astringent winter tea with a pleasant bitter taste considered soothing to stomach digestion. (Steep 1 teaspoon dried leaves for 5 minutes.)

BEACH PLUM (*Prunus maritima*) is a native perennial of the rose family. This low, straggling, spring-flowering shrub is indigenous to the North Atlantic coastal regions. It prefers sandy soil and is capable of withstanding the rough maritime climate. Its small, juicy fruits are within easy reach for autumn picking.

BLUE COHOSH, Squaw Root, Papoose Root (*Caulophyllum thalictroides*). This is a shady woodland tall-stemmed plant with small greenish flowers in April and May and round bluish seeds in August (an excellent coffee substitute when roasted). A boiled decoction of the root was a noted Indian remedy for fever, while many tribes used the warm tea made from the root infusion to aid in childbirth.

BLUE COHOSH
Caulophyllum thalictroides

BUFFALO BERRY
Shepherdia canadensis

BLUEBERRIES *(Vaccinium angustifolium* and various spp.) are a member of the widespread heath family, most of which favor acid soil and light shade. With as many uses to the Amerindians as they have to us today, blueberries were primarily enjoyed raw, preferably "picked before the dew is off." Dried or charred for preservation against winter needs, they were essential to many of the hunting and gathering cultures. They are also the source of a wonderful blue-gray dye; mixed with nutgalls, they produce a rich brown dye or ink.

BUFFALO BERRIES *(Shepherdia canadensis* with 3 var. native only to the U.S.) are a favorite food of black bears, quail, and song birds. Indians dried these like currants, to be used with buffalo meat. They have small yellow flowers with green oval leaves that are silvery underneath. Small, round orange-scarlet berries are translucent and contain saponin. The berries are sweetened by frost.

CHOKECHERRY
Prunus virginiana

CHOKECHERRY *(Prunus virginiana)*, WILD BLACK CHERRY *(P. serotina)*. One of the most widely distributed trees on the North American continent. Long clusters of flowers blossom in late spring and usually produce abundant red to black fruits, tart and tasty, about the size of large peas; excellent raw. Avoid eating the leaves and the kernels, as they are toxic.

FALSE SOLOMON'S SEAL, False Spikenard, Scurvyberries *(Smilacina racemosa)*, is a showy woodland plant of the lily family, noted for its terminal blossom clusters, which bloom in the spring and ripen in autumn to small clusters of aromatic red berries. These are delightful eaten raw or used as seasonings; they are somewhat cathartic and should be eaten in moderation.

GROUND-CHERRY, Chinese Lantern, Strawberry Tomato, Husk-Tomato *(Physalis pubescens)*, is a widespread annual weed of the nightshade family. These ornamental vines produce the bright-orange papery husk (resembling an Oriental lantern) that droops by autumn. Each husk contains one bright-orange, smooth, many-seeded berry, which is much like a tiny tomato, about $1/2$ inch in diameter. The berry's milky, pleasant flavor when fully ripe makes it a delight to eat fresh. But unless the berries are fully ripe, they have an unpleasant taste. This worthwhile fruit complements any dish or relish and was dried by many tribes for winter seasonings. Suitable for preserves, jams, jellies, pies, and sauces, ground-cherries do require pectin or the addition of a tart, more acid companion fruit.

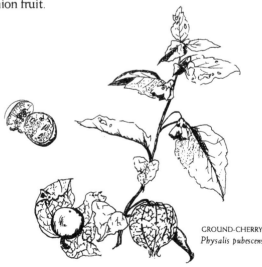

GROUND-CHERRY
Physalis pubescens

HIGHBUSH CRANBERRY or Squawbush *(Viburnum trilobum — not* related to the cranberry) is a tall shrub 6 to 10 feet high. The leaves are opposite, toothed, and terminate in three lobes, slightly resembling the maple. The white flowers are in clusters. Bright-red berries sweeten after frost, are high in vitamin C, and cling during the winter. The bark is a New and Old World medicinal antispasmodic used to treat asthma, epilepsy, and convulsions. It is gathered in the spring.

JUNEBERRY, Shadbush, Serviceberry *(Amelanchier canadensis* and var. spp.). These deciduous shrubs are native to temperate North America. Our earliest blooming spring shrubs, their juicy blackish berries are usually ripe in June. They must be harvested early, as they are highly prized by birds and woodland creatures.

JUNIPER BERRIES *(Juniperus communis* and spp.). These gray-blue aromatic berries were prized in Northwest Coast cultures as a secret ingredient of so many of their varied and succulent recipes. The distinctive flavors of salmon, deer, elk, and bear were enhanced by this woodsy fragrance. Also a popular winter flavoring used by Eastern Woodlands tribes, juniper berries were widely used in tea and to flavor natural medicines and smoking mixtures.

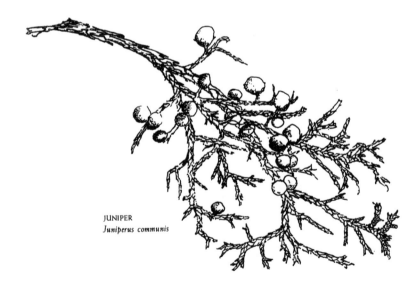

JUNIPER
Juniperus communis

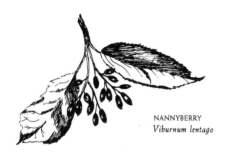

NANNYBERRY
Viburnum lentago

NANNYBERRY, Sheepberry, Wild Raisin (*Viburnum lentago*), is a spring-flowering viburnum shrub. The white blossom clusters give way to flat clusters of oval, green summer berries ripening to blue blackberries on coral-red stems. The drooping fruits are juicy, contain a solitary stone, and are sweetened by early frosts.

NIGHTSHADE (*Solanaceae* spp.). Bittersweet berries of the Solanaceae (nightshade) family are toxic fresh, especially when underripe. These fruits contain a poisonous alkaloid, solanine, which decreases to a non-toxic state in the ripe fruit and is completely destroyed by heat in cooking. Northeastern tribes cooked the ripe hulled berries in their meat stews. They make a tasty seasoning.

PARTRIDGEBERRY or Squaw Vine (*Mitchella repens*). This is a creeping evergreen with fragrant white flowers, April to June, in pairs. The scarlet berries are very bland and long-lasting and contain tannin (a substance which preserves tissue). Steeped as a tea, they were used as a tonic as well as an astringent. They have diuretic properties. A tea made of the leaves was used by many tribes (Cherokees, Penobscots) to speed and ease labor in childbirth.

SPICEBUSH, Wild Allspice, Feverbush (*Lindera benzoin*). This deciduous native shrub of our eastern woodlands prefers damp ground. Its honey-yellow spring blossoms give way to small, spicy yellow-to-red fruits which are something of a delicacy, as not many shrubs set fruit. The berries have excellent keeping qualities if dried; grind coarsely and use in place of conventional pepper.

WILD PLUM (*Prunus americana*) is another native perennial, widespread across temperate North America. Growing as a coarse shrub or small tree, it favors woodland borders, thickets, and the banks of streams. Its spring flowers give way to small red-to-yellow fruits, which are enjoyed throughout late summer, growing sweeter in autumn.

WINTERGREEN, Checkerberry, Teaberry (*Gaultheria procumbens*), is a tiny creeping shrub of infertile woodlands, growing especially under evergreens. The leaves were the original source of oil of wintergreen but have been displaced by the wider use of black birch twigs, which contain greater quantities of this oil. Both the leaves and the berries are refreshing eaten raw. They contain a compound similar to aspirin and can be effective in reducing fever and relieving minor aches and pains.

WINTERGREEN
Gaultheria procumbens

BEACH PLUM JAM (*yields eight 6-ounce jars*)

1 quart select beach plums	8 cups sugar
1 cup water	sterile glass jars

Cook the beach plums in the water in a covered saucepan over low heat for 15 minutes, or until soft. Remove from heat; cool slightly. Seed the plums, but do not mash. Return the fruit to the juice in the saucepan. Add the sugar while boiling; stir constantly for 15 minutes.

Skim the froth from the jam. Ladle the jam into glass jars, and seal immediately with ¼ inch liquid paraffin.

STEWED WILD CHERRIES (serves 8)

1 quart wild black cherries, stoned, *1 cup maple syrup*
 cracked, and cherry kernel saved *1 cup cider*

Simmer the wild cherries with their kernels plus the syrup and cider in a large covered crock, stirring occasionally, for 30 minutes. Serve either hot or cooled over puddings, or to flavor cornmeal dishes.

WILD GRAPE BUTTER
(OR WILD PLUM OR APPLE BUTTER)

Pick the wild grapes before the first light frost. Stem and wash them, then cover them with water in a large covered pot and bring to a boil. Simmer for 30 minutes or until their skins pop. Stir and mash the grapes as they cook. Pour off the grape juice to sweeten with honey, and drink.

 Sieve the remaining grape pulp to remove the seeds, and puree. Add an equal measure of maple sugar or honey, blending all in a bean-pot. Bake in a preheated 325° F oven, stirring occasionally, for 3 hours. Seal in hot, sterilized jars.

 Applesauce and grape puree may be combined to create yet another tasty butter variation. Wild plum puree and apple butter are also a good combination.

DRIED APPLES, PUMPKIN,
PLUMS, ETC.

Peel and core the harvested fruit. Slice thinly $\frac{1}{2}$ to $\frac{1}{4}$ inch thick and spread to air-dry on white cloth or muslin, away from the sun, over screens or boards. Turn twice daily. Keep the fruits from touching. Depending on the atmospheric conditions, it can take 6 to 10 days before the fruit is fully dehydrated. The process can be effectively hastened by drying near a fire or in a very low oven. Store in airtight containers.

 Dehydration of seasonal fruits and vegetables was, and still is, the most efficient way of putting most of these foods by — safely. Furthermore, these foodstuffs occupy much less space when reduced by natural water loss and are the least changed chemically. They make very nutritious sweet snacks.

INDIAN PUDDING (serves 12)

2 cups raisins or nannyberries
2 cups fine cornmeal
4 cups water
$^1/_2$ cup nut butter (see page 9)

$^1/_2$ cup honey
$^1/_4$ cup Juneberries, fresh or dried
$^1/_4$ teaspoon ground ginger
$^1/_2$ teaspoon nutmeg

Toss the raisins (or nannyberries) and cornmeal together gently. Bring
the water to a boil with the nut butter in a large saucepan. Gradually
add the cornmeal-raisin mixture and simmer, stirring until it thickens
— about 15 minutes. Add the remaining ingredients, blending thoroughly. Pour into a 2$^1/_2$ quart greased casserole. Set the casserole in
a pan of water, 1" or 2" deep, and bake in a preheated 325° F oven for
2$^1/_2$ hours. Cool thoroughly before serving. Serve with nut milk (see
page 7) or additional nutmeg for topping.

JUNEBERRY
Amelanchier canadensis

BAKED STUFFED APPLES (serves 6)

6 whole, firm apples, cored almost
    through to the bottom
$^1/_2$ cup dried currants or raisins or fresh
    blueberries

6 spicebush berries, dried and crushed
$^1/_2$ cup honey

Arrange the apples (in their skins) in a greased baking dish. Blend together the berries and honey and heat. Stuff each apple center pocket
with the hot mixture, drizzling some over the skins. Bake in a 300° F
oven for 30 minutes, basting once. Serve hot.

Sauces

CRANBERRY SAUCE (yields about 1 quart)

2 pounds cranberries
1 cup dried black walnut meats, chopped

1 cup maple sugar
1 cup cider

Combine all ingredients in a large kettle. Bring to a boil. Cover, reduce the heat, and simmer for 30 minutes, or until the cranberries' skins pop and the mixture looks glassy. Cool slightly, chill, and serve.

CRANBERRY AND WALNUT SAUCE (yields about 3 cups)

1 pound wild cranberries
2 cups water
½ pound dried black walnut meats, chopped

1 cup maple syrup
2 tablespoons cornstarch, with enough water to make it a thick paste

Place the cranberries and water in a covered pot, bring to a boil, and simmer until the berries pop. Add the chopped walnuts and syrup, simmer for another 10 minutes, then thicken with cornstarch paste, stirring to blend thoroughly.

Serve either hot or chilled with turkey, game, or other fowl.

CREAMED BEECHNUT SAUCE (yields about 2 cups)

2 cups water, with 1 tablespoon wood ashes (see page 4)
4 tablespoons beechnut butter (see page 9)

4 tablespoons fine cornmeal
½ cup dried beechnut meats

Bring the water and ashes to a boil, then simmer. Add the nut butter and blend until smooth. Gradually stir in the cornmeal, blending until smooth and thick. Add the nutmeats, and simmer for 2 minutes more. Serve hot to dress and complement roasts, fried fish, or your favorite vegetables.

Tree Essences

MAPLES *(Aceraceae)* are the most distinctive trees and shrubs in North America. There are 12 native species, and over 150 species of maples known. These handsome deciduous trees produce paired, winged fruits and usually have simple opposite leaves; their seeds ripen in spring and early summer. Maple trees are tapped in late winter/early spring, when the days begin to warm but the nights remain frosty cold. The sugaring season can last 3 to 6 weeks (until the trees bud and blossom) with the sap flowing sweet and water-clear. At blossomtime the sap turns to pale amber, and the taste definitely changes. Though sugaring may continue, the product is less desirable, and continued sapping-off would impair the health of the tree. Many myths and legends about the sacred maples have come to us from the Indians. The Mohicans believed that the melting snow caused the spring sap to run in the maples; they considered the snow to be the dripping oil of the Great Celestial Bear, who had been slain by the winter hunters.

Maple Syrup was the Eastern Woodlands Indians' principal confection. Most early accounts of explorations into these cultures mention the use of maple syrup as well as the tapping of various trees near winter's end. Maple syrup and its sugars were greatly favored, and were used to flavor cooked vegetables and fruits and to mellow the flavors of various native stews.

Natural Sugars can be derived from the sap of several other native trees, much the same as the Indians refined them from the maples. In the early spring the three major species of birches were tapped: BLACK BIRCH, Cherry Birch or Sweet Birch *(Betula lenta)*, YELLOW BIRCH *(B. lutea)*, and WHITE BIRCH *(B. papyrifera)*. A number of beverages, liquors, vinegars, syrups, and sugars are easily rendered from these trees.

MAPLES

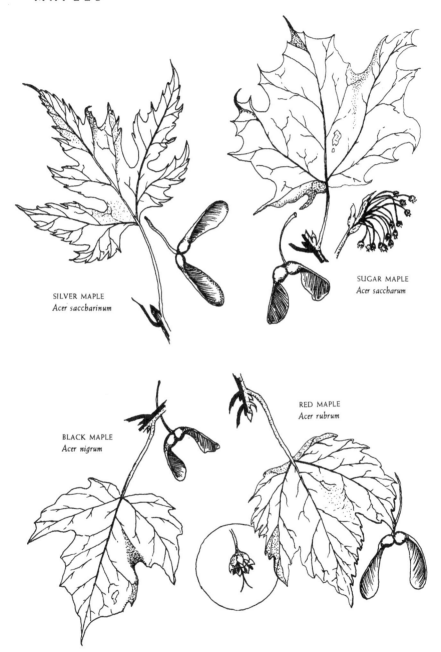

SILVER MAPLE
Acer saccharinum

SUGAR MAPLE
Acer saccharum

BLACK MAPLE
Acer nigrum

RED MAPLE
Acer rubrum

GREAT BULRUSH *(Scirpus validus)*, native to North American marshes and freshwater ponds, was highly valued by the Indians. A totally usable food plant, the younger, smaller roots were dug in the fall and early spring, then bruised and boiled down for the rich sugars and starches they contain.

BLACK WALNUT *(Juglans nigra)* and BUTTERNUT *(Juglans cinerea)* also produce quantities of spring sap for beverages, syrups, sugars, and so on.

HICKORY, or Swamp Bitternut *(Carya* spp.), is tapped and utilized much the same way as birch sap.

Vinegars are relatively easy to produce by exposing fermenting saps, syrups, or fruit or vegetable juices to air for a short period of time, usually a few days, depending on temperatures and atmospheric conditions. Fermentation is indicated by frothing and a fizzing noise. It is a complex action whereby the living organism of yeast breaks down the natural sugars into carbon dioxide and alcohol. This interreaction between yeast and sugar continues until the volume of alcohol reaches 12 to 14 percent. At this point the yeast's action is inhibited by the alcohol it has produced, and fermentation stops. When the mixture is exposed to air, acetic acid bacteria oxidize the alcohol to give vinegar.

GREAT BULRUSH
Scirpus validus

CATBRIER
Smilax rotundifolia

Additional Wild Flavorings

BLACK MUSTARD *(Brassica nigra)* is a widespread native perennial used by the Indians as a potherb and seasoning. Its seeds are gathered as they ripen in summer and are dried and ground to be used in place of conventional pepper. It is the principal source of table mustard.

CATBRIER *(Smilax* spp.*)* is a widely distributed perennial climbing vine. Its pounded roots yield a fine gelatin with a mild taste similar to that of wild sarsaparilla.

COLTSFOOT *(Tussilago farfara)* is a spring-blooming perennial of swamps and stream banks found all across northern North America and sought for its versatile leaves, which may be used as a salt substitute. Roll the large, broad coltsfoot leaf into a tight ball and dry thoroughly before a fire; then burn. The resulting ashes are very salty and can be used to season many dishes to taste. Highly prized by numerous Indian tribes, coltsfoot was especially in demand among various vegetarian peoples, to such a degree that it became the object of intertribal warfare among West Coast tribes.

CORIANDER *(Coriandrum sativum)* is a pungent herb of the parsley family, cultivated for centuries for its flavorful seeds. It is still cultivated by the Zunis, who use the fragrant foliage in salads, and the seeds to season meats and chilies.

GARLIC MUSTARD *(Alliaria officinalis)* is a persistent biennial herb of our countrysides and open woods, where it has naturalized (after introduction from Eurasia). This tall, white blossoming botanical may be used to lend a garlic flavor to many dishes; it is a fine vegetable raw or slightly steamed. Use its leaves, blossoms, and young seed pods throughout the spring and summer.

GARLIC MUSTARD SAUCE (serves 4 to 6)

2 cups fresh garlic mustard leaves,
    chopped coarsely
1/2 cup nut oil (see page 7) or corn oil

1 teaspoon ground dried spicebush
    berries

Blend all ingredients together thoroughly. Cook in a heavy iron skillet over moderate heat for 5 minutes or until the garlic mustard is limp and warmed through. Serve over fish.

MILKWEED (*Asclepias syriaca*) blossoms and buds make fragrant flavorings and thickeners for meats, soups, and stews. For use as a seasoning they should be dried.

MINT LEAVES (*Mentha* spp.) complement almost all wild foods and game, but are especially good for seasoning meats.

ONION, GARLIC, and LEEK (*Allium* spp.), all of which may be found growing wild, are flavorful and nutritious raw or cooked with native food preparations.

PURPLE AVENS or Water Avens (*Geum rivale*) is a low, blossoming perennial of swamps, meadows, and bogs, widely spread across North America and sought for its chocolate-flavored roots. The roots are acid and slightly astringent, but when well sugared, they are a tasty seasoning.

SASSAFRAS (*Sassafras albidum*), the fragrant deciduous shrub/tree, native to northeastern North America, was much prized and well used by the native Americans. The aromatic bark, roots, and leaves were used in teas and medicinal drinks. The Choctaws taught the early settlers to grind dried sassafras leaves into a powder that would sweeten and thicken their stews. This subsequently became the flavorful essence of Creole cooking, the filé that forms the base of gumbo.

FILÉ POWDER

Gather young sassafras leaves and spread them to dry in a layer on a screen. When leaves are crisp and crumbly, grind them until powdery, sieve and store in glass jars. Use 1 tablespoon filé powder per pot of stew or gumbo. Remove pot from heat and slowly add the powder, stirring well. *Do not add filé while the gumbo is cooking*, or it will become stringy and unappealing.

SHEEP SORREL (*Rumex acetosella*) is a widespread weed favoring sour soil. Its leaves are useful as a seasoning and thickener; boiled, they make a flavorful beverage similar to lemonade. Sorrel especially complements fish and potatoes. This is one of the major ingredients in an old Ojibwa herbal cancer formula currently marketed under the name of Essiac.

SHEPHERD'S PURSE (*Capsella bursa-pastoris*) is a vigorous wild plant spread all across our country and used by many tribes as a flavorful potherb and peppery seasoning. California Indians used the seeds as a source of ground meal. The seeds are gathered as the small pods ripen in autumn, and are used in soups and stews.

SWEET COLTSFOOT (*Petasites palmata*) was sought as a potherb, tobacco, medicine, and tea. Like coltsfoot (*Tussilago farfara*), its ashes may be used as a salt substitute.

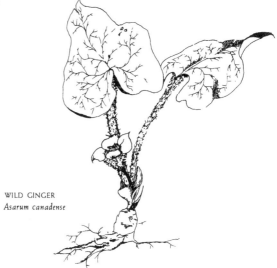

WILD GINGER
Asarum canadense

WILD GINGER (*Asarum canadense*) is a low-growing woodland plant found throughout the northern United States. Its long, slender roots are a sought-after flavoring, confection, and medicine. They are easily dug and are used fresh or dried for their unique flavoring qualities. In some states wild ginger is on the protected species list; if harvesting is permitted, do so sparingly.

WILD SARSAPARILLA (*Aralia nudicaulis* and spp.) is a native perennial plant widely used by many tribes for a variety of preparations, but principally for its flavorful rootstock.

MILKWEED
Asclepias spp.
(See pages 28,159.)

II

❧

NATIVE
SOUPS

"Crow first brought them a kernel of corn in one ear, and a bean in the other, from the Great God Kautantowits field in the Southwest."

. . . from a Narragansett traditional origin story, 1643

Soups complement and extend a meal; they are a delicious means of stretching limited quantities of foodstuffs. The best soups are the homemade stocks derived from fresh or dried produce and herbs. The native Americans evolved numerous concoctions of the wonderful foods inhabiting their regional environments.

JERUSALEM ARTICHOKE (*Helianthus tuberosus*) is a native sunflower that develops edible tubers. It grows 3 to 10 feet tall, is slender, branching, and persistent, and thrives in dense clumps in the wild (as well as in cultivated areas). It has slender, pointed leaves and produces many flowerheads, 2 to 3 inches in diameter, with small quantities of edible seeds. This plant has been a popular vegetable among the Indians for many centuries. Because of its hardiness and tastiness it was also cultivated extensively by the colonists and was enjoyed as a delicacy.

Jerusalem artichoke tubers are harvested in late fall; shaped like knobby sweet potatoes, they grow from 3 to 5 inches long. Their sweet juiciness is reminiscent of water chestnuts and potatoes. A truly versatile vegetable, the tubers can be used like either of these or like carrots. More nutritious than potatoes and lower in starch, these tubers are so digestible that they are considered excellent food for babies and invalids (and everyone in between). They are delicious raw, eaten in salads, briefly cooked and pickled, or boiled, roasted, creamed, or fried, like potatoes. They make excellent food for diabetics.

JERUSALEM ARTICHOKE SOUP (serves 8)

1 pound Jerusalem artichokes, scrubbed *2 tablespoons dillseed*
6 cups water *1 tablespoon chopped fresh dillweed*
3 scallions, sliced (including tops) *3 eggs, beaten lightly*

Boil the Jerusalem artichokes in the water in a covered saucepan for 25 minutes, or until tender. Drain, reserving the liquid, and slice the artichokes in half. Scoop the meat out of the skins and mash until it makes a smooth puree. Combine the puree, scallions, water, and seasonings, and simmer for 15 minutes.

Pour several spoonfuls of hot soup into the beaten eggs, stirring well. Slowly add the egg mixture to the hot soup, stirring over low heat for 1 more minute; serve.

EVENING PRIMROSE (*Oenothera biennis*) is a favorite biennial flowering plant with edible leaves and roots. Gather first-year roots before the plant blossoms.

EVENING PRIMROSE ROOT SOUP (serves 6)

2 cups quartered evening primrose roots *6 bayberry leaves, dried and crumbled*
2 cups diced Jerusalem artichokes *$^1/_2$ teaspoon grated dried spicebush berries*
2 quarts water *3 wild leeks, diced*
3 wild onions, halved *2 tablespoons chopped fresh dillweed*

Combine all ingredients (except the dill) in a large soup kettle. Cover and simmer for 40 minutes, add the dill, and simmer for 10 minutes more. Season to taste and serve hot.

SQUASH (*Cucurbita* spp.) was almost as important as corn to the Iroquois and other Eastern Woodlands tribes. It was versatile and nourishing and was also ceremonially important. The rattles created and used by the medicine societies were fashioned of the summer crookneck squash and the long-necked calabashes (gourds). Squash was generally baked whole, especially the rich, sweet-meated hard-shelled varieties: buttercup, acorn, and butternut. Favored seasonings were honey, maple syrup, and animal fats. The yellow summer varieties of squash were mostly boiled (often with their blossoms, to thicken the broth) and blended into smooth, fragrant soups.

YELLOW SQUASH SOUP (serves 8)

2 pounds or 2 medium yellow squash,
    cubed
2 scallions or wild onions, sliced
    (including tops)
1 tablespoon honey
1 tablespoon sunflower seed oil (see
    page 8)

1 quart water
1 tablespoon chopped fresh dillweed
garnish: shelled sunflower seeds or toasted
    squash seeds

Simmer the squash, scallions, honey, and oil in the water in a large covered pot for 30 minutes, or until the squash is tender. Cool slightly, mash to a smooth puree, and add the dill. Return to heat and simmer for another 5 minutes. Add more water to thin if desired. Serve either hot or cold with garnishes.

CLOVER SOUP (serves 6)

2 cups clover blossoms and leaves, fresh
    or dried
2 small wild onions, chopped
4 tablespoons sunflower seed butter (see
    page 8)
1 quart water
12 groundnuts, or 3 medium potatoes,
    quartered
chopped fresh dillweed to taste
spicebush berries, dried, grated over soup
    to taste

Sauté the clover blossoms and leaves and the chopped onions in the sunflower seed butter. Add the water, and groundnuts, and seasonings. Simmer, covered, for 20 minutes. Serve hot.

WILD ONION
Allium cernuum

SCALLION SOUP (serves 6)

8 scallions, sliced (including tops)   6 cups water
8 dried juniper berries   1 tablespoon chopped fresh coriander

Combine all ingredients in a large pot and simmer, covered, for 40 minutes. Serve hot.

SUNFLOWER SEED SOUP (serves 6)

2 cups shelled sunflower seeds   6 cups water
3 scallions, chopped (including tops)   1 teaspoon chopped fresh dillweed

Simmer all ingredients in a large covered pot, stirring occasionally, for 30 minutes. Serve hot.

FRESH TOMATO (OR POTATO) SOUP (serves 10)

4 pounds ripe tomatoes or potatoes,   1 tablespoon sunflower seed oil (see
   diced   page 8)
1 cooking apple, peeled, cored, and   1 tablespoon fine cornmeal
   quartered $^1/_2$ teaspoon chopped fresh basil
2 yellow onions, chopped   2 bayberry leaves
$^1/_2$ cup fresh mint leaves, chopped   1 cup chopped fresh dillweed
2 quarts water

Place all ingredients except the last three in a large kettle. Cover and simmer slowly, stirring occasionally, for 2 hours. Add the basil, bayberry leaves, and dill, and simmer for 10 minutes more. Serve hot.

CORN CHOWDER (serves 8)

3 cups dried corn kernels   2 tablespoons nut butter (see page 9)
6 cups water or meat stock $^1/_2$ pound fresh mushrooms, sliced
1 potato, diced   1 tablespoon chopped fresh dillweed
1 onion, chopped   garnish: chopped dillweed or seasonal
1 green pepper, chopped   herbs of your choice

Soak the corn in the water (or stock) overnight in a large, covered kettle. Bring to a boil, then simmer, covered, for 15 minutes. Add the remaining ingredients (except the mushrooms and dill) and simmer for another 30 minutes. Add the sliced muchrooms. Steam with the lid on for another 5 minutes. Garnish, and serve hot.

CORN SOUP (serves 8)

kernels from 2 ears dried flint corn
8 cups water
2 scallions, chopped (including tops)
10 juniper berries, dried

one 2-inch strip fatback, thinly sliced
½ pound dried bear meat or venison or
 beef, etc.

Soak the corn in 2 cups of the water overnight in a large, covered kettle. Add the remaining ingredients, bring to a boil, and simmer, covered, for 3 to 4 hours until the corn is tender. Serve hot.

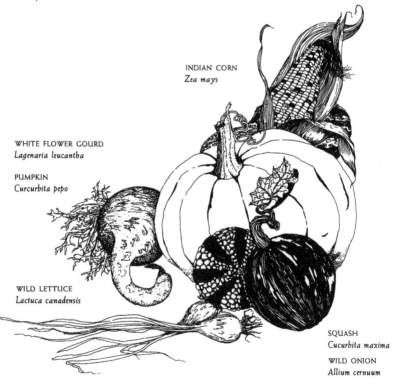

INDIAN CORN
Zea mays

WHITE FLOWER GOURD
Lagenaria leucantha

PUMPKIN
Curcurbita pepo

WILD LETTUCE
Lactuca canadensis

SQUASH
Cucurbita maxima

WILD ONION
Allium cernuum

BLACK WALNUT AND PUMPKIN SOUP *(serves 4 to 6)*

1 small pumpkin (about 12 inches in
    diameter)
1 cup black walnuts, chopped
maple syrup (to taste)

1 quart water
garnish: roasted pumpkin seeds and
    chopped walnuts

Roast the whole washed pumpkin in a preheated 325° F oven for 1 hour (or until the skin wrinkles and is easily pierced with a sharp stick); remove the pumpkin and cool slightly. Cut the pumpkin open and spoon out the seeds (save and spread in a pan to toast). Spoon out the pumpkin meat into a saucepan and mash it with the walnuts and syrup, adding enough water to liquefy to the desired soup consistency. Mix well and simmer, covered, for 3 to 5 minutes. Serve garnished with roasted pumpkin seeds and a spoonful of chopped walnuts.

    This excellent taste combination is very high in vitamins and minerals and is a rich source of carbohydrates and proteins.

HAZELNUT SOUP *(serves 6)*

2 cups ground dried hazelnuts
5 cups water
1 tablespoon honey

2 scallions, diced (including tops)
2 tablespoons chopped fresh parsley

Simmer all ingredients together in a covered saucepan, stirring frequently, for 1 hour. Serve hot in small servings, as this is a rich soup.

TROUT STEW *(serves 10)*

two 3-pound trout, cleaned
2 large potatoes, quartered
2 large onions, quartered
2 quarts water
10 juniper berries

1 pound spinach or purslane, chopped
11 fresh mint leaves
2 tablespoons nut butter (see page 9)
garnish: chopped fresh parsley and
    dillweed

Combine the first five ingredients in a large covered kettle and simmer for 30 minutes. Carefully remove the fish; peel, bone, and return the trout meat to the kettle. Continue to simmer for 20 minutes more. Mash the juniper berries with a spoon against the side of the kettle. Add the greens and nut butter and simmer for 10 minutes more. Serve steaming hot with chopped fresh parsley and dillweed.

EASTERN BOX TURTLE

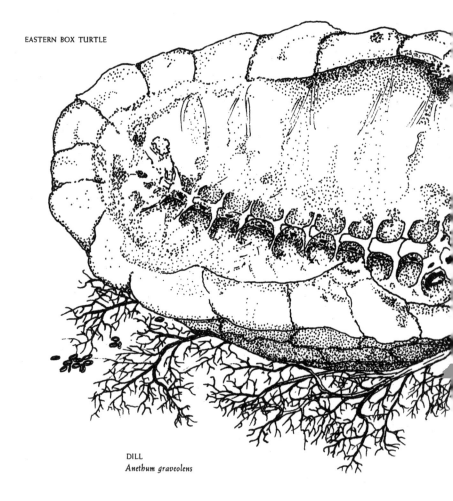

DILL
Anethum graveolens

TURTLES and turtle eggs were prized by many tribes. Favored species were the snappers, wood turtles, and painted turtles, and the giant sea turtles far south. Turtle broth was considered a remedy for sore throats and was a special food for young babies. The turtle shells became musical instruments (rattles), ceremonial symbols, and serving bowls long before there were pottery or wooden eating vessels. Easy hunting, the turtle has long been associated with all Indian cultures.

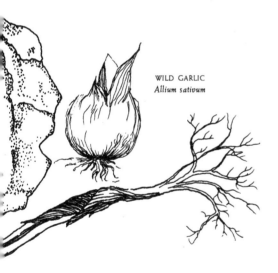

WILD GARLIC
Allium sativum

TURTLE SOUP (serves 4)

1 pound turtle or terrapin meat
2 scallions, sliced (including tops)

3 quarts water
1 tablespoon chopped fresh dillweed

Combine all ingredients in a large pot and simmer for 2 hours. Remove the meat, cool slightly, dice; return the meat to the broth. Add more water as necessary. Simmer for 1 more hour, or until tender. Serve hot.

Morning ritual
Wild mushrooms steam on low fire
a meditation.

Wild Mushroom Soup

A morning meditation while brewing fine coffee—
I cut wild mushrooms into thin wedges,
Soft white meat of young Dryad's Saddle,
Moist fragrance of cucumber and watermelon,
Brings a mystery from woodlands into
My country kitchen—a gift from foraging.
The prodigious month of May!
Sprinkle with sea salt, drizzle with olive oil in
Shallow water bath, steaming, slow-cooking, I
Weave these blessings into memory's kitchen;
Simmered over an hour, careful reduction,
Seasoned to taste, the best wild mushroom soup!

Dryad's Saddle or
Pheasant's back,
Polyporus squamosus Fr.
Polyporaceae
Most common in May,
Large scaly, fleshy (white),
yellowish-brown cap
dense white meat, odor of
watermelon & cucumber;
found on living or dead elm,
Poplar, willow, beech, birch.

III

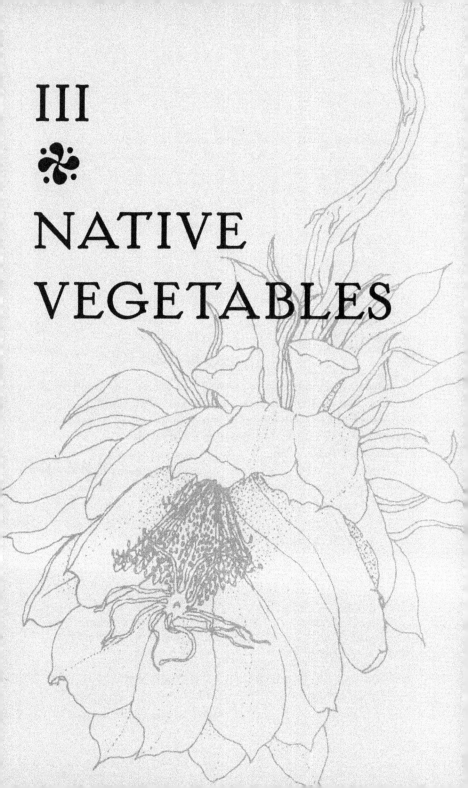

NATIVE
VEGETABLES

"Our elders recognized the spiritual elements thought to be present in corn, beans, and squash. These vegetables were planted when the moon was 'growing' — never after the full moon."

... Gladys Tantaquidgeon, Mohegan Medicine Woman, 1989

The early Americans' relationship to their foods and methods of harvesting was also intricately interwoven with their human and spiritual relationships. The Indians' kinship to the plant world was a product of centuries of accumulated knowledge. Much can be understood about a culture through analyzing its seasonal diet.

These select recipes "skim the surface" in order to focus on the Amerindians' respect for their environment and their resourcefulness. Most of these botanicals are widely available and possess great food value.

JERUSALEM ARTICHOKE SALAD (serves 6)

1 pound Jerusalem artichokes, scrubbed and diced
2 scallions, diced finely (including tops)
$^1/_2$ cup nut oil (see page 7)
$^1/_2$ cup cider vinegar
1 tablespoon honey
1 tablespoon chopped fresh mint leaves
2 cups salad greens

Place the Jerusalem artichokes and scallions in a large salad bowl. Add the nut oil, vinegar, honey, and mint leaves. Toss thoroughly. Marinate at room temperature for 1 hour. Add the salad greens, toss again, and serve.

JERUSALEM ARTICHOKE
Helianthus tuberosus

(ENLARGED.)

SPICED JERUSALEM ARTICHOKES (serves 8)

1 pound Jerusalem artichokes,
    scrubbed and sliced
½ cup nut oil (see page 7)
2 cloves wild garlic, chopped

2 tablespoons chopped chives
2 tablespoons chopped fresh dillweed
¼ cup cider vinegar

Boil the Jerusalem artichokes in water to cover for 20 minutes. Drain. Combine the Jerusalem artichokes and the nut oil, garlic, chives, and dill in a skillet; sauté, stirring, for 15 minutes. Add the vinegar and simmer for 5 minutes longer. Serve hot.

ROAST JERUSALEM ARTICHOKES (serves 8)

1 pound Jerusalem artichokes
nut oil (see page 7)

Wipe the Jerusalem artichokes with nut oil and wrap them individually in foil, or place them directly, unwrapped, in the glowing coals of a wood fire. Roast for 10 minutes, turn, and roast for 10 minutes more. Serve hot, split in half, with nut butter (page 9) or nut oil (page 7) to accent the taste.

LAMB'S QUARTERS (*Chenopodium album*) is a nutritious member of the goosefoot family, a relative of spinach. It is one of the earliest spring greens to harvest. This wild relative is tasty all summer long and into autumn, when the leaves are still delicious. Brought centuries ago from Europe, this hardy annual has spread throughout our country.

A multitude of tiny black seeds (up to 75,000 per single plant) are easily harvested in late summer. These nutritious "poppy seeds" from lamb's quarters can be used as seasoning, garnishes, and cereal or flour additives.

This bountiful cosmopolitan plant seems to be cultivated in some areas, it grows so profusely.

LAMB'S QUARTERS
Chenopodium album

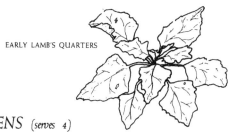

EARLY LAMB'S QUARTERS

LAMB'S QUARTERS (GOOSEFOOT) GREENS (serves 4)

4 cups lamb's quarter leaves
1 tablespoon nut butter (see page 9)

½ cup water
diced scallions (to taste)

Combine all ingredients in a covered saucepan and simmer for 5 minutes, or until the greens are tender. Serve hot.

NASTURTIUM (*Nasturtium officinale* and spp.), a member of the watercress family, is a tasty and colorful addition to any summertime cold plate. As a garnish, the nasturtium is hearty and highly nutritious. The blossoms, buds, leaves, and seeds taste like radishes. "When the covered wagons moved west across the Plains, the settlers found a kind of nasturtium growing wild. They named it Indian Cress because tribes of the area used both the blossoms and leaves to give their green salads a special pungency."*

NASTURTIUM SALAD (serves 4)

1 cup young nasturtium leaves
1 cup nasturtium buds and blossoms

2 cups mixed greens
1 scallion, chopped (including tops)

Dressing

⅓ cup sunflower seed oil (see page 8)
¼ cup cider vinegar

1 tablespoon honey
1 teaspoon chopped fresh dillweed

Combine the dressing ingredients in a glass jar and shake to blend. Let stand at room temperature for a while to develop flavor.

Combine all the salad ingredients in a large bowl and toss. Dress, toss again, and serve.

*Yeffe Kimball and Jean Anderson, *The Art of American Indian Cooking* (Garden City, N.Y.: Doubleday & Co., Inc., 1965), p. 117.

SALAD OF WILD GREENS (serves 6)

2 scallions, sliced (including tops)
1 quart watercress sprigs
1 quart wild lettuce leaves

1 cup wood sorrel leaves and blossoms*
1 cup fresh mint leaves
1/2 cup chopped fresh dillweed

Dressing:

1/2 cup vinegar
1/2 cup nut oil (see page 7)

Toss all the salad ingredients together in a large wooden bowl and dress.

PURSLANE
Portulaca oleracea

PURSLANE SALAD (serves 8)

2 quarts purslane, washed twice
1 cup boiling water
1 medium onion, sliced thinly
2 ripe tomatoes, cubed

1/4 cup chopped fresh dillweed
1/2 cup cidar vinegar
1/3 cup nut oil (see page 7)

Steam the purslane in the boiling water in a covered saucepan for 5 minutes. Drain and cool. Add the remaining ingredients to the purslane in a large wooden bowl. Toss thoroughly. Serve.

*Wood sorrel should be eaten in moderation because of its high oxalic acid content which can bind calcium in our bodies and eliminate it.

YOUNG MILKWEED SPEARS (serves 6)

2 quarts young milkweed spears (picked
   before 10 inches tall and before
   leaves unfurl, plant becomes toxic
   as it matures)

1 tablespoon wood ashes (see page 4)
3 cups water
garnish: nut butter (see page 9) or nut
   milk (see page 7)

Steam these young plant tops (do not boil) with the wood ashes in 1 cup
water in a covered saucepan for 4 to 5 minutes. Pour off this first bath,
rinse thoroughly, and steam again in 1 cup clear, fresh water without
wood ashes for 4 to 5 minutes. Rinse and steam again in 1 cup water for
4 to 5 minutes. Serve either hot or chilled (like asparagus) with complements of nut butter or nut milk topping.

MILKWEED BUDS AND BLOSSOMS (serves 4)

1 quart freshly gathered milkweed buds
   and blossom clumps
1 clove wild garlic, chopped

½ cup water
1 tablespoon maple syrup (optional)

Steam the milkweed buds and blossoms with the garlic in a covered
saucepan for 15 minutes. Stir thoroughly and add maple syrup if desired. Serve either hot or cold; this spicy, fragrant vegetable is delicious
either way. Also excellent served as a seasoning and flavor enhancer to
other vegetable and fish dishes.

STEAMED YOUNG MILKWEED PODS (serves 8)

3 quarts young (tiny) whole milkweed
   pods, up to 1½ inch long only*
2 cups boiling water

1 scallion, diced (including top)
2 tablespoons maple syrup

Combine all ingredients in a covered saucepan and simmer (do not boil)
for 25 minutes, stirring occasionally. Serve either hot or cold. These
crisp, spicy pods make good garnishes and finger foods as well as a very
tasty vegetable. The taste is reminiscent of okra.

*Milkweed pods this size can be harvested for almost 6 weeks through July and early August.

MILKWEED PODS VINAIGRETTE (serves 10 to 12)

1 quart young whole milkweed pods (under ¹/₂ inch long)	2 cups small white onions, peeled
1 cup milkweed buds and blossoms (optional)	1 quart water
	¹/₂ cup maple syrup

Combine all ingredients in an enamel pot and bring to a boil. Simmer, covered, for 25 minutes. Stir occasionally. Drain and rinse with cold water. Place ingredients in a crock and prepare marinade.

Marinade:

2 cups chopped pimentos	1 quart cider vinegar
1 cup chopped fresh dillweed	¹/₂ quart corn oil

Blend all ingredients together thoroughly and pour over mixture in the crock. Stir gently. Cover and refrigerate overnight to enhance flavors before serving. This tasty, colorful dish is a favorite in July and August, one worth putting by in extra amounts for winter enjoyment!

BUTTERED NETTLES (serves 6)

1 scallion, diced (including top)	2 quarts young nettle tops*
2 tablespoons sunflower seed oil (see page 8)	¹/₂ cup boiling water
	¹/₃ cup sunflower seed butter (see page 8)

In a medium saucepan, sauté the scallion in the sunflower seed oil over medium heat for 3 minutes. Add the nettles, boiling water, and seed butter. Stir thoroughly, and simmer, covered, for 20 minutes. Serve steaming hot with the broth. A highly nutritious vegetable and soup stock.

BUTTERED BEECH LEAVES (serves 4)

2 cups young beech leaves† (newly collected, as they wilt rapidly)	1 clove wild garlic, crushed
³/₄ cup boiling water	1 tablespoon nut butter (see page 9)

*Cooking destroys the nettles' stinging properties.
†Beech leaves should be picked by the leaf stalk (petiole); eat the leaf blade and discard the stalk.

Combine all ingredients in a medium saucepan, stir thoroughly to blend; cover, and simmer for 8 minutes. Serve hot as an appetizer or side vegetable. Eat with the fingers.

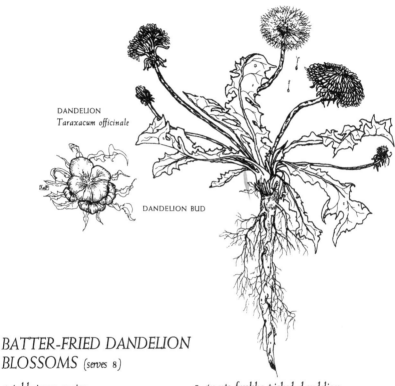

DANDELION
Taraxacum officinale

DANDELION BUD

BATTER-FRIED DANDELION BLOSSOMS (serves 8)

1 tablespoon water
2 eggs
¹/₄ cup nut oil (see page 7)

2 quarts freshly picked dandelion
blossoms, washed and dried*
1 ¹/₂ cups fine cornmeal

Add the water to the eggs and beat well. Heat the nut oil to sizzling in a cast-iron skillet. Dip the dandelion blossoms, one at a time, into the egg, and then into the cornmeal. Sauté, turning often, until golden. Drain on brown paper. Serve either hot or cold, as snacks, a vegetable side dish, or a tasty garnish.

*For full, showy blossoms, pick just before using, as blossoms close shortly after picking. The dandelion blossom responds quickly to temperature changes; it opens only in clear weather and bolts as soon as temperatures approach 90° F. Notice the dandelion's yellow-blossoming abundance in spring, its disappearance during the summer, and the return of a few fall flowers as temperatures cool.

WILD RICE WITH HAZELNUTS
AND BLUEBERRIES (serves 12)

2 cups wild rice, washed in cold water
5 cups water
2 wild onions, diced

1 cup shelled dried hazelnuts, diced
1 cup dried blueberries

Combine the rice, water, and onions in a large kettle, bring to a boil, then cover and simmer for approximately 40 minutes, or until most of the water is absorbed. Add the hazelnuts and dried blueberries, mixing thoroughly. Steam, covered, for an additional 20 minutes, stirring occasionally. Serve hot.

SUCCOTASH (serves 8)

1 onion, chopped
1 green pepper, chopped
1 cup water

2 cups shelled lima beans
2 cups yellow corn
2 tablespoons nut butter (see page 9)

Simmer all ingredients together in a large covered kettle for 20 minutes. Serve hot.

This was one of the easiest Indian recipes adopted by the first settlers. The hearty mixture of boiled beans and corn was usually sweetened with bear fat.

LEEKS AND NEW POTATOES (serves 6)

10 whole new potatoes
3 large leeks, quartered
1 teaspoon maple syrup

2 cups water
one 1½-inch cube fatback

Combine all ingredients and simmer, uncovered, until tender, about 25 minutes. Serve hot in bowls with the broth, as a porridge or vegetable.

STEAMED CATTAIL STEMS (COSSACK ASPARAGUS) (serves 4)

During the spring as the cattails are sprouting upward, before flower stalks emerge, pull upward on the center of the plant, removing the white, syrupy core. Pull 16 stalks. Then remove the outer portion of fronds and cut off the top leaves, saving the inner, white, tender core. This nutritious vegetable is tasty raw, sliced like onions into salad, or eaten alone.

   To cook: Cover the stalks with boiling water and simmer for 10 minutes, or until tender. Serve with nut oil (see page 7) and cider vinegar dressing, or topped with nut butter (see page 9).

   The clear, syrupy juice of this perennial vegetable of the marshlands is an important thickening agent: Added to soups and stews or other vegetable broths, it acts as a "corn-starch." The cattail roots are an important source of starch and carbohydrates.

CATTAILS
Typha latifolia

POKEWEED
Phytolacca americana

BUTTERED POKE SPROUTS (serves 6)

According to Euell Gibbons, poke is "probably the best known and most widely used wild vegetable in America." Poke is best when very young, when the leaves are just unfolding at the top of the sprout. *At its most advanced, mature stages, the leaves, berries, seeds, and large taproot are toxic and can be poisonous.*

Gather, wash, and trim 12 to 16 tender young poke sprouts. Place in a large kettle, cover with the boiling water, and boil for 10 minutes. Pour this cooking water off and discard. Cover the sprouts again with fresh water; add 1 tablespoon wood ashes (see page 4) and 2 cloves wild garlic, some bacon fat (if desired). Simmer slowly. Serve steaming hot, dressed with nut butter (see page 9) or nut oil (see page 7), and cider vinegar to taste.

FRESH CHICKWEED SALAD (serves 8)

2 pounds young chickweed leaves and
    stems
2 teaspoons honey
4 teaspoons sunflower seed butter
    (see page 8)

2 teaspoons sunflower seed oil (see
    page 8)
1/2 cup cider vinegar

Place the washed chickweed in a medium saucepan and cover with boiling water. Simmer, covered, for 3 minutes. Remove from heat and pour off the water. Pour cold water over the greens to set the color and stop the cooking process. Drain at once in a colander.

Combine the remaining ingredients in the bottom of a large salad bowl. Blend to make a smooth dressing. Add the prepared greens. Toss to coat thoroughly, then chill for 1 hour to set the flavor before serving.

By itself, cooked chickweed is a fine addition to fritters, griddle cakes, and any number of dishes. It should be eaten in moderation because of its high nitrate content.

CHICKWEED
Stellaria media

STEWED TOMATOES (serves 10)

3 pounds ripe tomatoes, cored
12 scallions, chopped (including tops)
2 green peppers, chopped
¹/₄ cup water
¹/₄ cup fine cornmeal

¹/₄ cup chopped fresh dillweed
¹/₄ cup chopped fresh basil
1 tablespoon sunflower seed butter (see page 8)

In a covered kettle, simmer the tomatoes, scallions, and peppers in the water for 40 minutes. Stir in the remaining ingredients, mixing thoroughly to break up the softened tomatoes. Simmer for another 10 minutes; serve hot.

BOILED CORN PUDDING (serves 10)

12 large ears corn, shucked
2 quarts water
¹/₄ cup nut butter (see page 9)
1¹/₂ cups fine cornmeal

1 tablespoon honey
1 teaspoon chopped fresh parsley
1 egg, beaten

Steam the ears of corn in the water in a large covered kettle for 10 minutes. Remove the corn (reserving the water), cool slightly, then trim the kernels from the cob. (Save and dry the cobs for fire starters.) Reserve the corn in a large bowl.

Mix the nut butter, cornmeal, honey, and parsley together thoroughly. Measure $^1/_2$ cup hot liquid from the corn pot and beat this into the mixture, then beat in the egg until light. Fold in the corn and mix well. Bring the corn water to a bubbling boil, the drop in the corn pudding batter by tablespoonfuls. Reduce heat and simmer, covered, for 15 minutes; drain and serve as a vegetable. This makes a good potato substitute.

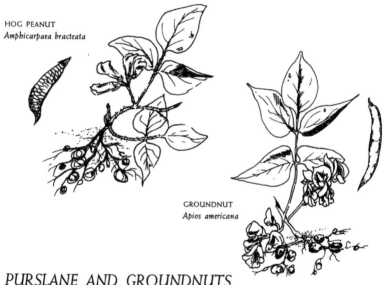

HOG PEANUT
Amphicarpaea bracteata

GROUNDNUT
Apios americana

PURSLANE AND GROUNDNUTS OR HOG PEANUTS (serves 10)

1 quart groundnuts or hog peanuts, washed
1 leek, sliced
3 cups boiling water

1 quart purslane, washed twice
2 small fresh dillweed fronds, chopped
$^1/_2$ cup sunflower seed butter (see page 8)

In a covered kettle, simmer the groundnuts and leek in the water for 20 minutes. Partially drain. Add the purslane, dill, and sunflower seed butter. Stir and blend thoroughly. Steam for 5 more minutes. Serve hot.

BAKED SWEET POTATOES (serves 6)

6 medium sweet potatoes, scrubbed and
   skins rubbed with nut oil (see
   page 7)

nut butter (see page 9)

Bake the oiled potatoes for 1 hour in a preheated 400° F oven, or in the ashes of a hot fire (turning to prevent charring). Serve with nut butter.

BAKED PUMPKIN (serves 8)

1 small pumpkin, 12 inches in diameter
2 tablespoons honey
2 tablespoons cider for seasoning

2 tablespoons nut butter (see page 9)
$\frac{1}{2}$ cup cider for basting

Place the whole washed pumpkin in a baking dish in a preheated 350° F oven for 1 $\frac{1}{2}$ hours. Remove, cool, cut a 6-inch-diameter hole in the top. Remove the pulp and seeds; save the seeds. Remove the pumpkin meat and mix with the next three ingredients; return to the shell. Replace the pumpkin top and return the pumpkin to the oven to bake, basting occasionally with additional cider, for 30 minutes more. Serve the whole pumpkin, scooping out individual portions at the table.

Toast the reserved seeds on a flat tray in a 350° F oven for 30 minutes and serve as a complement.

BAKED BUTTERNUT SQUASH (serves 8)

2 butternut squash
4 tablespoons nut butter (see page 9)
4 tablespoons honey

4 tablespoons maple syrup
nutmeg and cinnamon or vegetable or
   meat stuffing (optional)

Bake the whole washed squash in a preheated 325° F oven for about 40 minutes, or until the skins wrinkle and are easily pierced, turning once or twice. (They may be baked in the hot ashes of a fire.) Remove, cool slightly, cut in half, and scoop out the pulp and seeds. Dot each portion of squash with a dab of nut butter and drizzle with honey and maple syrup. (Season lightly with spices, if desired, or stuff with cornmeal, cooked rice, or meat mixture.) Return to the oven and bake for 30 minutes, or until tender. Serve hot. Toast the seeds on a flat tray in the same oven for 30 minutes and serve as a complement.

BEANS (*Phaseolus,* various spp.) were as highly regarded as corn by many native Americans. They carefully cultivated and hybridized as many colors as possible. Beans could vary from white and yellow to red and blue, black, magenta, purple, and multicolored. As in the variously colored corn kernels, colored beans signified the six cardinal points: north, south, east, west, zenith, and nadir.

Beans were prepared in a multitude of ways: They were soaked, flattened, and fried into cakes; served cold as salads, or in salads; simmered slowly with meats; made into spicy chilies, stews, soups; and ground and dried as flour. The most colorful varieties were dried and used in games.

BAKED BEANS (BOSTON) (serves 8)

1 pound dried red beans	1 teaspoon dried mustard
2 quarts water	1 green pepper, diced
1/2 pound salt pork, cut into 4 pieces	4 tablespoons maple sugar
1 pound dried lima beans	2 onions, quartered
1/2 cup molasses	1 cup cider

Place the beans in a large kettle, cover with water, add the salt pork, and simmer, covered, for 2 hours. Add more water as needed. Drain the beans, saving 1 cup of the cooking water. Stir the remaining ingredients into the beans; blend thoroughly.

Pour the beans into a large cooking crock and bake, covered, for 1 1/2 to 2 hours in a preheated 325° F oven. Just enough liquid should bubble up in the beans and caramelize. Serve hot.

POPCORN (yields about 2 quarts)

1/3 cup sunflower seed oil (see page 8)	1/4 cup nut or seed butter (see page 9)
1/2 cup popping corn	2 cups shelled peanuts

In a saucepan with a lid, heat the oil to the "popping point." Test by dropping in 1 kernel of corn; then add the remainder. With the lid held on securely, shake the pan until the corn stops popping. Pour immediately into a large bowl. Place the nut (or seed) butter and the peanuts in the still-warm pan and return to the heat to melt the butter and lightly coat the nuts. Toast and stir. Then pour over the popcorn and serve.

SQUASH VINE AND BLOSSOMS
Cucurbitaceae family

FRIED SQUASH (OR PUMPKIN) BLOSSOMS *(serves 8)*

1 cup milk
1 egg
1 tablespoon flour
1 teaspoon ground dried sassafras leaves
3 dozen male blossoms,* picked just
*   before they open, mashed*

½ cup oil
garnish: chopped fresh mint leaves or
*   dillweed*

Blend the milk, egg, flour, and seasoning in a bowl with a fork. Beat the batter until smooth. Place the mashed blossoms in the batter, stir gently, and allow to soak for 10 minutes. Heat the oil in a cast-iron skillet until hot. Fry the batter-coated blossoms, a few at a time, until golden, turning once. Drain on brown paper. Serve hot, garnished with mint leaves or dill.

---

*The male blossoms are the larger, infertile blossoms without an ovary (the swelling at the base of the flower).

REED GRASS (*Phragmites communis*) is one of the tallest marsh plants in North America. This perennial grass, introduced from Eurasia, played a vital role in the lives of the American Indians, as well as the colonists. The tall aerial parts of the Common Reed were used for arrow shafts, weaving, thatching, mats, and insulation; the seeds were a grain source for gruels, cereals, and breads; the early shoots were fine as a raw or cooked vegetable; and the roots and rhizomes, an excellent sugar source, were dug and roasted year-round.

PHRAGMITES GRUEL (*serves 2*)

½ cup phragmites seeds   *maple syrup or nut milk (see page 7)*
3 *wintergreen berries*   *to taste*
2 *cups boiling water*

Collect 12 to 15 seed heads of the phragmites (in late summer or autumn). Remove the tiny seeds by hand, and crush (hulls and all) with the wintergreen berries for flavor. Add to the boiling water in a medium saucepan, cover, and cook slowly until it becomes a thin, red mixture — about 30 minutes. Sweeten with maple syrup or nut milk if desired, or simply enjoy this nutritious, whole-grain cereal by itself.

ARROWHEAD, Duck Potato, Wapato, Katniss (*Sagittaria latifolia*), is a prodigious aquatic plant that was a staple food of the American Indians all across our continent. One of our most valuable native foods, arrowhead roots are delectable and nutritious, resembling new potatoes. They can be eaten raw, though they contain a bitter, milky juice that becomes sweet and tasty when the tubers are dried or cooked. Prepare these wild tubers exactly like potatoes. Dried and ground into flour, they are useful in many other food forms.

REED GRASS
Phragmites communis

CARAMELIZED ARROWHEAD TUBERS (serves 6 to 8)

25 egg-sized arrowhead tubers   8 tablespoons sunflower seed butter
½ cup maple syrup   (see page 8)

Clean the tubers and boil them (unpeeled) in a covered pot for 20 minutes or until soft. Cool and peel. Heat the maple syrup in a heavy skillet over low heat, cooking slowly so as not to burn, until it is golden brown. Stir in the sunflower seed butter and blend well. Add the tubers, rolling to coat them well. Serve hot.

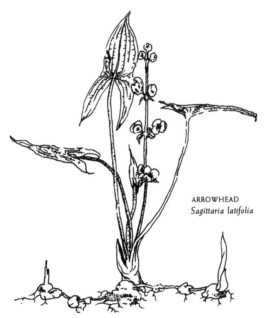

ARROWHEAD
Sagittaria latifolia

SOLOMON'S SEAL or Sealwort (*Polygonatum pubescens*). This herb is found in profusion in rich, shaded woods. Many of the New England tribes dried the spring-harvested shoots for future needs; they later taught the French and English colonists to do the same. The macerated roots and rhizomes were valued as an astringent and diuretic tonic. The Iroquois also used the thick rootstocks to pound into breads and ate the tender young shoots as spring greens and food extenders.

FALSE SOLOMON'S SEAL, False Spikenard, Scurvyberries (*Smilacina racemosa*). A widespread and graceful woodland plant favoring shaded woods and moist environments, false Solomon's seal provides a healthful and re-

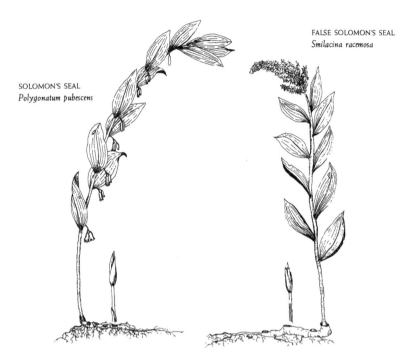

SOLOMON'S SEAL
Polygonatum pubescens

FALSE SOLOMON'S SEAL
Smilacina racemosa

freshing trailside nibble. The Indians used the entire plant throughout its growing season. The young shoots may be enjoyed as steamed asparagus in early spring; the young leaves, before blossomtime, are excellent in raw salads or lightly steamed as a potherb; the aromatic and starchy rootstocks may be cooked like potatoes or pickled. (To rid the rootstocks of their bitter taste, they should first be soaked for several hours in water and wood ashes, then rinsed and boiled in fresh water for 30 minutes to eliminate the lye.)

INDIAN CUCUMBER or Cucumber Root (*Medeola virginiana*) is a slender, perennial woodland herb and a delicious vegetable. It is principally sought for its crisp, starchy rootstock, which has the delicate taste of cucumber. Enjoyed raw in salads, as a lone vegetable, or pickled, this plant was used by numerous tribes. Harvest sparingly and only when found growing in abundance.

There are many plants native to this continent but not necessarily acclimatized to the Northeast that cannot be overlooked. Their importance to us in the twentieth century is heightened when we reflect on their centuries of usefulness to the Amerindians.

PRICKLY PEAR, Indian Fig, Beavertail, Devil's Tongue, Tuna (*Opuntia vulgaris* and var. spp.). These common broad-leafed spiny cacti are hardy and acclimatized from coast to coast. The fruits that form after the showy yellow blossoms were enjoyed in many cultures; they are still seasonal favorites in many parts of the country and are high in calcium. They are enjoyed fresh in salads, chopped in omelettes and stews, and in juices, jellies, and pickles.

NIGHT-BLOOMING CEREUS, Deerhorn Cactus, Christ-in-the-cradle, Reina de la Noche (*Peniocereus greggii*). This huge, plain cactus is cultivated today essentially for its large, showy white blossoms with special fragrance that open only after sundown, each for one night's duration. Across most of the Southwest to Mexico, this rangy plant is found growing among the creosote shrubs. The Amerindians dug these large roots to bake or boil as a starchy vegetable.

NIGHT-BLOOMING CEREUS BLOSSOM
Peniocereus greggii

JOJOBA, Coffee Bush, Wild Hazel, Goat Nut, Deer Nut (*Simmondsia californica*). This southern evergreen shrub favors dry, coarse desert soils, and as a native botanical cultivar of the southern tribes it has an impressive number of uses. This leathery-leafed bush produces acornlike nuts that have been food, medicine, and beverage material for the Amerindians for centuries. These fruits are almost 50 percent oil, and this oil is of enormous commercial value.

Botanical Charts

Caution: A few of these plants might be found growing in the company of toxic near-look-alikes. Do not mistake any other wild lilies for the edible daylily, and do not mistake the poisonous dogbane for milkweed.

Never take all of the plants growing in one area.

Key: *Harvesttime:*   *Usage*
        Sp = *Spring*   *F* = *Food*
        S = *Summer*   *T* = *Technology*
        F = *Fall*   *C* = *Charm*
        W = *Winter*   *D* = *Dye*
                    B = *Beverage*
                    M = *Medicine*

Note: All season here refers to the typical growing seasons of these particular plants, which vary across the country. The plant parts dictate their own harvesttime.

I. Wild Vegetables and Flavorings (Raw)

These plants are delightful additions to salads and delicious to eat or nibble without cooking. Remember that their nutritive value is at its maximum when they are eaten very shortly after picking.

Plant	Plant Part Used	Usage	Harvesttime
1. Barberry	leaves, berries	M, B, D, F	Sp
2. Blackberry	shoots & leaves	M, B, F	All year
3. Brooklime	leaves, stems	M, F	Sp, S
4. Burdock	leaves, leaf stalks	F	Sp, S
5. Calamus	shoots	M, F	Sp
6. Catbrier	shoots, leaves	B, F	Sp, S
7. Cattail	shoots, stems, pollen	T, B, F	Sp, S
8. Chickweed	leaves	F	Sp, S, F
9. Chicory	leaves	B, F	Sp
10. Chive, Wild	leaves	M, F	All season
11. Cleavers	shoots	T, B, F	Sp
12. Clover	leaves, blossoms	M, B, F	All season
13. Coriander	leaves, seeds	F	All season
14. Dandelion	leaves, blossoms	M, B, F	Sp
15. Daylily	tubers, blossoms	F	All season
16. Dewberry	shoots, leaves	M, B	Sp, S
17. Dill	leaves, seeds	M, F	All season
18. Garlic, Wild	leaves, bulbs	M, F	All year
19. Great Bulrush	shoots, pollen	T, F	Sp, S

Plant	Plant Part Used	Usage	Harvesttime
20. Horseradish	young leaves	M, F	Sp
21. Indian Cucumber	roots	F	All season
22. Jerusalem Artichoke	tubers	F	F
23. Lamb's Quarters	leaves, seeds	F	All season
24. Leek, Wild	bulbs, leaves	F	Sp
25. Milkweed	young sprouts	T, M	Sp
26. Mint, Wild	leaves	C, M, B, F	All season
27. Mustard, Wild Black	leaves	F	Sp
28. Nasturtium	leaves, buds, blossoms	F	All season
29. Onion, Wild	bulbs, greens	M, D, F	All season
30. Pasture Brake Fern	fiddlehead	C, F	Early Sp
31. Pennyroyal	leaves	M, B, F	All season
32. Purslane	leaves, stalks	F	All season
33. Raspberry	shoots, leaves	M, B, F	All season
34. Rose	blossoms, hips	C, M, B, F	All season
35. Sheep Sorrel	leaves	F	Sp
36. Shepherd's Purse	leaves	F	Sp, S
37. Thistle	leaves	T, F	Sp
38. Violet	leaves, blossoms	M, F	Sp, S
39. Watercress	leaves, shoots	F	All season
40. Winter Cress	leaves, shoots	F	All season
41. Wood Sorrel	leaves, blossoms	F	All season

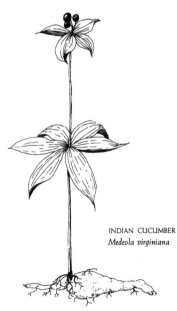

INDIAN CUCUMBER
Medeola virginiana

II. Wild Vegetables (Steamed)

The shoots, leaves, and plant parts of these wild potherbs should be served like spinach or asparagus. The young leaves and shoots at the tops of the stems are the mildest and tenderest. These should be rinsed in cold water and steamed in a minimum of plain or lightly seasoned water. *Do not overcook.* These are delicious dressed with natural vinegars and nut oils or butters.

Plant	Plant Part Used	Harvesttime
1. Bracken Fern	fiddlehead	Early Sp
2. Brooklime	leaves, stems	Sp, S
3. Catbrier	leaves, stems	Sp, S
4. Cattail	shoots, flowers	Sp, S
5. Chickweed	whole plant	Sp, S
6. Cleavers	shoots	Sp
7. Coltsfoot	leaves	Sp, S
8. Dandelion	leaves, buds	Sp
9. Daylily	buds, blossoms, tubers	All season
10. Ferns	fiddleheads	Early Sp
11. Green Amaranth	leaves, shoots	Sp, S
12. Horseradish	young leaves	Sp
13. Lamb's Quarters	leaves, shoots	All season
14. Milkweed	buds, blossoms, tiny pods	Sp, S
15. Mint	leaves, buds	All season
16. Plantain	young leaves	Sp
17. Purslane	leaves, shoots, stems	All season
18. Sheep Sorrel	leaves	Until late S
19. Thistle	leaves, stems (stripped)	Sp, S
20. Violet	blossoms, leaves	Sp
21. Watercress	leaves, shoots	All year
22. Wild Onion	bulbs, greens	All season

III. Wild Vegetables (Well Cooked)

Certain plants require more preparation and should be cooked in two or more changes of water. Longer cooking times help modify their bitterness or stronger flavor. Some botanicals contain poisonous substances that are soluble in the cooking water, destroyed by heat, and thrown away in the necessary water changes. Tougher, stringier plants, such as burdock, chicory and poke, can be tenderized by adding a pinch of bicarbonate of soda (or wood ashes) to the *first* cooking water. Though the vitamin content is minimized by such preparations, essential minerals do remain.

Plant	Plant Part Used	Harvesttime
1. Burdock	roots, stems, leaves	Sp, S
2. Chicory	leaves	Sp
3. Dandelion	roots, leaves	S
4. Jewelweed	shoots, leaves	Early Sp
5. Mallow	leaves, fruits	Sp, S
6. Marsh Marigold	leaves	Sp
7. Milkweed	shoots	Early Sp
8. Mustard	leaves	Sp
9. Nettle	tops, leaves	Sp, S
10. Ostrich Fern	fiddlehead	Early Sp
11. Pokeweed	shoots, leaves	Early Sp
12. Salsify	roots, leaves	All season
13. Shepherd's Purse	leaves	Sp, S
14. Winter Cress	leaves, stalks	All year

BURDOCK
Arctium lappa

IV. Natural Flours and Flour Extenders

Any of the following botanicals may be dehydrated and ground to make flour. The tastiest and most nutritious wild flours are those prepared from nutmeats. Seeds of the various botanicals can easily be used to make flour as well as cereals, gruels, and puddings.

The finest flour in nature, which needs no sifting or refining, is cattail and bulrush pollen. However, its fineness also makes it very hard to wet, so it is easier to mix the pollen with a greater portion of other flour.

Plant	Plant Part Used	Harvesttime
1. Acorn	nutmeats	F, S
2. Arrowhead	tubers	F, S
3. Beech	nuts	F
4. Black Walnuts	nuts	F
5. Butternut	nuts	F
6. Cattail	roots, pollen	All year (midsummer)
7. Corn	seeds	S, F
8. Daylily	tubers	S, F
9. Dock	seeds	F
10. Great Bulrush	roots, pollen, seeds	S, F
11. Green Amaranth	seeds	S, F
12. Groundnuts	tubers	S, F
13. Hazelnuts	nuts	F
14. Hickory	nuts	F
15. Jerusalem Artichoke	tubers	F
16. Lamb's Quarters	seeds	F
17. Potato	tubers	F
18. Purslane	seeds	F
19. Shepherd's Purse	seeds	F
20. Sunflower	seeds	F
21. Wild Leek	bulbs, greens	Sp
22. Wild Rice	seeds	F
23. Yellow Pond Lily	tubers	F

IV

NATIVE
FERNS,
LICHENS,
AND
MOSSES

"May we now gather our minds together as one and give greetings and thanks to the plant life for giving us food and medicine."

. . . OHONTEHSHON: 'A . . . from the Mohawk Thanksgiving Address,
Akwesasne Freedom School

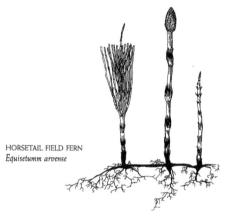

HORSETAIL FIELD FERN
Equisetumm arvense

Wild Ferns, lichens, liverworts, mosses, and ground pines represent some of the oldest plants on our planet. These non-flowering plants were the earliest colonizers of the land. They continue to bring us a mineral-rich earthiness for countless lifeways needs.

Ferns

One of the first green edible plants in spring is the newly emerging fiddleheads (curled crosiers) of ferns. High in oil and starch, this fine delicate vegetable is always best picked early in the day while fresh-flavored and when the long-stemmed crosiers snap crisply in your hand. The same fronds would be overgrown by afternoon. In New England, the fiddlehead season lasts only about 3 weeks in May, depending on the weather.

The Indians used more than twenty species of indigenous ferns as food. In early spring the new fiddleheads were gathered and enjoyed raw or cooked as a vegetable or simmered in soups and stews for their thicking qualities. Brought to a boil and then simmered for 30 minutes, the young, slender stalks can be seasoned and served as a delectable asparaguslike vegetable. The rhizomes are also an important food source: Roasted or baked, then ground Indian fashion, the fern roots can be worked with other substances into cakes or gruels, or

BRACKEN FERN
Pteridium aquilinum

dried and used as flour for breads. The rhizomes of bracken are best utilized this way. The older, full-grown fronds of most species are slightly toxic and inedible. Grazing animals have been poisoned by eating too many fern fronds.

Never harvest more than half of the fiddleheads from any cluster!

BRACKEN, Pasture Brake, Eagle Fern *(Pteridium aquilinum)*. This is our common, most widespread fern, rising singly from long, slender rhizomes in dry, sandy soils. The small fiddleheads are distinctly three-forked, easily picked and cleaned, and delicious raw, especially in salads. Lightly steamed, these fiddleheads are excellent pickled or used with other vegetables. The Indians pounded the rootstocks into flour for bread. *Caution:* The raw plant contains an enzyme that can destroy vitamin B_1 (thiamine). Do not eat it in large quantities.

CINNAMON FERN *(Osmunda cinnamomea)*. This tall, graceful fern of the swamps and moist woodlands was gathered as a favored spring potherb by many East Coast tribes for their soups and meat stews. Gather when about 8 inches tall; the crosier plus 2 inches of stem are desirable. Thoroughly wash and remove the bronze woolly covering (used by the Indians as an absorbent dressing for open sores and wounds). This species of fiddlehead is somewhat dry in texture and needs complementary seasonings.

HORSETAIL FIELD FERN, Scouring Rush, Shave Brush, Pewterwort, Mare's Tail *(Equisetum arvense* and 2 spp.). These dwarf survivors of the carboniferous woodlands seem to thrive in any soil. Three major tribes record distinct food usage of this fern. The Hopis dried and ground the stems with cornmeal and ate the mixture as gruel or baked it into a pone bread.

The stems contain silica, and the plant structure is abrasive enough to make this an excellent pot scrubber and equally good for brightening gunstocks and pewter. An interesting yellow-gray dye is created from the stalks.

As a spring food the young emerging stalks can be treated like asparagus. They are a rather pallid but mineral-rich early vegetable, known to be toxic and poisonous in sufficient amounts to livestock. The bitter taste of this wilderness food is removed when boiled in two to three changes of water.

Perhaps the horsetail's most beneficial use is as an astringent to wash and stop the bleeding of external wounds. Thus, a decoction made from boiling the stems into a body lotion is possibly their best recipe.

OSTRICH FERN *(Matteuccia struthiopteris)*. One of our largest ferns and very common in the East, the ostrich fern favors the rich, alluvial soil of river and stream banks and swamps. Two or three fern clusters can supply enough fiddleheads for a meal; *no more than half of the emerging crosiers are required*. These large, easy-to-clean fiddleheads may be enjoyed raw in salads or slightly steamed for 10 minutes.

SENSITIVE FERN, Bead Fern *(Onoclea sensibilis)*. This widespread common fern favors damp environments. The prolific pale reddish-green fiddleheads were spring favorites of the Iroquois, who also gathered and ate the rhizomes in lean times. The classic beaded fertile frond is this fern's hallmark. These beaded fronds are attractive in dried harvest arrangements.

SALSIFY
Tragopogon porrifolius

FIDDLEHEADS AND SALSIFY ROOTS (serves 6 to 8)

2 dozen salsify roots, peeled
¹/₂ cup boiling water
4 dozen ostrich fiddleheads
1 tablespoon cider vinegar
1 tablespoon sunflower seed oil (see
*   page 8)*

Place the salsify roots in a medium
pot. Cover with the water; add the
fiddleheads and the remaining
ingredients, and stir thoroughly.
Simmer, covered, for 10 minutes more.
Serve hot, or marinate further and serve
cold. A tasty and exciting vegetable
combination!

FIDDLEHEAD STEW (serves 8)

4 dozen fiddleheads
2 cups boiling water
1 teaspoon nut oil (see page 7)
¹/₂ cup nut butter (see page 9)

In a medium pot, cover the fiddleheads
with the water and nut oil. Reduce heat
and simmer, covered, for 20 minutes, or
until tender. Top with nut butter to
enhance the flavor, and serve hot, either
alone or on a nest of wild rice or
cornmeal (grits).

ROASTED RHIZOMES
OF BRACKEN FERN (serves 6)

Gather 18 good rhizomes of bracken; scrub, wash, and peel. Bake like potatoes in hot coals for 30 minutes. Serve hot. Virginia Indians used hickory ashes as seasonings for these wild vegetables.

ICELAND MOSS ·
Cetraria islandica

Lichens

Many species of lichens contain rock-dissolving bitter acids, which tend to be cathartic to the system when ingested. To lessen this cathartic quality somewhat and to enhance the edibility of certain species, soak the lichens for several hours or overnight. Change the water three or four times and add 1 tablespoon wood ashes (see page 4) or baking soda per pot.

Though lichens appear rather drab, dry, and forbidding, growing as they do in seemingly sterile ground or on rocks and tree barks, several notable species have been important survival foods for people and animals. Contemporary evidence indicates that the "manna from heaven" of biblical accounts was a form of lichen blown free from its rocky habitats and swirled into the valleys. Two species, *Lecanora affinis* and *L. esculenta*, are still eaten by desert tribes, and records confirm the extraordinary circumstances of these lichens providing food for large numbers of people and their herds of sheep or cattle. This type of occurrence has repeated itself at various times and in diverse areas throughout recorded history; at times large areas have been covered with a grayish-white layer of bitter, irregular "clumps," from 3 to 6 inches thick. Lichens were utilized by the American Indians throughout prehistory.

Lichens have various medicinal properties that have proved beneficial to many Indian tribes, and as a noteworthy dye base the lichens have produced dozens of lovely soft colors.

ICELAND MOSS *(Cetraria islandica)*. A common northern lichen, Iceland moss is found growing in broad-cushioned mats of olive green to purple, which pale to gray as they dry. The paper-thin branching growth prefers sandy soil and colder, more exposed terrain. It has long been sought as a medicinal and nutritive tonic to relieve bronchial problems. This lichen contains a large amount of starch, which is soluble in boiling water and gelatinizes on cooling. Aside from its nutritive value it improves both the appetite and digestion.

Iceland moss is used as flour and in soups, puddings, blancmange, and medicines.

ICELAND MOSS JELLY

Gather 2 cups Iceland moss and wash. Place in a pot, cover with 2 cups boiling water, cover the pot, and let stand for 3 hours. Stir, strain, and sweeten to taste with honey or maple syrup. Up to 1 pound fresh wild berries or $\frac{1}{2}$ cup citrus peel may be added. For children, the jelly may be boiled briefly in milk for greater palatability.

REINDEER MOSS *(Cladonia rangiferina* and spp.) is another common northern lichen forming large irregular carpets on sandy ground. The antler-like branchlets of silvery gray are hollow; they are rubbery and spongy when wet and brittle when dry. This appealing lichen has had many noteworthy uses since prerecorded time in soups, gruels, and blancmange. In a dried, powdered form it may be used like cornstarch and baked as bread.

Northern Indian tribes depended upon this food source for their winter survival. Caribou and reindeer continue to do so.

REINDEER MOSS
Cladonia rangiferina

CLUB-MOSS
Lycopodium clavatum

Mosses

CLUB-MOSSES (*Lycopodiaceae* family). This is one of the oldest plant groups, dating back perhaps three hundred million years. These dwarf spore-producing evergreens perennially spread by running rootstocks in dense woodland carpets. Many club-mosses have erect spore-bearing structures, which produce water-resistant spores. These have been used as dusting powder to prevent skin chafing, to treat eczema, and especially to dust on open wounds. High flammable, the spores have also been used in small fireworks and in photographic flashes.

Considered inedible, the club-mosses have significant medicinal and technological benefits. They seem to mirror the appearance of the pines, hemlocks, and cedars they so often grow beneath. Of the more than one hundred species, the most common North American ones are profiled here.

CLUB-MOSS, Vegetable Sulphur, Wolf's Claw, Stag's Horn Moss (*Lycopodium clavatum*). The Indians inhaled the yellowish spores to stop nosebleed and considered the plant a diuretic.

CHRISTMAS CLUB-MOSS, Running Cedar, Ground Pine (*Lycopodium complanatum*). Pale green and delicately spreading, this species was collected for decorative roping and ornamentation and was used as well in treatment of diarrhea, dropsy, and scurvy.

FIR CLUB-MOSS or Mountain Club-moss *(Lycopodium selago)*. A northern mountain species used medicinally as an emetic and sedative, and externally as an insect repellent on animals.

TREE CLUB-MOSS or Princess Pine *(Lycopodium obscurum)* is a multibranched miniature pine tree in appearance. The stems and leaves were used as mordants to fix dyes in woolens.

V

WILD
MUSHROOMS

"The life that we have asked and obtained from the creator, this we shall put to good use. It is ours, He has put us in control of it. Remember that Earthmaker put the means of obtaining the goods of life in control of every single spirit he created."

. . . from the Winnebago Medicine Society initiation, 1945

The fungi are unique and powerful plants in all their various forms: mushrooms, molds, blights, and rusts. They can feed and cure us, as well as induce visions and kill us. Those that are safe to eat make a nutritious and delectable vegetable group and are sought for their many flavors and textures. They are a fine addition to any meal, year-round. Wild mushrooms are rich in folic acid and are a particularly good source of B vitamins; when mushrooms are grown in light, vitamin D becomes quite abundant. Because some fungi are deadly, only a favored few are profiled here. Many edible varieties were eaten raw or cooked by the American Indians.

As a precaution, the beginner should avoid all wild mushrooms until proper identification can be made.

1. Start with a simple list of species and an excellent mushroom guide. *Identify carefully and thoroughly!*
2. When collecting several species at a time, *keep each type separate.* One poisonous Amanita can make the entire batch of edible species deadly.
3. Use only fresh, healthy mushrooms in order to avoid food poisoning. If you can't use them right away, they may be stored in an uncovered container in the refrigerator for up to 24 hours.
4. You might be allergic to some species. Even though a new mushroom seems absolutely delectable, eat only a small portion (no more than 1/4 cup) and wait at least 24 hours to be sure there are no side effects. When first trying a new mushroom, sauté in nut butter (see page 9) or scramble with an egg to savor its flavor.

COMMON MOREL
Morchella esculenta

COMMON MOREL or Sponge Morel (*Morchella esculenta*); BLACK MOREL (*M. augusticeps*). The deeply pitted spongelike cap is fused to the stem at the lower end (unlike the poisonous false morels, whose caps hang skirtlike around the stem). Favoring orchards, moist woods, and especially burned fields, the common morel is found throughout the northeastern United States. It is most common in May after heavy spring rains. The pale tan to grayish cap is oval to cone-shaped, and the entire growth is hollow inside. The stem is tall, stout, creamy, and often furrowed. Excellent stuffed or cut in long slices and sautéed briefly in nut oil (see page 7).

FAIRY RING MUSHROOM (*Marasmius oreades*) is a small, cap-shaped mushroom, white to pale yellow-brown, on a slender stem. The cap is broad, smooth, and moist; the flesh is thick and creamy pink to tan; the gills are broad and creamy white; the stem is long. Common in grassy areas where it often forms neat circles, it may be gathered June to September throughout most of the United States. It is quite a popular vegetable, with a delicious taste and fragrance. Fairy ring caps have a very choice flavor and dry well for preservation as distinctive food additives. Enjoy careful harvesting when this delectable species is found, and with proper irrigation the same area will produce mushrooms all summer.

MEADOW MUSHROOMS (*Agaricus campestris, A. arvensis*). The most common mushroom found in open pastures and lawns, the meadow mushroom is *never found in the woods*. These short, white to brown mushrooms were enjoyed by numerous tribes. The cap surface is silky and dry; the flesh is soft white to pale pink; the gills are free and crowded; the stem is short.

This species is a close relative to the commercially grown mushroom, and the flavor is similar. They may be collected June through October, although like most wild mushrooms they are best in late summer with the early fall rains. Excellent raw, marinated, or sautéed with eggs or rice.

MEADOW MUSHROOM
Agaricus campestris

OYSTER MUSHROOM (*Pleurotus ostreatus*). The delicious oyster-gray convex cap may be gathered through late fall into December in the Northeast, though the earlier, younger mushrooms are the most tender. Found in clusters attached to deciduous trees (usually elm, oak, beech, birch, or maple), these mushrooms have lilac spores, white, broad, radiating gills, and almost no stem. ANGEL WINGS (*Pleurotus porrigens*) are very similar to oyster mushrooms and are found in the same places; their caps and spores are white. Excellent sautéed or in stews, both mushrooms taste much like scrambled eggs.

OYSTER MUSHROOM
Pleurotus ostreatus

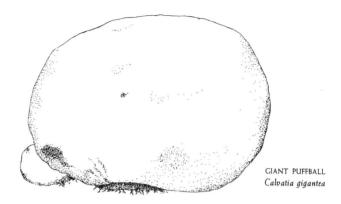

GIANT PUFFBALL
Calvatia gigantea

PUFFBALLS, Giant (*Calvatia gigantea*), are large, usually smooth, balloon-shaped mushrooms growing directly from the ground. Eight to fifteen inches in diameter and white when young, puffballs are found in the rich, disturbed soil of barnyards, pastures, and lawns. They grow singly or in clusters throughout the United States. *Warning:* Be sure the interior flesh is *pure white*, indicating it is fresh; if yellowish, the mushroom will be bitter. Discard if the inside shows a shadowy mushroom form or gills, which indicate that it may be the poisonous Amanita.*

Zunis gathered great quantities of puffballs to eat fresh or to dry for the winter. Many tribes cut this species into chunks and fried it like meat. All puffballs are edible in the young stage while the flesh is white; peel before cooking and prepare as you would cultivated mushrooms. Puffballs are one of the safest groups of fungi to harvest; one genus, *Scleroderma*, may cause slight sickness.

Some additional family members are: SKULL-SHAPED PUFFBALL (*Calvatia craniiformis*), PAPERY PUFFBALL (*Bovista pila*), CUP-SHAPED PUFFBALL (*Calvatia cynthiformis*), GEMMED PUFFBALL (*Lycoperdon perlatum*).

EDIBLE PUFFBALL

IMMATURE
POISONOUS AMANITA

*See the Reference Guide for suitable mushroom guidebooks. *Foraging for Wild Edible Mushrooms*, by Karen and Richard Haard, is especially useful.

SHAGGY MANE or Ink Cap (*Coprinus comatus*). When newly formed, this delicious, prolific mushroom resembles a closed, shingled umbrella and ing, self-digesting enzymes turn it into a black, inky mess. When a scaly; the flesh is white; the gills are white, free, and crowded; the stem is long. Found in lawns, waste places, and roadsides throughout the United States, it is a showy member of the ink cap group; upon ripening, self-digesting enzymes turn it into a black, inky mess. When a group of shaggy manes or ink caps is found, they should be harvested as soon as the dew dries in early morning. To wait until evening on a warm summer or fall day would be wasteful, for the mushrooms are likely to ripen and become inedible. They make an excellent cooked vegetable.

SULPHUR SHELF (*Polyporus sulphureus*) or CHICKEN-OF-THE-WOODS (*Laetiporus sulphureus*) are the same species and the latter Latin name is the correct current one. They are found in dry, open woods, throughout North America, on dead on injured deciduous trees. They grow in large, many-leveled yellow to orange brackets (shelves) with tiny pores on the underside. The cap is yellow to orange, broad, smooth, and fluted; the flesh is white; the pores are a sulphur-yellow. Harvest the tender outer portions in late summer and early fall. This mushroom is one of the finest edible mushrooms. Requiring longer cooking than most, this firm-textured species has the consistency of chicken breast meat when sliced and sautéed or simmered 30 minutes. Excellent in potages and casseroles.

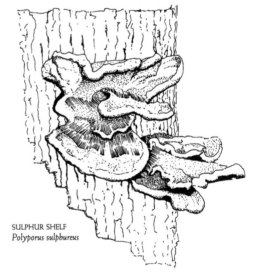

SULPHUR SHELF
Polyporus sulphureus

The Hen-of-the-Woods, (*Grifola frondosa*), is another ubiquitous polypore also known as the Maitake*, "The Dancing Mushroom" in Japan where enthusiasm for finding this specimen made people dance for joy – realizing that they could get a lot of money for this delicious healing mushroom. An amazingly generous mushroom, it is called *Grifone* in Italy, where knowledgeable mushroom gatherers realize this great food source can provide many meals.

The "Hen" is a closely-related cousin of the "Chicken" in the large Polypore family of fungi. Yet, the "Hen" looks entirely different, being a large clustered mass of fleshy gray-brown "petals" or spoon-shaped flutes branching out from a large whitish-gray base. This spectacular mushroom mass can grow to nearly 100-pounds per specimen in our northeastern woods. I have seen such specimens which can provide enough food for some families for the entire winter. This 'shroom looks almost like an exploded giant cauliflower growing at the base of some deciduous trees.

Today, scientific tests prove the anti-cancer, anti-diabetes, anti-tumor, anti-HIV/AIDS capacities in the Maitake are exciting, and this may surpass the legendary Shitake in overall health benefits, according to Japanesse research. Scientists have identified a polysaccharide compound which stimulates cellular immune activity. Many people take capsules of this dried mushroom as a potent adaptogen and tonic for health and longevity. Our ancestors simply ate it and saved it for reliable winter uses, as it is a tasty meat-substitute. Perhaps, this 'shroom is a powerful preventive medicine bringing the mineral-rich complexities from the forest into new healing light.

Many mushrooms, like these last two, are even better-tasting after they are dried - revealing a wholesome fragrance and rich taste. These are great meat-substitutes, and some seem to mimic the taste and fragrance of certain favorite meats, like the various chicken mushrooms, the tree oysters, the robust lobster, and beefsteak 'shrooms, and so many, many others.

One of the most common and attractive fungi found throughout North America on dead trees is the Turkey-tail, (*Trametes versicolor*), which is also a Polypore. These multicolored zoned, wavy, thin leathery growths are usually overlapping. They are also known as

---

*There is a corporation by this name in New Jersey devoted to bringing this prodigious healing mushroom into broad medical use.

Polyporus and *Coriolus versicolor,* according to noted mycologist Gary Lincoff. *Trametes* means "flesh" or "fabric," and these basal rosettes often appear like beautifully fluted fabric emerging from the host organism. Some are velvety.

These fungi have long been reliably cooked as survival foods, yet we woodland hikers just pick them and chew them like long-lasting gum as we walk through the woods. They have a wonderfully earthy taste. Our enthusiasm for these fungi continues to grow – based upon the growing body of scientific evidence that they are strongly anti-cancer, anti-AIDS, anti-diabetes, plus immuno-strengthening – especially in Japanese tests! Scientists are finding that these water-soluble fungi can even enhance the anticancer effects of chemotherapy drugs. These fungi are also being used to successfully treat "hepatitis, herpes, general immune suppression, and post-surgical recovery," according to scientific studies published by JHS Natural Products in Eugene, Oregon.

Perhaps, the most unique 'shroom in Indian America was and is the Corn Smut fungus or Maize Mushroom, (*Ustilago maydis*), which appears, as a wind-blown parasite, on ripening kernels of corn. When young (immature) and pearly gray-white, this is a delicious much-sought-after food, especially in the southwest and Mexico. This is the sacred *Huitolacoche* of the Maya. As this 'shroom darkens (ripening fully), it becomes a powerful medicinal substance which was used by Native midwives to speed and ease childbirth labor and to treat selective ailments and for ceremonial applications.

More than 60 different species of medicinal mushrooms are clinically used in Traditional East Asian Medicine (TEAM), and quite a few of these are currently applied throughout American complementary medicine channels. Most of these medicinal 'shrooms, and many more than we could know and name here, were used in American Indian healing strategies.

Cooking Wild Mushrooms

Preparation begins in the field with clean collecting habits. Brush off any dirt or debris and avoid wetting or mixing collections. Remember that water can spoil some mushrooms after harvesting, so wash only when truly necessary. Because mushrooms deteriorate rapidly, they should be cleaned and par-boiled as soon as possible after collection.

For best natural flavor and texture, never overcook or overspice mushrooms. Indeed, the raw mushroom retains a delicate flavor and aroma that often change or dissipate in cooking.

An excellent use of raw sliced mushrooms is in a savory wild-salad bowl. A natural next step is to marinate the fresh mushrooms. *If they are left covered and at room temperature,* the deterioration of the wild mushrooms by bacteria may quickly lead to food poisoning.

Another **note of caution:** certain mushrooms, like the *Coprinus* family and the Honeys, (*Armillarias* spp.), can cause nausea and sickness when mixed with alcohol. Enjoying a dish of finely prepared mushrooms with a glass of wine or beer might produce disagreeable aftermaths for some folks. Not everyone experiences this, yet those who do, find it quite unpleasant.

MARINATED MUSHROOMS
AND WILD LEEKS (serves 8 to 10)

4 cups fresh, firm mushrooms (shaggy   ½ cup sunflower seed oil (see page 8)
    manes, meadow mushrooms, etc.)   1 tablespoon chopped fresh parsley
2 cups wild leek bulbs   1 teaspoon dillseed
½ cup cider vinegar

Simmer the mushrooms and leeks in a small amount of boiling water for 5 minutes. Drain, cool, and place in a crock or glass jar. Cover with the remaining ingredients blended into a sauce and store in the refrigerator, loosely covered, for 24 hours or more before serving.

PICKLED MUSHROOMS (serves 8 to 10)

1 cup of water   1 teaspoon crumbled dried bayberry
1 cup cider vinegar   leaves
1 teaspoon coltsfoot ashes, optional (see   1 tablespoon flavored pickling spices
    page 27)   4 cups steamed wild mushrooms, drained
1 small onion, diced   (use about 6 cups raw mushrooms)

Combine all ingredients (except the mushrooms) and simmer, covered, for 5 minutes. Remove from heat and cool. Place the mushrooms in a large glass jar and strain the pickling broth over them; cover the jar and refrigerate for 24 hours or more before serving. These should keep safely in the refrigerator for days.

SAUTÉED MUSHROOMS (serves 8 to 10)

4 tablespoons nut oil (see page 7)
    or nut butter (see page 9)
2 teaspoons lemon juice
1/2 teaspoon coltsfoot ashes, optional (see page 27)
1/2 teaspoon chopped fresh wild marjoram
1/2 teaspoon wild mustard seeds
5 cups fresh mushrooms, sliced

Warm the nut oil (or nut butter) and lemon juice in a broad cast-iron skillet. Add the remaining ingredients and sauté over medium heat for barely 5 minutes, or until tender. Serve warm to complement any meal.

MEADOW MUSHROOM PIE (serves 8 to 10)

3 cups fresh meadow mushrooms, chopped
3 tablespoons nut butter (see page 9)
1 egg, beaten
4 cups mashed potatoes
2 tablespoons chopped fresh dillweed
1 tablespoon coltsfoot ashes, optional (see page 27)
1 tablespoon chopped fresh parsley
1 tablespoon chopped onion
1/2 cup water
1/4 cup fine cornmeal

Sauté the mushrooms in the nut butter until golden — about 5 minutes. Combine the egg and mashed potato and press to cover the bottom and sides of a deep baking dish evenly. Blend 1 tablespoon of the dill, the coltsfoot ashes, the parsley, the onion, and the water with the mushrooms and gently turn the mixture into the potato crust. Sprinkle the top with the cornmeal and additional dill. Bake in a preheated 375° F oven for 30 minutes. Serve hot.

SHAGGY MANE
Coprinus comatus

SHAGGY MANE PIE (serves 6 to 8)

4 cups large fresh shaggy manes, caps
  only
4 cups fine cornmeal
1 cup cattail flour (see page 66)

2 tablespoons chopped fresh chives
¼ cup nut oil (see page 7)
4 eggs, beaten

Cut the mushroom caps into ½-inch slices, place in a pot, and almost cover with water. Bring to a boil and simmer, covered, for 10 minutes. Remove from heat and cool in the broth. Mix together the cornmeal, cattail flour, and chives. Grease a glass baking dish or crock with some of the nut oil and alternately layer the mushrooms with the flour mixture. Cover with the eggs, drizzle the remaining nut oil over the top, and bake in a preheated 375° F oven until set — about 40 minutes.

Preserving Wild Mushrooms

Although many mushroom enthusiasts follow the "black bear" approach of eating fresh mushrooms in abundance, wild mushrooms may be kept by freezing, canning, and drying. The latter is the simplest method and is especially good for those species put by for use in soups, gravies, casseroles, and sauces.

Do not wash mushrooms that will be dried. Brush off the dirt and trim; large ones should be cut in half and sliced into ½-inch segments, or you may chop them. Spread the pieces to dry away from sunlight in any clean, ventilated setting. Keep the pieces from touching (as you would any herbs and fruits in the drying process).

Alberto C. Meloni, Executive Director of The Institute for American Indian Studies in Washington, CT holding a fresh-harvested 36-pound "Hen of the Woods" Mushroom (*Grifola frondosa*), called "Grifone" in Italy, and the "Maitake" in Japan. This delicious meaty mushroom is quite sought-after because of its anti-cancer, anti-tumor, anti-diabetes, anti-HIV benefits. Only in North America can a specimen sometimes grow to be 100 pounds! Young students in an IAIS summer camp were treated to many gourmet preparations of this mushroom.

Ruth & Dan Cippolla beaming over a 20-pound specimen of the "Chicken of the Woods" or Sulphur Shelf mushroom (*Laetiporous sulfurus*), another meaty delicious Polypore. More than 50 pounds of this fungi were harvested from one fallen tree one early September morning. This, too, is a gourmet delight!

Maize Mushroom (*Ustilago maydis*), a most delicious delicacy when under-ripe (young). An ancient ceremonial food of the Mayas and Aztec Peoples. Corn: the sacred and robust "gold of the Americas" – in so many various colors, forms, and tastes.

Squash blossom stew, baked beans, wild rice, pollen, juniper berries, plus goldenrod, mountain mint, and pennyroyal for teas.

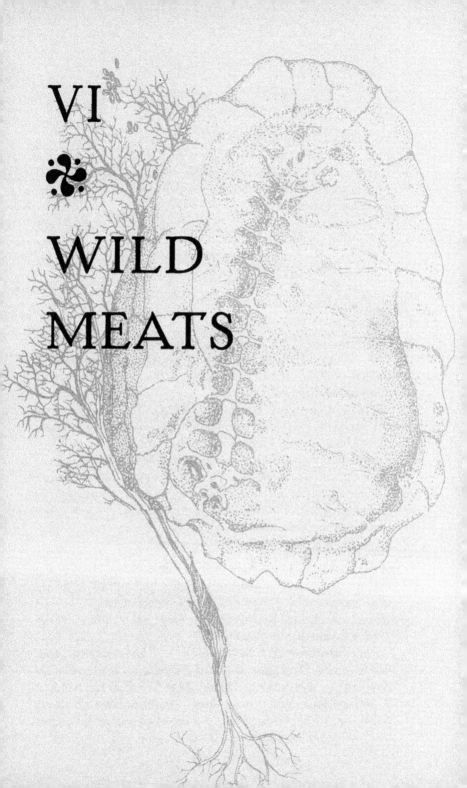

VI

WILD
MEATS

". . . our fathers had plenty of deer and skins, our plains were full of deer, as also our woods, and of turkies, and our coves full of fish and fowl. But these English having gotten our land, they with scythes cut down the grass, and with axes fell the trees; their cows and horses eat the grass, and their hogs spoil our clam banks, and we shall all be starved."

. . . Miantonoma, Narragansett, 1642

It is essential that wild game be prepared properly for cooking. The animal should be cleaned immediately, or the meat might absorb a bad flavor from the last meal ingested.

The animal should be hung in a cool place and enclosed in a cheesecloth bag to protect it from flies. Small animals and birds should hang for 48 hours in order for body heat to dissipate.

If not needed immediately, small game may be frozen in cartons or bags of water with a little vinegar. This protects the meat from freezer burn and makes it juicier and more tender. With defrosting, this marinade melts away; if it was lightly spiced in advance, it can be reserved to begin the preparation process.

Most eastern tribes enjoyed only one full meal a day, a combination of breakfast and lunch, which they ate before noon. This was the time for hearty food, a robust rack of game or broiled fish, a crisp salad, baked pumpkin or squash, crunchy hazelnut cakes. The men ate first, usually from wooden or earthenware bowls. Afterward, the women and children ate what was left.

John Bartram visited the Iroquois in 1743 and described a feast he was served: "This repast consisted of three great kettles of Indian corn soup, or thin hominy, with dry'd eels and other fish boiled in it, and one kettle full of young squashes and their flowers boiled in water, and a little meal mixed . . . last of all was served a great bowl full of Indian dumplings, made of new, soft corn, cut or scraped off the ear, then with the addition of some boiled beans, lapped well up in Indian corn leaves, this is good hearty provision."*

BRUNSWICK STEW (serves 12 to 14)

The Jamestown settlers gave the name to this particularly favorite "game soup" prepared by the women of the Powhatan, Cherokee, and Chickahominy tribes. The seasonal mixture of game or fowl was usually squirrel, rabbit, or turkey accompanied by corn, beans, and tomatoes. It is a grand way of absorbing leftovers.

one 5-pound capon or boiling chicken	2 cups shelled lima beans
2 dried bayberry leaves	10 dried juniper berries
3 sprigs parsley	1/2 teaspoon dried oregano
1 stalk celery	2 cloves wild garlic
2 potatoes, cubed	6 ripe tomatoes, quartered
2 large onions, cubed	1 tablespoon fresh basil
2 cups corn kernels	

Simmer the whole chicken, with water to cover, in a large covered kettle, with the bayberry leaves, parsley, and celery stalk, for 2 hours. When the meat seems tender, remove the chicken from the pot; cool slightly. Separate the meat from the bones and return the meat to the broth.

Add all remaining ingredients to the kettle, except the tomatoes and basil, and simmer for 30 minutes, or until the vegetables are tender. Add the tomatoes and basil and simmer for 10 minutes more. Serve at once, with corn dumplings (see recipe below) if desired.

CORN DUMPLINGS (serves 12)

2 cups fine cornmeal	1 cup nut milk (see page 7)
1 teaspoon crushed dried mint leaves	2 tablespoons nut oil (see page 7)

Blend all ingredients together into a soft dough. Drop the dumplings by spoonfuls into the steaming stew broth during the last 15 minutes of cooking time. Cover the pot and steam.

*Yeffe Kimball and Jean Anderson, *The Art of American Cooking* (Garden City, N.Y.: Doubleday & Co., Inc. 1965), pp. 166-167.

ROAST SADDLE OF VENISON
WITH WILD RICE (serves 12)

one 5-pound saddle of venison, dressed
    and severed for easy carving
dried juniper berries

peppercorns
6 to 8 strips thick-sliced bacon

Basting Marinade:

2 tablespoons honey or maple syrup
2 cups cider

Stud the saddle of venison with juniper berries and peppercorns. Lay the bacon strips over and secure with toothpicks. Stand the saddle on a rack in a large roasting pan.

Prepare the basting marinade by simmering the honey (or maple syrup) in the cider in a small saucepan until it is well dissolved and steaming.

Roast, basting often, for 1½ hours in a preheated 350° F oven. Cool the roast for 20 minutes. Carve, serving 1 rib per portion.

Serve on a bed of wild rice, together with the pan drippings.

STEWED WILD RABBIT
AND DUMPLINGS (serves 10)

one 5-pound wild rabbit, dressed and
    cut up for stewing
³/₄ cup corn oil
1½ cups fine cornmeal
2 quarts water
2 tablespoons wood ashes (see page 4)
    or ¼ cup cider vinegar

12 dried juniper berries
12 small onions
8 carrots
2 sprigs fresh dillweed

Rub each piece of rabbit with a little oil and lightly dust with the cornmeal. Brown each piece in hot oil, in a large kettle, turning until evenly seared. Add the water and ashes (or vinegar) and simmer, covered, for 1½ hours. Add the remaining ingredients and simmer for 30 minutes more. Serve hot.

Dumplings:

2 cups *fine cornmeal*
1 tablespoon *wood ashes, optional (see page 4)*

1 egg, *beaten*
1 tablespoon *nut butter (see page 9)*
1 cup *water*

Thoroughly blend all ingredients together. Drop the dumpling batter by spoonfuls into the simmering rabbit gravy. Cover and steam for 15 more minutes. Serve hot.

SPICEBUSH
Lindera benzoin

RACCOON PIE (serves 10 to 12)

1 large *raccoon*
4 cups *water*
2 cups *vinegar*
2 tablespoons *coltsfoot ashes, optional (see page 27)*
¹/₄ cup *pickling spices*
2 onions, *diced*

4 potatoes, *chopped*
4 carrots, *chopped*
2 green peppers, *diced*
1 tablespoon *maple syrup*
1 tablespoon *dried spicebush berries*
4 tablespoons *cornstarch*
biscuit dough

Raccoons and muskrats are dark-meat animals, and when properly prepared, they make excellent and tasty dishes. All layers of fat, inside and out, must be removed before cooking. The small round scent glands located under the armpits of the front legs and in the small of the back on either side of the spine must also be removed.

Cut the dressed raccoon into serving-sized pieces and place these in a mixture of the water, vinegar, coltsfoot ashes, and pickling spices for 8 hours, or overnight. Drain, reserving this brine, and place the meat in a large stewing kettle. Cover with fresh water and add 1 cup of the reserved brine. Cook for 1 1/2 hours, or until tender. Then add the onions, potatoes, carrots, and peppers. Simmer until the vegetables are tender.

Remove the meat and the vegetables from the broth and place them in a large baking dish. Thicken the broth with cornstarch, and season to taste with the maple syrup and spicebush berries. Blend thoroughly, then pour this mixture over the meat and vegetables. Cover the top with your best biscuit dough. Slice a vent in the top. Bake the pie in a preheated 450° F oven until golden brown — about 20 minutes.

Muskrat pie and rabbit pie may be prepared in much the same way, varying the vegetables and the seasonings to taste.

PARTRIDGE OR ROAST DUCK STUFFED WITH APPLES AND GRAPES (serves 4 to 6)

2 partridge or one 5- to 6-pound duck, dressed

2 cups cider for basting

Stuffing:

giblets
1/2 pound fresh mushrooms, chopped
2 cups Concord or wild grapes, halved and seeded
6 to 8 whole potatoes, unpeeled (optional)

4 green apples, cored and chopped
2 cups shelled dried hazelnuts
1 tablespoon juniper berries
pinch of dillweed
6 medium whole onions (optional)
6 carrots, cut into thirds (optional)

Simmer the giblets in 2 cups water for 40 minutes. Lift out the giblets, cool slightly, then chop and return to the liquid in the pot. Add all the stuffing ingredients and mix together thoroughly.

Clean the fowl, removing any pin feathers and singeing to remove any hairs. Stuff the neck and body cavities; skewer and truss. Prick the skin well all over with a sharp fork to allow the excess fat to run off. Place the fowl on a rack in a large roasting pan, surrounding with the potatoes, onions, and carrots if desired.

Roast for 1 hour in a preheated 400° F oven, pricking the skin and basting it with the cider every 20 minutes. Reduce the oven temperature to 350° F and continue roasting for 2 hours more, pricking the skin and basting twice more.

TURKEY WITH OYSTER-CORNBREAD-RAISIN STUFFING* *(serves 12)*

one 12-pound turkey, dressed

Stuffing:

giblets

8 cups crumbled cornbread or johnnycakes	2 tablespoons chopped fresh parsley
	1/2 teaspoon chopped fresh savory
5 scallions, diced (including tops)	18 oysters, shucked and chopped (reserve liquid)
10 medium-sized fresh mushrooms, chopped	1 egg
1 cup shelled dried black walnuts	1 clove garlic, crushed
1 cup raisins	5 tablespoons giblet broth
1 cup sunflower seed butter (see page 8)	1/2 cup drippings
5 tablespoons oyster liquid for basting	3 tablespoons cornmeal

Prepare the cleaned, dressed turkey for stuffing. In a covered saucepan, simmer the giblets in 1 1/2 cups water for 30 minutes. Remove, cool, and chop. Return to the cooled broth and save for gravy.

Thoroughly mix all the stuffing ingredients together in a large bowl. Lightly stuff the neck and body cavities of the turkey; do not pack. Skewer the openings together and truss the legs together.

Place the turkey, breast side up, in a large roasting pan. Rub the bird generously with 1/4 cup of the sunflower seed butter.

Roast the turkey, uncovered, in a preheated 325° F oven, basting every 30 minutes with a mixture of 5 tablespoons of the oyster liquid and the juices from the bird. Also dot every hour or so with spoonfuls of the remaining 3/4 cup sunflower seed butter. Roast for approximately 6 hours, allowing 40 minutes per pound as a guide. The bird is done when the legs move easily at the joint.

Giblet gravy should be made in a saucepan over medium heat, after the turkey is finished and being carved (but prior to serving). Add 1/2 cup of the seasoned drippings from the turkey to the giblets and broth. Bring to a boil, add the cornmeal, and simmer, stirring continually until the gravy thickens and is creamy. Serve hot.

*Courtesy of Ella Thomas/ Sekatau of the Narragansett peoples.

QUAIL WITH HAZELNUTS (serves 4)

4 quail, dressed
1/4 cup sunflower seed oil (see page 8)
1 cup fine cornmeal
1/4 cup nut butter (see page 9)
1 cup hot water

2 tablespoons wood ashes, optional (see page 4)
1 cup wild grapes, seeded
1/2 cup shelled hazelnuts, chopped

Rub the quail inside and out with the sunflower seed oil and roll in the cornmeal to coat the skins lightly. Melt the nut butter in a skillet and sauté the quail, turning often, over medium heat, until they are well browned. Add the water, ashes, and wild grapes, cover, and simmer over low heat for 45 minutes, stirring once or twice to blend.

Toast the hazelnuts in a shallow pan in a 350° F oven, until light brown — about 10 minutes. Serve each quail on a bed of rice or tender greens, and spoon over each bird the hot, toasted hazelnuts.

STUFFED ROAST GOOSE (serves 10 to 12)

one 10- to 12-pound goose, dressed
2 cups cider for basting

whole onions (optional)
apples (optional)

Stuffing:

goose giblets
1/4 pound fresh mushrooms, chopped
2 cups fine white cornmeal
1 tablespoon chopped fresh dillweed

2 cups dried currants or fresh cranberries, chopped
1 tablespoon honey
1 teaspoon chopped fresh spicebush leaves

Simmer the goose giblets in 1 quart water for 40 minutes. Lift out the giblets and cool slightly, then chop. Return the giblets to 1 1/2 cups of the broth and combine with the rest of the stuffing ingredients. Mix thoroughly.

Clean the goose, remove the pin feathers, and singe off any hairs. Stuff the neck and body cavities. Skewer and truss. Place the goose, breast side up, on a rack in a large roasting pan. Surround with whole onions and apples if desired. Roast, uncovered, in a preheated 350° F oven for 4 1/2 hours. Prick the skin well with a fork and baste with the cider and drippings every 30 minutes.

Gravy:

Reserve the drippings in the bottom of the roasting pan after removing the goose (to stand and cool before carving). Tip the pan and skim off the fat. Return the pan with the drippings to low heat. Add 2 tablespoons cornstarch to $1/2$ cup water, then add to the hot drippings, stirring until thick and bubbling. Keep hot and serve beside the goose, for use over the meat, vegetables, or wild rice.

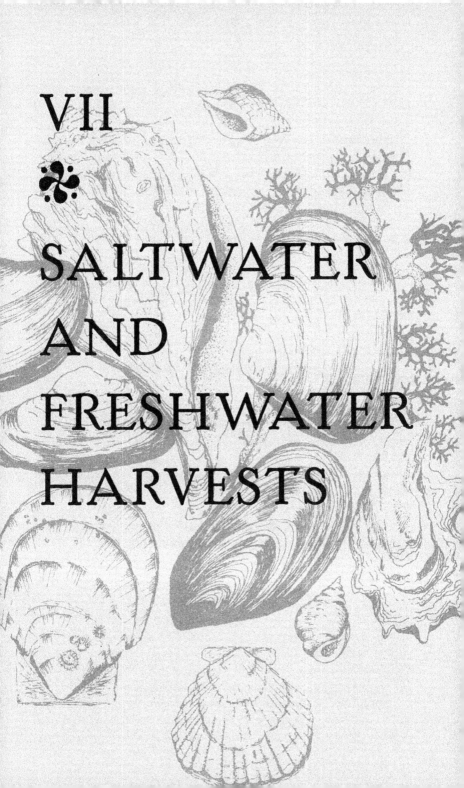

VII

SALTWATER AND FRESHWATER HARVESTS

"Maushop was fond of whale meat and would eat a whole whale at a meal. Near the entrance of his den he could reach out over the cliffs, pick up a whale that had been washed ashore, and swing it over to his fire which was burning continually. The blood and grease from the whales stained the cliffs beautiful colors."

... Gay Head Wampanoag traditional origin story, 1930

Seasonally many northeastern Indian tribes migrated to the bays and Atlantic coastal areas, seeking the abundance of foods from the sea and salt marshes. Accompanied by feasting and ceremonial celebrations, these periods offered a welcome change from the Indians' woodland diet. Many of the seafood classics we enjoy today evolved during these coastal migrations.

The earliest migration was for the April fishing season for shad, harbinger of spring, and foretold by the blossoming shadbush (shadblow).

SHAD is a variety of saltwater fish related to the herring but having a meatier body. They spawn in the rivers that come together along the North Atlantic coast. A valuable spring food to the Eastern Woodlands Indian tribes, shad is still considered a delicacy today.

Shad is very bony, each fish containing up to seven hundred bones in its body, and great care is necessary to clean and debone them into 4-inch fillets before preparing them for broiling, baking, or stewing.

BAKED SHAD WITH WILD LEEKS
AND NANNYBERRIES *(serves 6)*

1 medium shad, split and boned
2 tablespoons nut butter *(see page 9)*
1 tablespoon chopped fresh parsley
1 cup wild leek bulbs

1 cup nannyberries or raisins
1/2 cup cider vinegar
garlic mustard sauce *(see page 28)*

Place the shad in a long greased baking dish. Mix the remaining ingredients (except the sauce) loosely together. Stuff the shad with half the mixture, sprinkle the rest over the outside, and bake in a preheated 375° F oven for 45 to 60 minutes. Baste once or twice with the juices.

Serve with herb rice and garlic mustard sauce.

BONELESS BAKED SHAD *(serves 8)*

one 3- or 4-pound shad
1 quart water
1/4 cup cider vinegar
3 tablespoons shelled sunflower seeds

1 tablespoon sunflower seed butter *(see page 8)*
ground dried spicebush berries to taste
1 cup chopped fresh sorrel leaves

Boil the shad in the water and vinegar in a large enamel kettle for 20 minutes. Drain, rinse, and place in a heavy roaster. Season with the sunflower seeds, sunflower seed butter, and spicebush berries and pour 1/4 cup water around the fish. Cover tightly and bake in a preheated 250° F oven for 5 hours. By this method the smaller bones are completely dissolved, leaving the fish tender and delicious. Serve on a bed of fresh sorrel leaves.

PLANKED SHAD *(serves 8)*

Prepare initially as for Boneless Baked Shad (see recipe above), but after steaming for 5 hours, remove the head, tail, and fins. Slit along the backbone and open gently into two halves (skin side down) on a well-greased oak plank. Season to taste and broil for approximately 20 to 30 minutes. Serve with boiled groundnuts, chopped potatoes, or wild rice and chopped fresh drillweed. Serve hot on a bed of sorrel or garlic mustard leaves.

SHAD ROE AND MILT

Shad is principally sought in its spawning season for the creamy male sperm (known as milt or soft roe) and the female sac full of eggs (known as hard roe). Both may be marinated raw in the refrigerator 2 weeks in a blend of vinegar, onions, spices, and oil, or they may be parboiled for 3 to 12 minutes in slowly simmering water, then quickly fried in nut butter to a golden, delicate doneness. When preparing hard roe, the membrane surrounding the eggs must be pricked several times with a needle to prevent it from bursting and scattering the minute eggs.

HERRING OR MACKEREL
ROE AND MILT (serves 8)

A rich, delicious treat that must be delicately handled in preparation.

Save the sac of roe and milt from 2 fish; wash lightly then chill or freeze until preparation time.

Place the roe and milt, one at a time, in a medium pot of boiling water (with 1 teaspoon cider vinegar added) and simmer for 5 minutes. Remove and carefully drain, sauté quickly, on all sides, in nut butter, or broil in a greased baking dish for 15 minutes.

This delicacy is usually served as an appetizer and may be placed on a bed of fresh sorrel or violet leaves, and flanked with hard-boiled eggs and chopped fresh dillweed.

BLUEFISH is found, at various seasons, along the entire length of the Atlantic coast. Its name is derived from the bluish tinge of its skin and flesh. This dark-meated fish is rich and flavorful and may be prepared in a variety of ways.

SHEEP–SORREL
Rumex acetosella

BAKED BLUEFISH *(serves 6)*

1 large bluefish
1 teaspoon ground dried juniper berries
1 teaspoon coltsfoot ashes, optional *(see page 27)*
3 tablespoons shelled sunflower seeds
1 teaspoon celery seeds

1 tablespoon chopped fresh dillweed
1 tablespoon chopped onion
2 tablespoons nut oil *(see page 7)*
1 cup chopped fresh sorrel leaves
½ cup wild onions, coarsely chopped

Clean and split the bluefish. Place in a well-greased pan; season inside and out with a mixture of juniper berries, coltsfoot ashes, sunflower seeds, celery seeds, dill, and onion. Sprinkle generously with nut oil and bake in a preheated 375° F oven for 1 hour. Serve steaming hot on a bed of fresh sorrel leaves and wild onions.

Bluefish cheeks are considered a delicacy by most Amerindians.

BAKED STUFFED BLUEFISH *(serves 6)*

one 4-pound bluefish, split and cleaned
2 tablespoons oil
pepper
choice of herbs to taste *(tarragon, cumin, sage, dillweed, etc.)*
1 cup chopped fresh mushrooms
1 cup shucked oysters and liquor
1 cup shelled chestnuts, chopped

1 scallion, chopped *(including top)*
1 clove garlic, crushed
1 tablespoon maple syrup
2 cups cornmeal
1 cup cider
¼ teaspoon ground dried sassafras *(young leaves)*

Wipe the clean fish inside and out with the oil. Season with pepper and choice of herbs.

Mix the remaining ingredients (except the cider and sassafras) into the cornmeal; blend thoroughly and stuff the fish cavity.

Lay the oiled, stuffed, and seasoned fish on a large aluminum foil sheet in a long roasting pan. Fold and wrap the foil tightly around the fish, allowing a vent slit for steam to escape. Bake for 1 hour in a pre-heated 350° F oven, basting several times through the vent hole with the cider. Sprinkle with sassafras at the very end, after removing from heat.

COD, which gave its name to New England's best-known cape, is one of the most valuable and versatile fish, abundant year-round in our coastal waters. A mainstay of the coastal Indians' diet, cod was also favored by the colonists. Fresh cod is best during late fall. The head and shoulders are usually gently boiled (wrapped in cheesecloth), and the remaining fish is sliced and fried or broiled.

Scrod is young cod, no more than two pounds in size, and is usually broiled.

BROILED SCROD (serves 4)

Clean and split the scrod, removing the head, tail, and backbone. Place the fish, flesh side up, in a greased pan. Sprinkle with sunflower seed oil (see page 8) and dillseed. Broil for about 20 minutes, or until golden. Serve hot with wild greens and cranberries.

CODFISH BALLS (serves 10)

3 pounds fresh cod or salmon or halibut
4 cups diced unpeeled potatoes
2 cups water
¼ teaspoon ground pepper
2 tablespoons oil

2 teaspoons maple syrup
choice of herbs to taste (dillweed, parsley, marjoram, etc.)
4 cups oil or fat for deep frying

Boil the fish and potatoes in a covered pot for 25 minutes. Drain and mash. Add the remaining ingredients (except the oil for deep frying) and shape into 2-inch balls. Deep fry in hot oil (or fat), stirring until golden. Drain on brown paper and serve either hot or cold.

COD TONGUES AND CHEEKS

Boil these delicate morsels for just a few minutes and serve with your favorite sauce, or dip in nut milk, roll in cornmeal, and sauté. Serve either hot or cold on a nest of fresh wild leek greens.

PICKLED FISH (serves 12)

one 4-to 5-pound fish
2 medium onions, thinly sliced
3 cups cider vinegar
12 dried juniper berries, crushed
12 peppercorns

1 tablespoon chopped fresh dillweed or 1
   tablespoon dillseed
1 tablespoon wood ashes, optional (see
   page 4)

Mackerel, herring, cod, halibut, tuna, striped bass, swordfish, and others may be well preserved by pickling. Clean and section the fish into medium-sized segments and place these on a bed of thinly sliced onions in a crock or glass container. Simmer the cider vinegar with the juniper berries, peppercorns, and chopped fresh dillweed (or dillseed), for 10 minutes. Stir in the wood ashes. Pour this mixture over the fish and onions to cover (add more vinegar if necessary). Cover and let stand in a cool place or in the refrigerator for 2 days to 2 weeks before serving. After 2 days the vinegar and spices should have softened and almost dissolved all internal bones. Serve cold, complemented with a wild salad composed of seasonal favorites. (The lemony sourness of sorrel makes it a fine companion to most fish.)

CREAMED OYSTERS (serves 8)

1 cup sunflower seed butter (see
   page 8)
2 cups fine cornmeal
2 cups small shucked oysters

$^1/_4$ cup hickory milk (see page 7) or
   medium cream
$^1/_2$ tablespoon ground dried spicebush
   berries

Melt the seed butter in a saucepan. Add the cornmeal, stir, and blend until crumblike. Spread 1 cup of this mixture evenly across the bottom of a shallow baking dish. Add the oysters, evenly spaced on the bed of cornmeal. Sprinkle with the hickory milk or cream and season with the spicebush berries. Top with the remaining cornmeal crumbs. Bake for 20 minutes in a preheated 350° F oven. Serve hot.

SPICED OYSTERS (serves 8)

2 cups large shucked oysters and liquor
cider vinegar
$^1/_2$ tablespoon chopped onion

$^1/_2$ tablespoon ground dried spicebush berries
2 cups water

Scald the oysters in their own liquor briefly, until just plump. Strain and reserve the liquor; add an equal amount of cider vinegar. Mix this liquid with the onion and spicebush berries and add to the water in a saucepan. Simmer for 10 minutes, skim, and strain over the cooled oysters. Let stand in a cool location or refrigerate for 24 hours before serving.

BAKED CLAMS (OR OYSTERS) ON THE HALF SHELL

freshly opened clams or oysters on half shell
cornmeal
oil

ground pepper
chopped fresh parsley
chopped sea lettuce

Place the clams (or oysters) in their half shells in a baking dish. Sprinkle with a mixture of the remaining ingredients. Bake in a preheated 325° F oven for 20 minutes, or until golden. Serve hot.

OYSTER PATTIES *(serves 4 to 6)*

2 cups mashed potatoes or Jerusalem artichokes
2 eggs, beaten
1 small onion, minced
1 tablespoon coltsfoot ashes, optional (see page 27)
2 tablespoons nut milk (see page 7)

1 tablespoon chopped fresh parsley
1 teaspoon mustard seeds
dillseed to taste
12 dozen shucked oysters
garnish: additional chopped fresh parsley and sorrel leaves

Blend all ingredients (except the oysters) into the mashed potatoes (or Jerusalem artichokes) and form into little cakes. Gently split each cake with a small spoon and push 1 or 2 oysters into the center, then press the cake back into shape. Brush each cake with additional nut milk and sprinkle the moist tops with dillseed. Bake in a preheated 375° F oven until golden — about 30 minutes. Garnish with parsley and lemony-flavored sorrel leaves. Serve hot.

CLAMBAKE (serves 6)

2 dozen fresh oysters, in the shell, cleaned

six 1- to 1½-pound fresh (green) lobsters

6 ears corn, in the husk

6 medium potatoes, unpeeled

3 dozen fresh mussels, in the shell, cleaned

2 dozen fresh clams, in the shell, cleaned

2 quarts water

2 whole scallions

Place the oysters in the bottom of a very large, deep kettle. Add 3 of the lobsters, 3 of the ears of corn, the 6 potatoes, then the 3 remaining ears of corn and the 3 remaining lobsters. Place the mussels and clams in and around the other foods. Pour in the water, and place the scallions on top. Cover the kettle and bring to a boil. Lower heat and simmer for 1 hour, or until the potatoes are tender. Serve hot.

STEAMED CLAMS (2 cups per person)

Refrigerate freshly dug clams overnight in seawater to which ¼ cup cornmeal has been added. By morning the clams will have flushed most of the sand and grit out of their systems.

Place the clams in a heavy kettle, cover with water, and add a celery stalk and 1 teaspoon dillseed for flavor. Bring to a boil over medium heat, cover the kettle, and remove from heat. Steam off heat for 20 minutes. Serve hot with drawn butter or your favorite sauce.

CLAM CHOWDER (serves 6 to 8)

1 large onion, chopped

2 large cloves garlic, crushed

¼ pound butter

2 dozen clams, steamed, shucked, and diced

2 large unpeeled potatoes, diced

2 cups clam broth

2 cups light cream or milk, or 2 cups stewed tomatoes

2 cups diced celery

garnish: ground pepper and chopped chives to taste

Sauté the onion and garlic in the butter in a deep kettle until golden. Add the remaining ingredients and simmer slowly until the potatoes are tender — about 30 minutes. Serve hot, garnished with pepper and chives. Oysters or mussels may be substituted for the clams.

BROILED MUSSELS (serves 4)

4 dozen mussels, in the shell, scrubbed
    well
2 cups boiling water
2 cups mussel broth
1 clove garlic, chopped

1 cup fine cornmeal
1/4 cup chopped fresh parsley or sea
    lettuce
1/2 cup oil

Steam the mussels in the water for 10 minutes, until tender. Place the mussels on the half shell in a flat pan, pour the broth over them, and sprinkle with the garlic and cornmeal. Top with the parsley or sea lettuce. Sprinkle oil over all. Broil until lightly browned.

STEAMED MUSSELS OR MUSSEL SOUP (serves 4)

2 quarts mussels, in the shell, scrubbed
    well
1 quart boiling water
1/2 pound butter

1 cup chopped celery
1/2 cup chopped leeks (including tops)
1 cup cider vinegar

Place all ingredients in a heavy pot and cover with boiling water. Cover and steam until the mussels are fully opened — about 10 minutes. (Overcooking will make the mussels tough and less flavorful.)

Serve hot in bowls with its own buttered broth, seasoned with ground pepper and chopped fresh parsley.

STEAMED MUSSELS AND HALIBUT (serves 4)

2 dozen blue Atlantic mussels, in
    the shell
2 center slices of halibut (about 2
    pounds)
1 cup cider vinegar

1/4 cup chopped fresh parsley
1/4 cup oil
2 scallions, chopped (including tops)
1/2 teaspoon dillseed
pinch of ground pepper

Scrub the mussels well with a stiff brush. Line a shallow baking pan with a 2-foot-long strip of heavy-duty aluminum foil. Coat the center of foil lightly with oil. Place the 2 halibut steaks on the foil, surround and top with the mussels and a mixture of the vinegar, parsley, oil, scallions, dillseed, and pepper. Wrap and seal the package tightly to steam the enclosed ingredients. Bake in a preheated 350° F oven for 45 minutes.

Remove from oven, cool slightly. Open the package and serve portions over plates of wild rice or corn mush, with wild grapes, currants, or cranberries.

CONCH (WHELK) STEW (serves 6 to 8)

1 or 2 channeled or knobbed pear conches (whelks), in the shell, scrubbed well	1/2 cup cider vinegar
	2 ripe tomatoes, diced
	pinch of ground pepper
3 quarts water	pinch of dillseed
2 stalks celery, chopped coarsely	pinch of dried sage

Boil the conches in the water with the celery and vinegar for 30 minutes. Drain and reserve the broth. When cooled slightly, pull the meat out of the shells and slice off the long, muscular foot. Discard the remaining body. Cut the foot into thin slices and return the meat to the simmering broth. Add the tomatoes and herbs. Simmer and blend for 10 minutes more. Serve steaming.

QUAHOG FRITTERS (serves 8)

2 dozen quahogs, in the shell, cleaned	1 tablespoon wood ashes, optional (see page 4)
2 1/2 cups boiling water	
2 cups fine cornmeal	1 tablespoon coltsfoot ashes, optional (see page 27)
1 egg, beaten	
1 teaspoon dillseed	1/4 cups corn oil for frying

Steam the quahogs in the water in a covered kettle until they open. Drain and reserve the broth. Remove the quahogs from their shells and chop. Place them in a bowl with 1 cup of the broth and add the remaining ingredients, blending thoroughly into a light batter. Drop by tablespoonfuls onto a hot greased griddle; fry quickly, flipping once, until golden.

Serve with wild greens and the remaining shellfish broth.

SCALLOPS are delicate, fluted shellfish native to North Atlantic waters. The large deep-sea scallop is readily available, while the smaller bay scallop is in shorter supply. In general, only the adductor muscle, which holds the mollusk's shells together, is eaten.

Most coastal Indian tribes enjoyed the whole shellfish, freshly opened and raw. Traditionally they ate all they could immediately; especially abundant catches were kept over a period of days by cooking and spicing, or smoking and drying.

FRIED SCALLOPS (serves 4)

2 pounds shucked bay or deep-sea
  scallops
1 egg, beaten

2 cups fine cornmeal seasoned to taste
  with ground dillseed and wood
  ashes (see page 4)
¼ cup nut oil (see page 7)

Dip the clean, dry scallops into the egg, then roll in the seasoned corn-meal. Heat the oil and fry for about 2 to 5 minutes, or until golden. Serve on wild rice with chopped fresh sorrel leaves and parsley.

LONG ISLAND SCALLOP STEW (serves 6)

2 cups nut milk (see page 7) or
  medium cream
1 tablespoon coltsfoot ashes, optional
  (see page 27)

2 dozen bay scallops, shucked
2 tablespoons fine cornmeal

Combine all ingredients and simmer for 20 minutes. Serve on a platter of chopped fresh sorrel leaves and chopped dillweed.

SPICED RAW SCALLOPS (serves 4)

3 dozen bay scallops
2 tablespoons sunflower seed oil (see
  page 8)
1 clove garlic, chopped

1 small onion, diced
4 dried bayberry leaves
1 cup cider vinegar

Combine all ingredients, blend, and chill overnight. Serve over chopped fresh parsley, dillweed, and mint leaves.

SEA HARVESTS

KNOBBED PEAR CONCH

ROCK PURPLE

IRISH MOSS
Chondrus crispus
SURF CLAM

BLUE MUSSEL

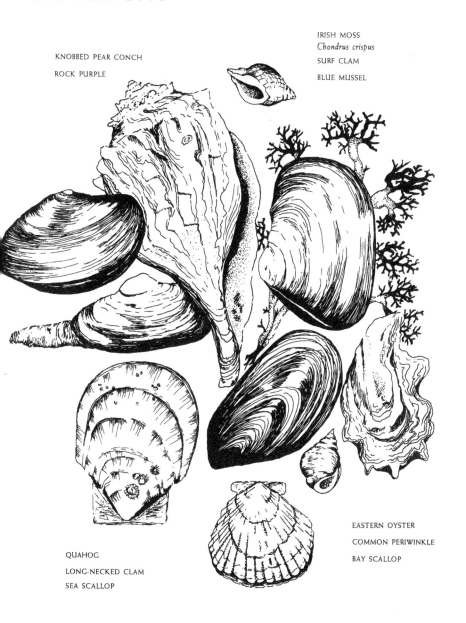

QUAHOG

LONG-NECKED CLAM

SEA SCALLOP

EASTERN OYSTER

COMMON PERIWINKLE

BAY SCALLOP

SHRIMP AND SCALLOP PIE (serves 8 to 10)

80 raw shrimp
30 bay scallops
1 teaspoon chopped fresh parsley
1 cup water
2 cups fine cornmeal
4 ripe tomatoes, chopped

1 cup chopped celery
1 tablespoon nut oil (see page 7)
4 dried bayberry leaves, crumbled
3 cloves wild garlic, chopped
1 tablespoon dillseed

Combine all ingredients (except for the dillseed) and blend well. Place
in a greased baking dish, sprinkle the top with the dillseed, and bake for
40 minutes in a preheated 350° F oven. Serve either hot or cold with
herb rice and tomatoes sprinkled with parsley.

ROAST SEA SCALLOPS
AND VEGETABLES (serves 8)

1 cup sunflower seed oil (see page 8)
1 tablespoon coltsfoot ashes, optional (see
    page 27)
1 teaspoon chopped fresh dillweed
2 dozen cherry tomatoes
1 dozen small green peppers, halved

2 dozen groundnuts or Jerusalem
    artichokes, scrubbed
2 dozen meadow mushrooms or chunks
    of giant puffballs
4 dozen sea scallops

Blend the sunflower seed oil, coltsfoot ashes, and dill; set aside. Alter-
nate vegetable pieces with scallops on 8 skewers. Brush all the pieces
with the seasoned oil; roast over a moderate fire for 15 to 20 minutes,
turning and basting occasionally with what remains of the oil. Serve
with fresh greens and wild rice.

SEAWEEDS are included among the algae. They are most prolific on
rocky shores, where many are firmly anchored. Many species have
air-filled bladders, so that when the tide comes in, the fronds float up
toward the light. The many seaweeds have uses as food, medicines,
and industrial ingredients. They are rich sources of minerals and vitamins.

DULSE *(Rhodymenia palmata)* is a sea alga found worldwide and has been a source of salt for centuries. Especially abundant in New England coastal waters (intertidal/subtidal zones), this flat, smooth red plant grows to about 1 inch long and washes onto beaches year-round. The rubbery dulse is easily dried, rolled, and stored for use as salty "fingers" to carry on hikes and camping trips as a mineral-rich chew.

EDIBLE KELP *(Alaria esculenta)* is olive-green to brown and 1 to 10 feet tall on short, cylindrical stems. It is found on submerged ledges and is washed ashore year-round. Brew it like a tea to render into a soup broth or chop it and add it to salads. All the kelps have an extremely high mineral content and make an excellent fertilizer.

IRISH MOSS *(Chondrus crispus)* is found all along the North Atlantic shore. It may be gathered all year round and dried and stored for use. The prepared jelly is a highly nutritious food, free of sugar and starch, high in sulphur and iodine, and excellent for restricted diets.

IRISH MOSS JELLY

Gather 1 cup Irish Moss and wash. Cover with 6 cups boiling water and boil for 30 minutes in a covered pot, stirring occasionally. Strain. Boil briefly in milk and flavor with wild fruits. Chill to serve.

LAVER *(Poryphyra vulgaris)* is a very thin, shiny ruffled frond about 1 foot long that washes ashore and may be harvested all year. It makes an excellent broth and a nutritious jelly; boiled until tender, it may be eaten as a vegetable. Or dry it and eat like dulse. A condiment may be created by cooking the fronds in water and lemon juice.

DULSE
Rhodymenia palmata

SEA LETTUCE. (*Ulva lactuca*) is a bright green, thin frond that is routinely washed up on shore. Use it dried and powdered as a saltlike seasoning or chop it and add it to salads. It is available all year round.

AMERICAN EELS are indigenous to the fresh and salt waters of the Atlantic and Gulf coasts of North America and are sought in both environments year-round. To the native Americans, eels were a highly prized, nutritious, and delectable food. Mature eels spawn in early spring, deep in the Sargasso Sea off Bermuda. During their early developmental stages they are widely dispersed by the coastal currents, but as they grow, they begin their migration into the estuaries along the coast. Eels are capable of crossing stretches of land in order to reach freshwater habitats, where they will remain (as elvers) for up to fifteen years. Finally maturing and undergoing a sexual metamorphosis, they begin their nocturnal migration back to the sea, to spawn in the depths of the Sargasso Sea.

SMOKED EEL STEW (serves 8)

one 1 1/2-pound smoked eel
4 potatoes, in their skins
4 yellow onions
1 tablespoon dried juniper berries
choice of herbs to taste

6 cups boiling water
garnish: ground pepper, chopped fresh
   parsley, and grated cheese
   (optional)

Clean and skin the eel; split and remove the backbone. Cut into 2-inch pieces. Simmer with the potatoes, onions, juniper berries, and herbs in the water in a large, heavy kettle for 1 hour. Skim off excess fat. Serve hot, topped with pepper, parsley, and grated cheese.

BAKED EELS (serves 10)

five 2-pound eels
3 cups groundnuts
3 cups wild leek bulbs
1/2 cup sunflower seed oil (see page 8)

1/2 cup cider or birch vinegar
1 tablespoon ground dried spicebush
   berries
1 teaspoon chopped fresh dillweed

Clean, skin, and split the eels; remove the backbones and cut into 3-inch pieces. Surround the pieces in a large pan with the groundnuts and wild leek bulbs. Sprinkle with the remaining ingredients and bake in a preheated 350° F oven for 30 to 40 minutes.

QUICK-FRIED EELS *(serves 10)*

five 2- to 3-pound eels
2 cups fine cornmeal
1 teaspoon ground dried spicebush berries
1 teaspoon coltsfoot ashes, optional (see page 27)

1 teaspoon chopped fresh dillweed
¹/₂ cup sunflower seed oil (see page 8) or nut' oil (see page 7)
garnish: chopped fresh dillweed or parsley

Clean, skin, and split the eels; remove the backbones and cut into 3-inch pieces. Drop them, 2 pieces at a time, into a "spice bag" containing a mixture of cornmeal, spicebush berries, coltsfoot ashes, and dill. Shake to coat each piece, then place the pieces in a hot cast-iron skillet containing sunflower seed (or nut) oil. Sear quickly on all sides to brown and seal in the juices.

Serve the fried eels on mounds of chopped ripe tomatoes, cooked squash, and rice. Garnish with dill or parsley. The meat can easily be eaten away from the tiny backbone vertebrae. It is tasty and juicy white meat.

Seasonally abundant freshwater fish and shellfish composed a significant share of the Eastern Woodlands Indians' diet. Prehistoric "midden heaps," or refuse deposits, yield the bones and shells of many species of freshwater fish, clams, and mussels.

TROUT, one of the salmon family, is perhaps the most delicate of all freshwater fish. The lake and brook trout are protein-rich and may be enjoyed in a variety of ways.

BAKED LAKE TROUT *(serves 2)*

one 3- to 4-pound lake trout
3 tablespoons sunflower seed oil (see page 8)

choice of herbs to taste (dillweed, parsley, basil, mint, etc.)
4 tablespoons fine cornmeal

Clean and split the trout; remove the head and backbone. Place in a greased baking pan, flesh side up, and sprinkle with the sunflower seed oil, herbs, and cornmeal. Bake in a preheated 350° F oven for 30 minutes.

TROUT CONSOMMÉ (serves 6)

8 cooked trout heads	10 juniper berries
5 cups boiling water	2 sprigs dillweed

Combine all ingredients in a pot and simmer for 30 minutes. Strain and serve hot, or chill and serve as an aspic garnished with hard-boiled eggs and herbs. This trout stock is also excellent to flavor vegetables.

CATFISH or BULLHEAD. A variety of fish (usually "whiskered") is grouped under this generic name, varying in size from one to a hundred pounds. If the fish is kept alive for twelve to twenty-four hours "after catch," until all the food in the stomach is digested, the flesh will be rich, sweet, and usually white.

FRIED CATFISH (BULLHEAD) (serves 10 to 12)

one 5- to 6-pound catfish	1 tablespoon chopped fresh dillweed
1 cup fine cornmeal	1/2 cup nut oil (see page 7)

Skin the fish before cooking; split; remove backbone. Roll the fish in the cornmeal seasoned with the dillweed, and fry in nut oil until golden. Serve with wild herbs and corn bread.

IROQUOIS SOUP — U'NEGA'GEI (serves 6)

two 3-pound fish (trout, bass, or haddock), cleaned but with the skin left on	2 tablespoons fine cornmeal
	2 tablespoons chopped fresh parsley
3 quarts water	1 clove garlic
4 large fresh mushrooms, sliced	1/2 teaspoon dried basil
1 large yellow onion, diced	garnish: fresh chopped dillweed and parsley
2 cups dried lima beans	

Place all ingredients in a large kettle and simmer, uncovered, for 30 minutes. Carefully lift out the fish, cool slightly; remove skin and bones. Flake the fish, then return it to the steaming pot (add pieces of fish skin if desired). Simmer for another 30 minutes, stirring frequently. Serve hot.

FISH BAKED IN CLAY

Pack any suitable fresh-caught fish (neither cleaned nor scaled) in a blanket of clay. Allow to dry for a few minutes by the fire; then bury this package in the hot coals, baking until the clay is hard (approximately 1 hour).

To serve, rake from the fire and hammer to break open the clay jacket. The cooked fish should split easily into 2 portions and the bones lift out. The intestines usually shrink into a tight ball and are easy to remove; the scales should be embedded in the clay. Sprinkle the steaming fish sections with your choice of herbs and nut oil (see page 7).

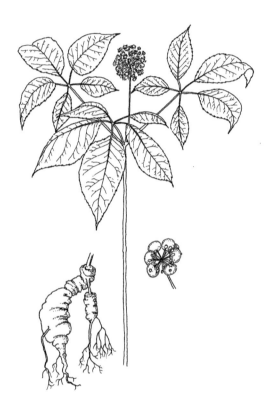

AMERICAN GINSENG
Panax quinquefolius
(See page 156.)

VIII

NATURAL BREADS

"Corn kernels were parched, then ground to a fine meal called yokeag, or 'traveling food.' Hunters and travelers would carry a small sack of this, which would serve as food until they could stop to cook. Today at our annual festival, yokeag is very popular because visitors like it sprinkled on ice cream, and some eat it as cereal."

. . . Gladys Tantaquidgeon, 1990, Mohegan Medicine Woman

ndians discovered the special properties of ashes mixed with foods or water. They saw that corn soaked in water with ashes became whiter and puffier and acquired a unique flavor. This became *hominy*, which was fermented into sour soup, fried with meats or wild greens, or baked into custardlike puddings. Hominy was also dried and pounded into grits, which became various other nutritious dishes.

HOMINY GRITS (serves 8)

5 cups water
1 cup hominy grits

1 tablespoon nut butter (see page 9)
1 tablespoon honey

Bring the water to a rapid boil in a saucepan. Gradually pour in the hominy grits, stirring; then add the nut butter and honey and stir. Cook for 20 minutes, or until all the water is absorbed.

Grits may be sweetened, if tastes dictate, or herb-seasoned instead. Hominy grits may be everything, from a steaming breakfast cereal to a lunch soup or side dish to a dinner vegetable.

FRIED HOMINY GRITS (serves 8)

1 recipe Hominy Grits, cooked and
    cooled (see page 118)

⅓ cup nut oil (see page 7)
    or bacon fat

Press the grits into 8 greased glasses; chill for at least 2 hours (preferably overnight). Unmold with the aid of a knife and slice into ½-inch-thick rounds. Heat the nut oil (or bacon fat) and brown for 8 minutes on each side. Serve hot as breakfast cakes. Great plain or topped with maple syrup.

Pones, "*Hoecakes,*" or "*Ashcakes*" are flattened cakes of cornmeal and water. These everyday breads of southern tribes were usually baked directly in the campfire on stones or wooden paddles, or tossed into the glowing coals. By observing Indian cooks, the colonists learned to create the Indian breads, using Indian methods.

CORN PONE (serves 6)

1 cup cornmeal
½ cup nut milk (see page 7) or water

1 teaspoon baking powder
2 tablespoons bacon drippings

Mix the cornmeal, nut milk (or water), and baking powder together thoroughly. Grease a hot skillet with the bacon drippings. Drop the batter into the skillet by tablespoonfuls, shaping into 6 pone cakes. Brown for 10 minutes on each side. Serve hot.

Indian women were creative and experimental cooks. They sweetened their cornmeal batters with fresh or dried fruits and berries if available or with fragrant herbs, powdered roots, or small quantities of wood ashes.

GRUEL (serves 8)

3½ cups water
1¼ cups white cornmeal

1½ teaspoon maple syrup

Boil the water, then add the cornmeal and maple syrup, mixing well. Heat slowly, stirring frequently, for 10 minutes, or until smooth and thick. Serve in bowls, topped with maple sugar and cream if desired.

FRIED GRUEL (serves 8)

1 recipe Gruel, cooked and cooled   ¹/₄ cup oil for frying
   (see page 119)

Chill the gruel in 2 round tin cans or glasses for 2 hours. Unmold with the aid of a knife and slice into rounds ¹/₂-inch thick. Heat the oil and brown the slices well on both sides. Serve hot as bread or topped with syrup as a breakfast dish.

CHIPPEWA BANNOCK (serves 6)

2 cups cornmeal   honey to taste or ¹/₂ cup berries
³/₄ cup water   ¹/₄ cup oil for frying
5 tablespoons fat or oil for seasoning

Blend the first three ingredients together and sweeten with the honey (or berries). Heat the oil in a large skillet and drop tablespoonfuls of batter into it, flattening them into cakes. Cook 5 minutes per side, or until golden. Enjoy either hot or cold. Good trail food.

INDIAN CAKE (BANNOCK) (serves 8)

1 cup white cornmeal   1 cup sour milk
¹/₂ cup cattail flour (see page 66)   1 egg, beaten
1 teaspoon wood ashes (see page 4) or   2 tablespoons honey
   baking soda   3 tablespoons corn oil
¹/₂ teaspoon ground ginger

Mix together the cornmeal and cattail flour in a large bowl. Gradually add the remaining ingredients, blending well and working into a sturdy dough. Turn into a well-greased loaf pan (8" x 4") and bake in a preheated 425° F oven for 30 minutes.

     The dough may also be shaped and flattened into a greased cast-iron skillet and cooked over an open fire, turning once. Gauge the cooking time according to the fire, usually 10 minutes per side. Delicious as a dinner or trail bread, it is enhanced by the addition of a handful or two of seasonal (or dried) berries included in the raw batter before baking.

NAVAJO FRY BREAD *(three 8-inch round breads)*

2 cups flour
1 teaspoon coltsfoot ashes, optional
   (see page 27)
¹/₂ cup ground sunflower seeds
2 teaspoons baking powder
2 tablespoons oil
1 cup milk or water, more or less *(depending upon altitude elevations, humidity, etc.)*

Work the first five ingredients into a dough ball, kneading until the texture is smooth. Place in a covered bowl or crock for 2 hours.

    Remove the dough and cut it into 3 portions. Roll them into circle shapes, about 8 inches round and ¹/₂-inch thick. Cut 2 large, deep parallel slits across the tops.

    Heat the oil in a heavy skillet and fry for 2 minutes on each side.

ELDERBERRY
Sambucus canadensis

ELDER BLOSSOM FRITTERS *(serves 8)*

2 cups fine white cornmeal
1 egg, beaten lightly
1 cup water
1 tablespoon maple syrup
¹/₄ cup corn oil for frying
16 elder blossom clusters, washed and
   dried

Prepare a light batter beating together the cornmeal, egg, water, and maple syrup. Heat the oil on a griddle and drop the batter by large tablespoonfuls onto it, immediately placing 1 blossom cluster in the center of each raw fritter and pressing lightly into the batter. Fry for 3 to 5 minutes, or until golden. Flip and fry for 3 minutes on the other side. Drain on brown paper. Serve hot, sprinkled with additional loose blossoms and maple sugar.

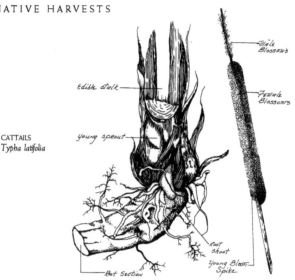

CATTAILS
Typha latifolia

Male Blossoms

Female Blossoms

Edible stalk

Young sprout

Root shoot

Young Bloom Spike

Root Section

Cattail Flour. During June the male blossoms, which are located above the female cattail bloom spike, produce quantities of bright yellow pollen. This nutritious, corn-flavored food substance is easily gathered by wading through cattail marshes and gently bending each bloom spike over a deep bowl or bucket and "dusting" the golden pollen in (thereby pollinating the plant at the same time). This gathering is best accomplished on a still, dry afternoon. Gather as much fresh pollen as you can use soon or put by. It is an important flour extender and makes a good addition to biscuit, bread, and cake batters. It should be added in an amount to replace an equal amount of flour deleted from a recipe.

CATTAIL POLLEN CAKES (serves 4)

1 cup sifted cattail pollen
1 cup fine white cornmeal or cattail
   flour (see page 66)
3 teaspoons finely chopped dried
   · spicebush leaves

1 tablespoon honey
2 eggs, beaten lightly
1 1/2 cups water or broth
2 tablespoons sunflower seed oil (see
   page 8)

Thoroughly blend all ingredients together into a smooth batter. On a very hot greased griddle, ladle the batter out into 4 large cakes. Cook for 3 to 5 minutes, until bubbles form on the surface, then flip and finish cooking. Serve hot with nut butter (see page 9) and maple syrup.

HAZELNUT CAKES (12 to 14 small cakes)

¹/₂ pound shelled dried hazelnuts, unblanched and ground finely or pureed	1 teaspoon maple syrup
	¹/₃ cup fine cornmeal
	¹/₃ cup oil for frying
2 cups water	

Boil the nuts in the water for 30 minutes, or until mushy. Add the maple syrup and cornmeal, stir well, and let stand for 20 minutes, or until thick.

Heat the oil in a skillet and drop the nut mixture by tablespoonfuls into the hot oil; brown on one side, flip, flatten into cakes, and brown on the other side. Drain on brown paper. Serve either hot or cold as a bread or breakfast treat.

PUMPKIN-HICKORY CAKES (yields 10 to 12 muffins)

2 cups fine cornmeal	³/₄ cup shelled dried hickory nuts, chopped
1 cup potato flour (see page 66)	
1¹/₂ cups stewed pumpkin meat, beaten smooth	1 egg, beaten with 1 teaspoon water
	¹/₂ cup maple syrup

Mix together the cornmeal and potato flour in a large bowl. Gradually add the remaining ingredients to the flours, blending thoroughly into a smooth batter. Pour into a well-greased loaf pan (9″ x 5″) and bake in a preheated 350° F oven for 1¹/₄ hours, or until a toothpick inserted into the center of the loaf comes out clean. Or spoon the batter into greased muffin tins and bake until golden on top — about 25 minutes.

JOHNNYCAKE "NOKEHICK"* (yields 16 to 20 johnnycakes)

2 cups johnnycake white stone-ground cornmeal	2 cups light or medium cream
	¹/₄ cup corn oil for frying
4 tablespoons maple syrup	
2 cups boiling water or 2 cups clam (quahog) juice	

*Courtesy of Ella Thomas/Sekatau of the Narragansett peoples.

Add the cornmeal and maple syrup to the boiling water (or clam juice), stirring well. Boil for at least 20 minutes, or until thickened. Cool slightly, then thin the batter with the cream until it is firm, not runny. Drop by tablespoonfuls onto a medium-hot, well-greased griddle. Flip after 6 minutes and cook for another 5 minutes.

Johnnycakes were eaten as a cracker and enjoyed with soups and stews. They were also crumbled and used to stuff game, poultry, and squash.

INDIAN CORNMEAL DESSERT* *(serves 10)*

1 cup johnnycake white stone-ground cornmeal	2 cups berries
2 cups cold water	1 teaspoon nutmeg
¹/₄ cup nut butter (see page 9)	³/₄ cup cream
1 cup blackberry, blueberry, or raspberry juice	³/₄ cup maple syrup
	3 eggs, beaten lightly

Soak the cornmeal in the water. Melt the nut butter in a large pot, add the cornmeal mixture, and slowly heat, stirring constantly, for 15 minutes, or until thickened. Add the berry juice, berries, and nutmeg and bring to a boil, stirring constantly. Add the cream and maple syrup, blending thoroughly. Add the eggs and remove from heat, stirring until the mixture stops bubbling. Serve either hot or chilled.

WILD STRAWBERRIES *(Fragaria vesca* and spp.) of June and July were considered a very special fruit by the Native Americans. Indian tribes celebrated this harvesting time with ceremonies and festivals.

These small, fragrant, wild fruits of the meadows and open woods were added to numerous dishes and pressed and dried for winter use.

*Courtesy of Ella Thomas/Sekatau of the Narragansett peoples.

WILD STRAWBERRY BREAD (serves 4 to 6)

1 cup fine cornmeal
1 cup flour
1 cup nut milk (see page 7) or water
2 tablespoons nut oil (see page 7)

1 egg, beaten
$^1/_2$ cup finely cut fresh strawberry leaves
1 teaspoon coltsfoot ashes (see page 27)
1 cup freshly picked wild strawberries

Combine the cornmeal and flour in a large bowl. In a separate bowl, mix together the nut milk (or water), nut oil, egg, strawberry leaves, and coltsfoot ashes. Add to cornmeal and flour mixture and blend well. Fold in the wild strawberries and turn the batter into a well-greased loaf pan (4" x 8"). Bake in a preheated 425° F oven for 40 minutes.

WILD STRAWBERRY
Fragaria vesca

*INDIAN HEMP
Apocynum cannabinum
(See page 158.)

IX

WILDERNESS
BEVERAGES

"When our people lived in the old way, we knew the right time and the right way to hunt and trap and harvest."

. . . Tall Oak, Wampanoag/Mashantucket Pequot Herbalist/Artist, 1974

Nature perennially provides a superabundance of flavorful botanicals for beverages that are healthful and rejuvenating, as well as refreshing. Natural beverages range from wild teas and tisanes to coffees, flavorings, and fruit drinks.

Indians depended largely on edible wild plants for their beverages. When the first settlers arrived, and for centuries afterwards as they were pushing their way westward, they followed suit. If these wild drinks had not been rich in Vitamin C, a vitamin which the body cannot store and which is necessary for the prevention and cure of scurvy, many pioneers could not have lived to open our frontiers.

At the time of the American Revolution, even in the communities where stores were well-stocked, many chose wild drinks rather than continue to use oriental tea, tinged with an English tax. When the Civil War tore the country apart, many northerners and southerners alike had to turn again to the wilds for their teas and coffees.*

Most early peoples instinctively used seasonally available wild botanicals to flavor drinking water, which was the most essential beverage of all. Many plants used in this way were somewhat tart or bitter, but bitterness was considered beneficial, a cleansing, strengthening tonic for the system. Natural saps from various trees and vines provided flavored sweetenings; and among many cultures sap alone was a delightful drink.

*Bradford Angier, *Feasting Free on Wild Edibles* (Harrisburg, Pa.: Stackpole Books, 1966), p. 161.

A growing knowledge of preferred beverage materials led to intriguing mixtures: blended herbal teas, tonics, fruit drinks, medicines, as well as the vinegars, beers, and wines. The fermentation process was known and practiced by most preliterate peoples, and numerous beverages were derived through fermentation, although the inherent alcoholic content was usually very low. Most drinks were imbibed for their specific beneficial effects, much as the medicines similarly used. Often only a fine line separated the two categories in native usage.

Some of the most common North American beverage botanicals are highlighted here, reflecting historical Indian and colonial usage. Many of these beverages can be enjoyed either hot or cold, and in abundance; others are better used in small amounts. In general, any beverage that requires a long steeping period may be reheated, provided it isn't boiled.

ACORN *(Quercus,* about sixty species). Acorn shells are roasted until they lose their astringent quality, then steeped in boiling water or sap for use as a wholesome coffee drink. Allowing 1 teaspoonful per cup, put the "coffee" in a saucepan and simmer for 15 minutes; strain and serve.

BARBERRY *(Berberis canadensis).* The American or Allegheny Barberry is a low, thorny shrub with yellow wood and inner bark. It has edible yellow six-petaled flowers yielding edible scarlet single-seeded berries, which are high in pectin. The young leaves are delicious raw as a trail snack or steeped in boiling water as a light tea (use 1 teaspoonful per cup and steep, covered, for 15 minutes). A nutritious acid "lemonade" is created by diluting the cooked berry juice, then sweetening it with honey or maple sap to taste.

BEARBERRY, Kinnikinnick, Mealberry, Upland Cranberry *(Arctostaphylos uva-ursi).* The dried leaves provide an astringent winter tea with a pleasantly bitter taste. Use 1 teaspoon per cup and steep, covered, for 15 minutes. This tea is considered soothing to the stomach.

BEECHNUT *(Fagus grandifolia).* Roast the husked beechnuts by an open fire (or in a preheated 300° F oven for 30 minutes) to crack the shells. Cool and shell the nuts, then dry further in moderate heat until they are brittle. Grind them fine with a rolling pin and place the "coffee" in a sealed jar until ready to use. To prepare: Allowing 1 teaspoonful per cut, put the "coffee" in a saucepan, cover with boiling water, and simmer for 15 minutes. Strain and serve.

BERGAMOT *(Monarda didyma)* is the red-blossoming Bee Balm or Oswego Tea, and WILD BERGAMOT *(M. fistulosa)* is its lilac- or pink-blossoming relative, along with six additional indigenous species of the mint family. The leaves, stems, and blossoms of these choice, vigorous herbs may be used in a natural tea, soothing for sore throats and settling for the stomach. Cover an entire stalk, minus the roots, in 2 quarts of boiling water; cover the pot and steep for 15 minutes. For an individual cup of tea, use 3 leaves and follow the same procedure. These herbs are a boost for ordinary teas and contain the antiseptic thymol.

BERGAMOT
Monarda didyma

BIRCH *(Betula,* over 14 spp.) is an important genus of deciduous trees tapped in early spring for their flavorful sap. Many tribes harvested this sap as a fresh, nutritious beverage. It was (and still is) used for birch beer and vinegars. By the end of "tapping season" the sap was the base for various teas, and botanicals were steeped in it for additional flavor and sweetness.

BLACKBERRY *(Rubus* spp.). The leaves make an excellent tea that relieves diarrhea. Steep several fresh leaves for 5 minutes in boiling water in a covered pot for a light, mild tea. Blackberry leaves were also an important ingredient in herbal tea mixtures. The fruits make an excellent juice for drinks. Raspberries, which come from the same family, may be used in the same way.

BLACK BIRCH, Cherry Birch, Sweet Birch *(Betula lenta).* The twigs and bark are a primary source of oil of wintergreen. A pleasing, golden woodland tea is derived by steeping fresh (or dried) bark chips and twigs in enough boiling water to cover for 15 minutes in a covered pot or cup.

BLUE COHOSH, Papoose Root, Squaw Root (*Caulophyllum thalictroides*). The bluish seeds are roasted, ground, and boiled to make an excellent coffee drink. Allowing 1 teaspoonful per cup, put the "coffee" in a saucepan and simmer for 15 minutes; strain and serve.

BORAGE (*Borago officinalis*). The leaves and blue blossoms are steeped in boiling water to make a soothing, healthful tea that is high in calcium and potassium. Muddle 2 to 3 fresh or dried leaves in the bottom of a cup; cover with boiling water and steep, covered, for 15 minutes. The same herbal parts may be steeped in wine to render a fine tonic.

CHICORY (*Cichorium intybus*). The leaves and blue blossoms are steeped to make a mild herbal tea that is a digestive aid, as well as a good "medicinal" to relieve mucus congestion. The roasted and ground root is brewed to make a caffeine-free coffee. Measure and brew like conventional coffee.

CLOVER (*Trifolium* spp.) and SWEET CLOVER (*Melilotus* spp.) have perennially provided fine teas. The leaves and blossoms of most species are choice food, tobacco, and tea materials. Steep ⅓ cup fresh (or 1½ teaspoons dried) blossoms for 5 minutes in 1½ cups boiling water; add honey to taste.

COLTSFOOT (*Tussilago farfara*) and SWEET COLTSFOOT (*Petasites palmata* and spp.) contribute their flowers and leaves to medicines, seasonings, tobaccos, and teas. An excellent herb (or medicinal) tea is prepared by steeping 2 teaspoons flowers and/or leaves in 1½ cups boiling water in a covered pot for 30 minutes. Strain and sweeten with honey. This flavorful tea was enjoyed often, especially to ease coughs, colds, bronchial asthma, and diarrhea.

COMFREY (*Symphytum officinale* and spp.). This coarse, introduced perennial herb has been used for centuries. The leaves and roots were brewed (or stewed) in boiling water (or mulled wine) to make a soothing tea. Both fresh and dried materials were used, internally and externally. This plant is still considered one of the finest healing herbs. Comfrey's huge hairy leaves provide the base for many mixed teas, lending a sturdy bouquet and flavor. One leaf is enough for an entire pot of tea; steep, covered, for 5 to 15 minutes, depending upon the strength desired.

DANDELION (*Taraxacum officinale*). This persistent, cosmopolitan herb (introduced from Europe to North America long ago) affords us many uses, reflecting centuries of both pioneer and Indian ingenuity. The blossoms are excellent for teas and wines; the roots (preferably second year or older) provide a delicious caffeine-free coffee. Dig, wash, and dry the lengthy taproot; slowly roast by a low fire or in a slow oven for several hours, until crisp and brown. Grind fine and store in an airtight container; this may be measured and brewed like conventional coffee.

DANDELION BUD
Taraxacum officinale

DEWBERRY (*Rubus* spp.) is a large group of perennial vines of the rose family. The black, shiny berries were used for fruit drinks and wines in late summer, but the prickly leaves were sought all season for tea. Muddle 3 to 5 leaves in the bottom of a cup, cover with boiling water, cover the cup, and steep for 5 minutes.

DILL (*Anethum graveolens*) is a strong-smelling introduced herb that escaped cultivation. Dill tea is made with water or white wine. Muddle 2 to 5 seeds in the bottom of a cup, cover with boiling water (or warmed wine), cover the cup, and steep for 15 minutes. Enjoy 1 to 2 cupfuls a day as a digestive aid and to stimulate the appetite.

DITTANY (*Cunila origanoides.*) This native perennial was utilized for hot beverages by numerous Indian tribes. A hot infusion of dittany leaves was drunk to ease cold symptoms. Add 1 tablespoon leaves to 1 1/2 cups boiling water; steep, covered, for 15 minutes.

ELDERBERRY (*Sambucus canadensis*). An indigenous shrub that had many native uses, elder flowers are excellent dried and steeped as a tisane (use 1 teaspoonful per cup and steep, covered, for 5 to 15 minutes) or added to other teas. Elder rob is a thick, sweetened syrup boiled down from the ripe purple-black berries. This was used as an elixir or was diluted with water to make a delicious fruit drink.

GOLDENROD *(Solidago* spp.) These hardy annuals/perennials were favored by many tribes for both utility and beauty. Collect the fragrant leaves and flowers on a dry day and air-dry. Add 2 teaspoons dried leaves and flowers to a small pot of boiling water, cover, and simmer for 15 minutes; strain and sweeten with honey or maple sap. This is a light, smooth tea.

GRAPE *(Vitis* spp.). Since prerecorded history the ripened grapes from numerous native wild vines have provided excellent beverages, from light teas to wines and vinegars. For a pleasant tea, crush a few grapes in the bottom of a cup and cover with boiling water; steep, covered, for 5 to 10 minutes.

Perhaps the grapevine's true virtue is its clear, watery sap, easily obtained by cutting or severing a sturdy portion of vine. This has saved lives in periods of drought, because the grapevine is capable of storing considerable amounts of liquid.

GROUND IVY
Nepeta hederacea

GROUND IVY, Gill-over-the-ground, Fieldbalm, Cat's-foot *(Nepeta hederacea).* Introduced from Eurasia, it is a perennial found in lawns, orchards, and gardens, in damp, rich, semishaded soil; it is widespread throughout the northern United States and southern Canada and April through June. The leaves and blossoms may be dried to make an enjoyable herb tea. Cover 1 teaspoon dried leaves with 1 cup boiling water; steep, covered, for 5 to 15 minutes.

ICELAND MOSS *(Cetraria islandica).* This pale, skeletal lichen is excellent tea material. Boil 1 teaspoon of the dried plant in 1 cup water, covered, for 30 minutes. Strain, sweeten, and cool. This is a smooth, palatable tea, hot or cold. It may be mixed with nut milk (see page 7) or fruit juice for a pleasing variation.

JUNIPER. (*Juniperus communis* and spp.). Juniper berries (among many other uses) may be roasted and ground to become a coffee drink or added to other coffee mixtures. Measure and brew like conventional coffee. For a large gathering of people, juniper tea may be prepared by combining 20 fresh sprigs juniper, $1/2$ cup blue juniper berries, 2 quarts water, and 2 tablespoons honey in a kettle or pot. Bring to a boil, cover, lower heat, and simmer for 10 minutes. Strain and serve. This pale, fragrant beverage is quite high in vitamin C.

LABRADOR TEA (*Ledum groenlandicum*) is a low, boreal, evergreen shrub, the woolly leaves of which make fine tea leaves. Dry the leaves, then muddle 2 to 3 leaves in a cup and steep, covered with boiling water, for 10 minutes. Sweeten to taste.

LIFE EVERLASTING (*Gnaphalium polycephalum*). A favored native Indian herb, the whole blossoming plant may be dried for use as a very palatable, mild tea. Use 2 quarts boiling water and steep, covered, for 15 minutes.

LINDEN or Basswood (*Tilia americana* and spp.). These large, useful deciduous trees have long been associated with many Indian cultures. The bark and inner fibers have many technological uses. The fragrant, cream-colored blossoms and inner bark are also excellent tea materials. Steep 1 teaspoon fresh (or dried) blossoms in $1 1/2$ cups boiling water in a covered pot for 10 minutes. Sweeten to taste. Excellent for colds.

LOVAGE (*Ligustrum canadense*) and SCOTCH LOVAGE (*L. scoticum*). These smooth perennial herbs provide excellent food and tea resources. Both the celerylike foliage and the large aromatic roots may be enjoyed fresh or dried (in moderate amounts). Add a small handful of leaves and roots to a quart of boiling water; steep, covered, for 15 minutes. Sweetening is hardly necessary. This pale, fragrant tea is mineral-rich and is a digestive aid.

MAPLE (*Acer* spp.). These trees were traditionally tapped by the Eastern Woodlands Indians in late winter and early spring for their clear, sweet sap, which is a bracing, nutritious drink. To refine its sweetness, the sap was simmered for hours until it yielded its amber syrup and sugar. This, in turn, was used to flavor many other beverages and foods. Extensively used as a seasoning prior to salt.

MINT (*Mentha* spp.) is fragrant perennial herbs, both wild indigenous and introduced varieties. Mint leaves are steeped fresh or dried in boiling water to render fine, light teas. Cover 1 tablespoon fresh leaves or 1 teaspoon dried with a cup of boiling water; steep, covered, for 5 to 15 minutes. Mint also enhances and boosts many other herbal and wild teas.

NEW JERSEY TEA *(Ceanothus americanus)* is a common indigenous herbaceous shrub of dry, gravelly soil. The leaves are highly prized for teas; steep 1 tablespoon fresh or 1 teaspoon dried in a cup of boiling water for 15 minutes and sweeten to taste. The dried root bark steeped in water was a fine sedative tea used by many eastern tribes. Some tribes used an infusion made of the whole plant to treat external skin disorders.

PENNYROYAL, Squawbalm, Squawmint, Pudding-grass *(Hedeoma pulegioides)*. This species was used frequently by numerous Indian tribes as a soothing tea to relieve headaches and cramps. Use 1 tablespoon fresh leaves and stems to 1 cup boiling water; steep, covered, for 15 minutes. Drink in moderation. A strong tea of this whole plant makes a good external skin wash for rashes and itching.

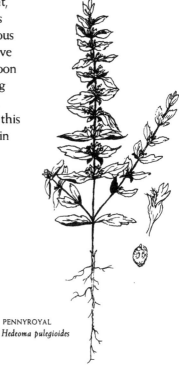

PENNYROYAL
Hedeoma pulegioides

PERSIMMON *(Diospyros virginiana)*. The leaves are dried and steeped in boiling water, 1 teaspoonful per cup, for 10 minutes to create a light tea, very similar in flavor to sassafras. The ripe fruits, after the first frost, are mixed with other fruits in drinks and flavorings.

RASPBERRY *(Rubus* spp.). See Blackberry.

ROSE *(Rosa* spp.). A large family of native and introduced varieties, the ripe hips are prized for teas. The hips are very high in vitamin C, and the whitish seeds are high in vitamin E (grind to extract). For rose hip tea, steep 2 teaspoons crushed whole rose hips (either fresh or dried) in 1 quart boiling water in a covered pot for 10 minutes.

SASSAFRAS *(Sassafras albidum).* This deciduous tree was considered a panacea by both Indians and colonists. The leaves, roots, and bark were favored tea essentials. Muddle 2 or 3 fresh young leaves in the bottom of a cup, cover with boiling water, and steep, covered, for 10 minutes; or cover 1 tablespoon dried roots and bark with 2 cups boiling water and steep, covered, for 30 minutes. Indians used the pale red root infusion to reduce fevers and as a "spring tonic." Sassafras roots are believed to be the first plant product exported from New England. The first shiploads sailed from Cape Cod.

SPICEBUSH
Lindera benzoin

SPICEBUSH, Wild Allspice, Feverbush *(Lindera benzoin).* For centuries this noted member of the laurel family has provided an agreeable beverage. A pleasing tea is brewed from the aromatic leaves, twigs, and bark. Cover 3 to 5 fresh leaves with 1 cup boiling water and steep, covered, for 10 minutes; or cover 1 tablespoon dried roots and bark with 2 cups boiling water and steep, covered, for 30 minutes.

STRAWBERRY *(Fragaria* spp.) was sought for its green leaves and delicious fruits. Use it as you would blackberry.

STAGHORN SUMAC
Rhus typhina

SUMAC *(Rhus glabra* and *R. typhina)*. Sought for its ripe red berry clusters in late summer and fall through winter, pink sumacade (Indian "lemonade") is made by bruising 1 cupful of the red berries and then soaking them for 15 minutes in 1 quart hot (not boiling) water; cool and strain. This pleasing beverage is high in vitamins and in malic acid, which gives it the light citrusy taste. It does not require sweetening.

SUNFLOWER *(Helianthus* spp.). The hulls and seeds were roasted and ground, then brewed into a coffeelike drink by various Woodlands tribes. Measure and brew like conventional coffee.

SWEET FERN or MEADOW FERN *(Comptonia peregrina)*. The highly aromatic dark green leaves of this indigenous deciduous shrub were brewed into a warming tea by many Woodlands peoples. Cover one 10-inch branch with 2 quarts boiling water and steep, covered, for 20 minutes. This tea is so mild and light it does not require sweetening.

SWEET VERNAL GRASS *(Anthoxanthum odoratum)* is a perennial found in dry fields and meadows, and is widespread throughout the eastern and north-central states. It is best harvested in the spring and used as a fragrant herbal tea base. Use 1 teaspoon dried grass to 1 cup boiling water; steep, covered, for 10 minutes.

WILD CHAMOMILE (*Matricaria chamomilla*) and PINEAPPLE-WEED (*Matricaria matricarioides*) are low-growing, lacy perennials. Their small greenish-yellow flowerheads are daisylike, with tiny white rays. The foliage and blossoms have the fragrance of pineapple when disturbed or crushed. The fresh or dried blossoms are steeped to make an excellent pale gold-en, pineapple-scented tea. Use 1 teaspoonful per cup and steep, cov-ered, for 5 minutes. This delicate beverage is calming and settling to the system, especially good to relieve flatulence or upset stomach. An infusion is also beneficial as a shampoo and hair rinse (especially for blonds). A strong, warm infusion is soothing for external ear treatments and can relieve earache. Finally, the same tea is a soil sweetener and will benefit the root systems of potted plants, particularly young seedlings.

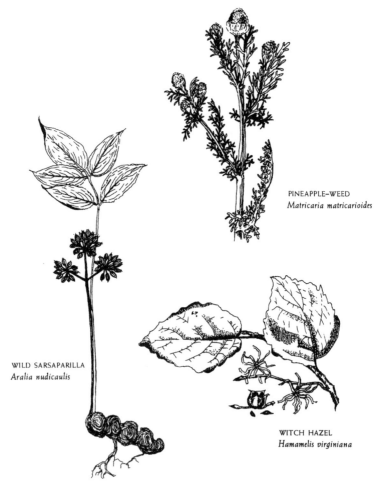

PINEAPPLE–WEED
Matricaria matricarioides

WILD SARSAPARILLA
Aralia nudicaulis

WITCH HAZEL
Hamamelis virginiana

WILD SARSAPARILLA (*Aralia nudicaulis* and spp.). This common woodland herb was sought for its aromatic roots, used to flavor beverages and medicines. A tea of the dried root was considered good for colds and rheumatism and was also used as a soothing external skin treatment. Steep 1 teaspoon dried, ground roots in 1 cup boiling water for 30 minutes.

WITCH HAZEL, (*Hamamelis virginiana*). Sought for its beneficial properties by many Indian tribes, witch hazel was used as a tea primarily by the Iroquois and Cayuga peoples. This fine, refreshing woodland tea has a warming, nutlike flavor. Steep 5 fresh leaves (or 2 teaspoons dried leaves) in 2 cups boiling water in a covered pot for 5 minutes.

NATIVE SEASONAL MENUS AND COMPLEMENTS

". . . so long as we enjoy the light of day, may we greet one another with love; . . . so long as we enjoy the light of day, may we pray for one another . . ."
. . . from a Zuni prayer by Sayataca,
the Bow Priest in the Night Chant, 1932

Wild foods are rapidly becoming endangered. As concerned conservationists and environmentalists, we see our wild resources dwindling in many regions. We must be much more conservative of these resources than our grandparents needed to be. As this Zuni prayer reminds us, we should celebrate each resource. Yet, we must also take sparingly from the edible wild, unless these resources are on your own private property. (See the cautions in Chapter 15, p. 200)

Here, we can focus on some of the common plants and other wild resources that are regionally abundant. Thousands of pounds of purslane, chickweed, nettles, burdock, sorrel, poke, yellow dock, dandelion, and milkweed go to waste each year because we have lost the art of using them to our healthy advantage. Select and clean each ingredient carefully. Remember to give something back in return for all that you take. A pinch of cornmeal, a prayer . . .

Perhaps, you will only choose 2 or 3 items from a certain menu to have with more conventional foods. Yet, here is a chance to develop your wild tastes and a fuller appreciation for the things your ancestors survived upon.

A SPRING CELEBRATION MENU
Steamed Fiddleheads of Ostrich Fern, p. 70
Sauteed Spring Morels, p. 79 or
Marinated Mushrooms with Wild Leeks, p. 85
Buttered Poke Sprouts, p. 52 with
Fresh Chickweed Salad, p. 52
Shad Roe and Milt, p. 102
Wild Strawberry Bread, p. 127 with
Sunflower Seed Butter, p. 9
Labrador Tea, p. 136 with
Maple Syrup, p. 24
Elder Blossom Fritters, p. 123

A SUMMER STRAWBERRY FESTIVAL MENU
Lots of fresh strawberries, wild and cultivated
Sauteed Fairy Ring Mushrooms, p. 79
Buttered Nettles, p. 48
Wild Strawberry Bread, p. 127 with
Strawberry-Mint Butter, p. 9 (using substitutions)
Beechnut-Strawberry Cakes, p. 12 (substituting with strawberries in place of currants)
Steamed Clams, p. 107 or
Clam Chowder, p. 107
Strawberry Water & Strawberry Tea, p. 138

A SUMMER GREEN CORN CEREMONIAL FEAST
Buttered Beech Leaves & Buttered Nettles, p. 48
Milkweed Buds and Blossoms, p. 47
Purslane Salad and Salad of Wild Greens, p. 46
Nasturtium Salad & Dressing, p. 45
Steamed Sweet Corn
Succotash, p. 50
Meadow Mushroom Pie, p. 86
Stewed Wild Rabbit and Dumplings, p. 92
Quahog Fritters, p. 109
Fried Catfish, p. 116
Indian Cake (Bannock), p. 122
Indian Cornmeal Dessert, p. 126
Goldenrod Tea, p. 135, and perhaps Cornmilk

A HARVEST MOON FESTIVAL
Shaggy Mane Pie, p. 87
Purslane and Groundnuts, p. 54
Baked Butternut Squash, p. 55
Fried Squash (or Pumpkin) Blossoms, p. 57
Boston Baked Beans, p. 56
Roast Saddle of Venison with Wild Rice, p.92
Baked Stuffed Bluefish, p.103
Indian Cornmeal Dessert, p. 126
Sweet Fern Tea or Sumacade, p. 139
Baked Stuffed Apples, p. 22

A NATIVE THANKSGIVING FEAST
Jerusalem Artichoke Soup, p. 33 or
Evening Primrose Root Soup, p. 33
Lamb's Quarters (Goosefoot) Greens, p. 45
Wild Rice with Hazelnuts and Blueberries, p. 50
Succotash, p. 50
Baked Pumpkin, p. 55
Pickled Mushrooms, 85
Brunswick Stew, p. 91
Turkey with Oyster-Cornbread-Raisin Stuffing, p. 95
Cranberry Sauce, p. 23
Creamed Oysters, p. 105
Indian Pudding, p. 22, with
Cranberry and Walnut Sauce, p. 23
Wild Grape Butter, p. 21 or
Beech Plum Jam, p. 20
Hickory Nut - Corn Pudding, p. 10
Cranberry - Walnut Cakes, p. 11

A MID-WINTER CEREMONIAL FEAST
Codfish Balls, p. 104
Oyster Patties, p. 106
Conch (Welk) Stew, p. 109
Shrimp and Scallop Pie, p. 112, with edible sea weeds
Irish Moss Jelly, p. 113

WILLOW

Spring Harvests: cattail shoots, wild polyganum spears (knotweed), wild lettuce, dandelion, wild violet salad bowl with Jerusalem Artichoke Roots, and salsify (oyster plant).

Summer Wild Edibles: tea herbs of yarrow and boneset flank a wooden platter of meadow mushrooms, wild strawberries, pumpkin seeds, corn fritters, bee pollen, and Sassafras bark.

Autumn Harvests: honeysuckle basket of wild grapes, clay bowl of acorns, black walnuts, butternuts, chestnuts, hickory nuts, with clam shell of ripe spicebush berries in center; surf clam shell full of wild raisins (nannyberries).

Sweet "green corn" ceremony. Pollen from the male flowers and corn silk, stigmas of the female flowers, are arranged in a prayer for renewed fertility and thankfulness. All plant parts are delicious and used in myriad ways.

X

NATIVE CEREMONIAL AND SACRED PLANTS

"Said Gluscabi to the people, "this blade will give strength to the mind, burn it and inhale the smoke. It will bring freshness to the mind and your heart will be contented . . . Remember her when the smoke of her bones rises before you, whatever be your work, stop in your labor until the smoke has all gone to the Great Spirit."

. . . Joseph Nicolar, Penobscot, 1895

Many plants have sacred meaning to various Native people and all plants have spirits and qualities to be acknowledged. Visions, dreams, ceremonies, and healing rites often illuminated certain plants as having powerful healing capacities. These occurances were considered holy. Certain rites and offering substances were and are given at these special times - to an altar, a particular plant, object, or place.

American Indians living close to their traditional beliefs consider that all life-giving forces deserve respect. Some see this as a continual dance of reciprocity: if we take something, the life of a plant or animal, then something must be given in return. This is most especially urgent in the case of foods and medicines - in order to gain their special nurturing blessings. People might offer a prayer, song, pinch of pollen, cornmeal, bearberry, or tobacco to the particular plant or animal's spirit before its life is taken. This is part of an ancient, detailed, heartfelt practice. In most instances, the offering substance is accompanied by a prayer or song, and often prayers are sung.

Corn has long been considered sacred throughout the Indian Americas. From its mystical beginnings cloaked in ancient horticultural wisdom more than 7,000 years ago in highland Mexico, it traveled along primal trade routes to so many different tribal groups in prehistoric times. Corn was often woven into many tribes' origin stories. The Cherokee had their Corn Mother, Selu, and the Mayans had their Corn Gods and Goddesses immortalized in pre-Columbian stoneware and pottery. Not every tribe were gardeners/farmers, but those who were not, frequently traded with or stole from their gardening neighbors.

Corn pollen and corn silk, from the male and female plant parts, are valuable in medicinal treatments and extremely sacred offering substances, especially during fertility and puberty rites. The ceremonial scattering of corn pollen symbolized fineness, fruitfullness, and, for many, the sun's great energies.

The corn leaves and stalks were fashioned into Native altars and used in sacred kiva rites and longhouse rites. Corn leaves and shucks were dried, braided, twisted, or woven into astonishing cornhusk ceremonial masks by the Iroquois, Delaware, Cherokee, and other tribes, who also made utilitarian objects from these materials. Corn shucks were and are used to wrap, tie, and encase small select servings of foods like tamales and some cornmeal breads.

Cornmeal has long been one of the most universal American Indian offering substances. Herbalists and medicine people often carry small amounts of sacred cornmeal (that has been blessed and prayed over) in a special pouch for use as traditional offerings.

Harvest ceremonies are sometimes enhanced by tying a kernel of corn, a dried bean, pumpkin seed, and sunflower seed into a tiny prayer bundle along with a pinch of sage or tobacco. Such small colorful prayer ties are sometimes given as special blessings to individuals who attend ceremonies and harvest rites. These same powerful prayer bundles can also bless the solstice and equinox rites and observations, and are well-prepared as gifts before spring planting and fertility rites.

The pollen of cattail and tule was sacred to many western tribes, especially the Apache and Navajo who used good amounts of this during their 3-to-5-day puberty rites. The Pomo and Karok and other California tribes, and some of the Great Lakes tribes, also collected and saved these plant pollens for their special ceremonial needs.

The spores of various Club Moss (*Lycopodium* species) were carried in special pouches and used like pollen for ceremonial and medicine rites. The spores of ripe puffballs (*Lycoperdon* and *Calvatia* species) were used ceremonially, dusted on the body, as well as medicinally. Prodigious quantities of windblown conifer spores dusted over northern lands and were collected and used by many tribes in healing and ceremonial rites.

Shredded Cedar bark and leaves and Juniper bark and leaves were and are sacred and used ceremonially by many tribal groups. These have long been popular for their fragrances and preservative qualities. Fine shredded cedar bark was woven or twisted into imaginative ceremonial masks, collars, capes, mats, and other adornments, especially among the Northwest Coast Peoples, whose totem pole and potlatch cultures are greatly admired.

All across the continent and range of the cedars and junipers, their fine peeled bark was sought for disposable diapers and sanitary napkins, as well as healing bandages and insulation. Cedar bark smudge (burning fragrant smoke) is still the most desirable insecticide and room purifier, and often blesses Native ceremonies and prayers.

Sagebrush (*Artemisia tridentata*) is one of the most sacred ceremonial substances as well as a common shrub west of the Mississippi River. Numerous other species of native sage in both the *Artemisia* and *Salvia* families are used extensively by Indians throughout the Americas. Some have come to commercial markets because of the growing need for them in sacred and ceremonial rites. Rocky Mountain Sage (*A. arbruscula*) and California Sage (*A. californica*) are extensively sought for ceremonial smudging, and leaves are chewed for relief of congestion and sore throat. There are 19 species of sage native to the greater California-West Coast regions, and a few species native to the northern regions, stretching back across Siberia into Asia.

Sand sage (*A. filifolia*) of the Desert South-West regions and Alaskan Sage (*A. frigida*) which grows down into Kansas and Arizona, are also used medicinally and ceremonially. The highly aromatic White Sage (*A. ludoviciana*) is also extensively used in smudging and medicines. Many more *native Salvia* species are used ceremonially, especially the southwestern Greaswood, or White

Sage (*Salvia apiana*) and the Great Plains Blue Sage (*S. azurea*). Scarlet Sage, or Texas Sage (*S. coccinea*) is cultivated for its stunning blossoms and foliage, as is the Pineapple-scented, red-flowered Sage (*S. elegans*) native to Mexico. All sages are members of the great mint family, Labiatae, noted for their aromatic qualities and cooling, fever-reducing principles.

Bearberry (*Arctostaphylos uva-ursi*) is a perennial trailing shrub that has long been highly esteemed by northeastern Indians for its fragrant dried leaves and bark. Pouches of dried bearberry were carried as ceremonial offering substance. This botanical was commonly called by its early Algonquian name *Kinnikinnik*, which also means mixture. A rich kinnikinnik might also contain dried sumac leaves, berries, and bark, willow, alder, and dogwood bark, goldenrod blossoms and leaves, and the dried leaves and blossoms of lobelia, everlasting, wild mints, meadowsweet, pussytoes, mullein, sunflower, yarrow, and wild lettuce. Additional regional botanicals might also be added. Kinnikinnik was sometimes burned and smudged, like incense, and prayed with much like tobacco and sweetgrass. Yet, it was also carried and offered dry with prayers, especially to medicinal plants and game animals before the harvests and hunts.

Sweetgrass (*Hierochloe odorata*) and Sweet Vernal Grass (*Anthoxanthum odaratum*) are two of the most special fragrant ceremonial grasses. All across Indian America, there are highly valued "sweetgrasses" - although not always the same botanicals. Some of the finest fancy baskets have sweetgrass woven through them or bound around their rims and lids. Fine quilled birchbark boxes are often finished with strands of fragrant sweetgrass. American Indian men and women often braided sweetgrass into their hair, and still do - for the perfumed good fortune and symbolic reverence it alone can bring. Sweetgrass was often carried and sometimes smudged for ceremonial prayer offerings. Sweetgrass is considered to be the hair of Mother Earth, and many of the shiny green blades grow to be more than 3-feet long by September, when it is usually harvested.

Many more sedges and rushes have fragrant qualities than the grasses, and as you move across the continent, western tribes' "sweetgrass" is usually a regional sedge or rush, yet it appears grasslike in every way, botanically. Sweetgrass was/is often braided or plaited in long braids and carried or wrapped with fine buckskin clothing, ceremonial masks, and other ritual objects. There is a strong Native belief that ritual objects must be "fed" and prayed over in order to renew their sacred energies.

White Birch and White Pine trees have long been considered special, and of sacred value to many Native people. Among the Iroquois, or Haudenausonee, "People of the Longhouse," in upper New York State and Canada, the White Pine symbolizes their White Roots of Peace – beneath which their weapons of war were buried centuries ago when they decided to follow their Peace Maker, Deganowida. They joined together to make the Five Nations. Later, in the 1700s they embraced the Tuscarora, who moved into their regions in 1722, and became the Six Nations. The Great Iroquois Confederacy has remained one of the strongest in the Northeast.

One of the most sacred plants throughout the Indian Americas is tobacco. Tobacco symbolized many things to different tribes and groups of Native people. Some tribes had and have tobacco societies and tobacco dieties, especially among the early Mayan, Aztec, and other Native Peoples in pre-Columbian Mexico and Central America, where there are more native wild species of tobacco. [See "Wild Smoking Mixtures" Chapter, 13 pages 186-192]. The fragrance and taste of tobacco smoke has long been considered sacred and therapeutic as it was used in healing ceremonies. The ceremonial smoking and sharing of tobacco symbolized the breath of life. The fragrant rising tobacco smoke carries prayers, thoughts, and chants to the Creator. Many tribes have creation stories about the origin of tobacco as a holy herb. Often, these intricate stories are as different as the people whose cultures they come from.

Many traditional folks wear tobacco pouches, which are often of finely-worked soft buckskin. Carrying and wearing tobacco is considered a protection from harm for many folks and can signify a follower of traditional pathways. It is usually a mark of respect to give an elder a gift of tobacco, especially wrapped in red cloth. Long before tobacco became a pricey recreational drug, during these past few centuries, it was primarily carried and reserved for ritual uses and to relax and sedate the ill and elderly.

Tobacco offerings are usually made during the daytime and a pinch of tobacco is offered to the object or spirit one wishes to bless.

Ceremonial prayers and opening events are usually prefaced with tobacco offerings to the four cardinal directions of north, south, east, and west – with prayers to each of these major directions. Many tribes also follow this with two or three additional directions: to the Sky World or Creator, to the Earth Mother, and to the Center (or self). With this grand sweep of ritual consideration, all living things are blessed with grateful praise.

Tobacco ties are prayerfully made before sweatlodge rites and Sun Dance Ceremonies. A tiny pinch of tobacco is prayed over and carefully tied into a small piece of red cotton cloth. Each tie contains a prayer. Some people may string together many prayer ties as they talk with the Creator about many special needs, especially for other people.

There are perhaps 70 species of tobacco native to the tropical and warm temperate regions. *(Nicotiana rustica)* and *(Nicotiana tabacum)* have been cultivated by Indian populations since early pre-Columbian times. *(N. acuminata)* originated in Chile and Argentina, *(N. glauca)* originated in Bolivia, and *(N. attenuata)* originated in California regions, where each had significant Native uses and were spread through trade.

"To replace what you have taken by making a tobacco offering is a recognition or acknowledgement of the life you take."

. . . *Trudie Lamb Richmond, Schaghticoke,* 1987

SMUDGING

"Powerful are the things we use."
. . . *Menomini, Great Lakes*

"Smudging" is the ritual act and art of "bathing" the body, mind, spirit, and emotions in sacred smouldering (smoking) herbs. Native Sagebrush or White Sage (not culinary or cooking sage) is typically used, and sometimes, it is mixed with tobacco, cedar, bearberry, juniper, or sweetgrass. Each of these sacred native herbs are respected for their symbolism and special meanings to different people.

In southern regions of Mexico and Central America, copal, so sacred to the Maya, Aztec, and other tribes, is used as smudge during rituals. Across the Desert Southwest, sage, mesquite, chamisa, or juniper are favored to smudge with during certain rituals. Today, lavendar, rosemary, or mugwort are frequently added to sage or sweetgrass to carry Eurasian gifts of "remembrance" and healing in therapeutic ways.

Smudging is an act of praying and sending prayers to the Creator. For countless centuries, smudging, the burning/smoking of aromatic herbs, has been an honored practice among American Indians and other tribal people. This is a means to cleanse away sadness or anger, remove negative energies, purify objects and locations and people, and bless ceremonies and special gatherings of people. The rising smoke carries our prayers toward the Sky World so the Creator and the spirits of our ancestors and loved ones can see that we remember to follow a good path in life.

We usually gather in a circle, if possible. First we offer smudge to the four cardinal directions: north, south, east, and west; and to Father Sky, Mother Earth, and "here" (our center). One person may smudge each individual, or the smudging may be passed around from one to another, each taking time with it to do their own prayers for cleansing. Often, we pass the smudge around the circle as each one smudges their next "neighbor" in a process of bonding and honoring each other. As we smudge and cleanse each other, we also care for each other.

I cup my hands (or use a feather or feather fan) and draw the fragrant smoke toward my eyes and up over my head – to clarify my vision and purify my thoughts and relax my mind, while sending my prayers upward to the Creator. Then, I draw more smoke with my cupped hands across my throat and heart and down and around my whole body, especially my hands and feet. I use a large abalone or clam shell, clay or pyrex dish to hold the smudge and pass this around my whole body.

XI

HERBAL TRADITIONS: MEDICINAL PLANTS AND NATURAL HEALTHCARE

"May all things move and be moved in me and know and be known in me.
May all creation dance for joy within me."

. . . Chinook prayer

YUPON HOLLY
(*Ilex Vomitoria*)

The uses of floral environments are deeply woven into people's way of life. Herbal traditions of every American Indian cultural group on this continent reach far back into prehistory. American Indians had an exceptional understanding of laxative, diurectic, emetic, birth control, childbirth aids, and fever-reducing therapeutics in native plants. Indians made use of the cardiac stimulating properties of native lobelias, dogbanes, milkweeds, and foxgloves. Native healers created formulas to successfully treat skin tumors, abcesses, and respiratory problems, and they pioneered the use of our first birth control formulas.

Today, millions of Americans take native plant extracts each day to treat heart disease, lower high blood pressure and high cholesterol levels, as well as relieve PMS and some of the problems of menopause. More and more trained midwives are delivering babies in the comfort of the home. New cancer and diabetes treatments are being revealed from common native plants and fungi. Contemporary society continues to benefit from the investigative prowess of our first American scientists, the American Indians, who discovered in their natural world the sources and secrets of healing.

Perhaps 80 percent of all medicinal plants harvested in North America are collected east of the Mississippi River, yet a shrinking number are wildcrafted (collected from the wild). More of the medicine plants and fungi are being cultivated and "farmed" for the burgeoning healthcare markets. American Ginseng is a major commercial farm crop in eleven states, where it is shade-grown. American Arnica, Prairie Cone Flower, St. John's Wort, Evening Primrose, and a growing number of native plants and fungi are dictating a new future in American farming, keeping us close to our land-based wisdom.

Continuing research also seeks new drugs and ways to produce them synthetically. Because some plant substances defy synthesis, modern medicine remains dependent on many of the same botanicals American Indians used for healing.

Native plants offer contemporary society many uses beyond healing. We are all aware, to some extent, of the impact cotton, tobacco, corn, allspice, avocado, squash, pumpkins, peppers, beans, chocolate, and vanilla have had on our civilization. Perhaps 75 percent of our modern foods were unknown to our European ancestors 500 years ago.

Various barks, roots, seeds, dried blossoms, and leaves of many native botanicals, along with a growing number of fungi, Jerusalem artichoke pastas, cattail and acorn flours appear on the shelves of our nation's healthfood stores and specialty markets. Sunflower seed butter, margarine, and oil, along with cotton seed oil seem to be surpassing corn oil products in contemporary markets. Yet corn, the true "gold of the Americas," is well woven throughout our lives, sweetening most of our beverages, ice creams, and dessert products, coating our paper plates, as sizing-coating our carpets, clothes, and some office products, and fermenting into fuels to drive vehicles of the future.

Witch hazel, jojoba, yucca, and aloe currently have tremendous cosmetic and industrial values. It would seem to be a renaissance of sorts, but these plants, and many others, have been sustaining the health, comfort, and life needs of people on this continent for countless centuries.

Some plants contain one or more toxic substances which could have a poisonous effect on human and animal systems. Others could prove harmful if used incorrectly, in quantity, or in the wrong season.

A * indicates plants with known toxic qualities. Plant chemistries vary widely, even those growing in the same areas, and the pollution of plant systems and environments is an ever-present problem.

AMERICAN GINSENG Centuries of over-harvesting have made American Ginseng (*Panax quinquefolius*) increasingly rare in the wild. For more than four centuries, roots of this perennial woodland herb have been shipped to the Orient for tremendous profits. American Ginseng is often sought in place of the more expensive oriental varieties as each are considered to be valuable restoratives. Ginseng requires three to five years growth to produce harvestable roots, and they are now extensively cultivated in shadehouses (grown under lathe) to supply steadily increasing demands.

American Indians in the northeast used the roots to treat convulsions, nervous disorders, colds, fevers, rheumatism and headaches. The root tea was used to ease childbirth and strengthen mother and baby. The powdered roots were a good styptic and wound dressing. Today, ginseng-root teas and formulas are costly and desirable tonics and stimulants. Extensive research shows that ginseng increases physical and mental efficiency and improves concentration while preventing overfatigue. In addition to benefiting the human immune system more effectively than synthetic stimulants, ginseng can be used longer and without side effects.

AMERICAN HELLEBORE*, or White Hellebore (*Veratrum viride**) is a tall, attractive, perennial herb of the wetlands. Even though it is highly poisonous, American Indian healers used the roots extensively to treat everything from toothaches to rheumatism, asthma, and high blood pressure. Some northeastern tribes used the pounded roots externally to shrink skin tumors.

American Hellebore and related species are valued today *in cautious use* as sedatives and cardiac depressants, as they lower blood pressure and dialate the arteries. Since the 1950s, certain alkaloids, acids, and mineral salts refined from the roots have been explored as potential antihypertensive agents. In closely monitored clinical use, they show great promise in treating, and in some cases preventing, heart failure, strokes, and kidney failure. Laboratory research continues to excite interest in their treatments for cancerous tumors.

BLACK ASH About 16 species of Ash trees are native to North America. American Indians valued the wood of the Black Ash *(Fraxinus nigra)* and White Ash *(F. Americana)* for splint basketry, tool handles, bowls, snowshoes, and lacrosse sticks. They steeped the leaves, buds, seeds, and twigs for various medicinal teas. The twigs were chewed as dentifrices and chew sticks.

The inner bark was chewed and applied as a poultice on sores and as a treatment for hemorrhoids. Women drank a strong tea made from the inner bark as a "thinning" beverage and diuretic, as it helped them loose weight. Strips or sheets of the outer bark, best slipped in spring, were shaped into vessels, and the pounded wood growth rings (splints) were plaited into diverse baskets. Today, the white ash wood is used commercially for tool handles, furniture, choice veneers, baseball bats, and fine paneling.

The old Iroquois wood ADIRONDACK means "bark eaters" and the tribes who lived in this great region did eat the inner bark of most deciduous trees because it was a reliable food resource and extensive "medicine chest" for human needs.

CATTAILS Ameican Indians had a multitude of uses for the ubiquitous marsh plants found in wet areas all across North America. Common Cattail *(Typha latifolia)* and Narrow-leaved Cattail *(T. angustifolia)* produce dense foliage useful for rope, insulation, baskets, mats, and caulking, as well as plentiful spring pollen for food, medicine, and ceremonial uses. Young flowerheads were and are delicious food, and when left to maturity, they bollow abundant cottony down used for disposable diapers, sanitary napkins, bedding, and insulation.

During winter, American Indians dug the creeping whitish roots for food and a treatment for diarrhea, gonorrhea, and intestinal parasites. They also applied the pounded poulticed roots to the skin for relief to minor burns and wounds. Indians separated the minute seeds from their downy fluff and worked them into salves to treat burns.

Cattails have enormous potentials today as absorbers and possible recyclers of toxic substances in soil and water. They are amazing fringe plants and are often grown around sewage treatment facilities, and border many airports and thruways. Cattails are also valuable renewable energy resources, as they can be compressed into fuel pellets, and their starch can be transformed into alcohol.

COTTON* The Cotton commonly cultivated today is an annual shrub with a boll of distinctive black seeds in white or light cotton fluff. Of the two New World species of cotton cultivated by pre-Columbian Indians, (*Gossypium hirsutum**), the oldest cotton grown in this hemisphere can be dated back to about 2500 B.C. in prehistoric Mexico. Ninety-five percent of all cotton grown in the world today is of this species. Cotton remains the world's most important plant fiber, the basis for more clothing than all other fibers combined.

In addition to its tremendous value for textiles, cotton was also used by the Alabama and Koasati people as a boiled root tea to ease childbirth labor. In the past decades, scientists have discovered that cotton seeds contain a toxic substance, *gossypol*. It has been developed and tested as a male contraceptive in China. Cottonseed oil is used today for shortening and margarine production. The nutritious seed meal that remains after the oil is extracted is a rich source of protein for Third World countries.

INDIAN HEMP* or Dogbane (*Apocynum cannabinum**) and Spreading Dogbane (*A. androsaemifolium**) are widespread perennial herbs whose slender stems and long pencil-thin pods were used for fiber and medicines. Both species provided strong durable fiber for cordage, latex (from broken plant parts) to help bind pigments for paints, and medicinal pod and roots useful for a broad range of treatments. The entire plant was used as a heart stimulant; chewed or consumed as a bitter tea, it was also effective against fevers, intestinal parasites, asthma, and pneumonia.

Fibers from these species have been found and identified in archaeological remains of prehistoric Indian fabric in the Midwest, which date back to 1000 B.C. These are the most rot-resistant fibers in wide use throughout ancient America. Although these plants are toxic and emetic if eaten, these botanicals yield beneficial diuretic teas.

Indian Hemp was also called rheumatism wood and rheumatism root, Choctaw root, wild ipecac, and wild cotton in various regions. These popular medicinal plants are currently being studied for their potential cardiovascular benefits, as they contain the cardiotonic glycosides, cymarin and apocannoside, which - have digitalis-like properties.

INDIAN TOBACCO*, of the Lobelia family, is an annual branching herb with acrid milky juice, whose delicate purple-blue blossoms (occasionally white) are common wildflowers. Fifteen species of Lobelia and numerous regional varieties grow in diverse habitats. Great Lobelia (*Lobelia siphilitica**) was so named in the 17th century because it was valued as a treatment for syphilis. Many American Indians dried the leaves and blossoms of Wild Tobacco (*L. inflata**) and used them as stimulants and expectorants. Indian Tobacco was also a popular asthma remedy; however, an overdose induces coma and may result in death.

Lobelias contain the alkaloid *lobeline* which, like nicotine, acts first as a stimulant and then as a depressant on the autonomic nerves. Today, this alkaloid is a common ingredient in a number of anti-smoking preparations because it induces nausea. *Lobeline* from *Lobelia Inflata* stimulates respiration and is used today to revive patients who have taken narcotic overdoses.

JEWELWEED (*Impatiens biflora*) is a colorful succulent herb that grows in moist rich areas and self-sows its seeds annually. American Indians valued this common orange-yellow spotted plant as a spring potherb and as a medicinal tea to treat colds. Jewelweed was also used as a diuretic, emetic, and cathartic. The fresh juice of the crushed whole plant was applied to bruises, sores, skin rashes, fungal infections, and sprains.

Pale Touch-Me-Not (*I. pallida*) has light yellow flowers and very similar uses. Both species yield vibrant yellow dye for wool, with rusty nails added to the syebath to produce deeper shades of orange. Jewelweed is one of nature's antidotes to poison ivy rash, and if rubbed on the exposed skin soon after contact with poison ivy, this treatment can prevent the dermatitis. The crushed plant also helps relieve the itch of insect and spider bites and other skin irritations. Today, it is being examined for its antibiotic qualities and as a fungicide for treating athlete's foot and ringworm.

MILKWEED* For countless centuries American Indians have explored a multitude of food, medicinal, and decorative uses for Common Milkweed (*Asclepias syriaca**). Archaeologists have discovered remnants of a milkweed fiber fishnet dating back to 300 B.C. in a prehistoric Indian site in Ohio. Like its botanical "cousins" the dogbanes, milkweed fibers are also very rot-resistant, making them excellent for hunting and fishing needs. Perhaps, 25 species of these perennial plants inhabit widely different ecosystems across the Americas.

American Indians ate the spring-emerging spears of common milkweed, well cooked, as an asparagus-like vegetable. Later, the buds, blossoms, and young pods were cooked for delicious vegetables, but otherwise, all plant parts are highly toxic. The milky latex that exudes from broken plant parts was a caustic skin treatment for ringworm and warts. Some tribes chewed this milky latex like chewing gum. They also drank a decoction of milkweed roots as an emetic and purgative to cleanse their systems, and this was also used to treat dysentry and asthma.

Some Indian tribes used milkweed decoctions to prevent conception. The vibrant orange-flowered Butterly Weed (*A. tuberosa*), also called Pleurisy root or Choctaw root, provided a bitter cold medicine and treatment for pulmonary troubles, as well as a fine red dye for basket fibers. Essential components in Indian medicine bags, the roots were used as treatments for everything from poison ivy rashes to heart problems. Milkweed is of continuing importance to contemporary medicine for its inherent cardiac glycosides.

OAKS are a large family with perhaps 58 species native to our continent north of Mexico, and over 150 Mexican species. Acorns develop through one of two growing seasons, with heavy crops occurring every two to four years. After being cracked and leached of their constipating tannins, acorns were pounded or ground into a meal which Indians used for breads, soups, patties, and mushes.

The White Oak (*Quercus alba*) of the northeast, and the California White Oak (*Q. lobata*) and Tan Oak (*Lithocarpus densiflora*) produce the sweetest edible acorns. Caches of acorns have been found in various New York state archaeological sites which date back to 3000 B.C. The high nutritional content and ability to withstand long storage made acorns the staple food among the Pomo and other West Coast tribes, as well as among many Eastern Woodland Peoples. Indians attached great spiritual values to oak trees, in addition to using parts of oaks for foods, medicines, baskets, bark trays, tanning leathers, and a range of dye colors.

The astringent tannins in oak bark teas and wound dressings were highly effective treatments for sore throats, coughs, colds, colic, rheumatism, and diarrhea. These constituents also healed sores and rid wounds of excess mucous secretions. The Winnebago, Pawnee, Dakota, and Omaha used oak root and bark teas to ease colic in children and treat numerous health needs. The Iroquois dusted the scraped powdered bark from oak burls (special growth areas on certain trees) on skin sores and tumors. Many tribes ate the inner bark of young oaks as survival food.

Oaks are abundant hardwoods with exceptional importance in today's lumber industry. The wood is a favorite choice for veneers, cabinets, flooring, furniture, barrels, and boats. Several species of oaks are favored as ornamental trees for urban parks and city streets, as they are very disease resistant and resilient to ground and air pollution. Constituents from oak bark and burls also provide powerful tumor and cancer fighting benefits, and researchers believe the oaks may possess anti-AIDS drugs.

OSWEGO TEA (*Monarda didyma*) is the tall red-blossoming Bee Balm native to our northeastern regions, and perhaps our showiest native mint. This was a choice herb among numerous tribes. These flowers, fragrant leaves, and square stems were brewed into soothing teas to treat sore throats, upset stomach, and rubbed on the skin to sooth poison ivy and other skin rashes.

Wild Bergamot (*M. fistulosa*) is a close relative with lilac to pink blossoms, and very similar uses. These showy native perennial mints were favored medicinal, fragrance, smoking, and culinary herbs among numerous Indians. The Delaware (Lenni Lenape) considered these ceremonial herbs and special perfumes, which they packed among their buckskins and finest objects.

When EuroAsian teas were unpopular after the Boston Tea Party and again during the Civil War, these plants were common and favorite substitutes. Both of these species are popular teas today and used in many tea and medicine formulas. Their fragrance closely resembles bergamot oil (derived from the rind of a small citrus fruit native to the Mediterranean region) used to flavor Earl Grey teas. These species, along with the related Horsemint (*M. punctata*) are a source of fragrant oils, and sometimes used as cardiac stimulants and antiseptic thymol, which effectively soothes mucous membranes. Today, the liquor of thymol is a key ingredient in the mouthwash Listerine.

POKE* American Indians and colonists frequently used the native perennial Poke (*Phytolacca Americana**) as an early spring potherb, medicine, dye, and ink. Tribes of the Virginia regions boiled the toxic berries and long taproot into teas to cure rheumatism. Concoctions of poke root were applied externally for various skin ailments and parasites. Indians used the dried root sections, strung in a simple necklace, to ease young children's teething discomforts. Indeed, dried poke roots were carried in the medicine bags of most herbalists.

Powdered poke roots were used in a poultice to treat skin cancers, thus giving us the common names for this plant of cancerroot and cancer jalap. Fresh green leaves were applied to wounds, swellings, and ulcers as curing poultices. Young leaves and spring stalks of poke, processed in several changes of boiling water, are annually consumed as spring potherbs across the south, and canned poke - as "poke salat" - is available throughout the year.

Many believed this spring tonic was also a powerful preventative medicine. This single species yields numerous alkaloids and complex chemicals, some of which are quite harmful to human systems. A pokeweed mitogen is being studied in antitumor immunity research, as it seems to stimulate cell transformation.

SAGEBRUSH* (*Artemisia tridentata*) is a tall gray branching perennial shrub native to dry open plains and scrub borders. More than 17 species of native sage grow in various habitats throughout North America, extending in some regions to sub-alpine locations. Perhaps another 19 species are native to the west coast regions alone. Yet sagebrush is one of the most widely distributed shrubs in western North America.

The pungent odor of sagebrush is an effective insect repellent; Indians burned/smoked branches of dried sage as a smudge to drive away insects and especially as a ceremonial ritual cleansing agent. The aromatic foliage was rubbed on skin and clothes, and placed under bedding and pillows to repel bedbugs, fleas, lice, and ticks. Indians also rubbed leather hides with sage during the tanning process, and when hides were smudged in thick sage smoke, they were softer and more water-repellent.

Sagebrush leaves and shredding bark provided excellent padding materials for babies diapers and cradleboards. Plains tribes often fashioned clothing and accessories from a fragrant shredding bark. Sage was used extensively as a deodorant for pillows, hides, clothing, moccasins, saddles, and also as toilet paper.

Pasture Sage *(A. frigida)* is the common low-growing shrub of the southern prairies, widely distributed throughout the west. Many tribes used it as a source of camphor. The coumarin glycosides of sage are the focus of some medical research today.

WILLOWS   The large willow family of shrubs and trees grow in cooler north-temperate zones, and perhaps 80 species are native to North America. Willows are key signs of wet areas and were frequently sought for the broad range of health problems provoked by dampness, such as colds, arthritis, rheumatism, and flu. Our native Black Willow *(Salix nigra)* is our tallest, most widespread east of the Rockies.

Throughout their history, American Indians have woven willow rods, or branches, into a great variety of lifeways necessities. Willow was favored to weave cradleboards, backrests, house mats, sleeping platforms, tightly-woven water bottles, and diverse baskets. Willow is also favored to build the sweat lodges.

Basket makers today still prefer willow withes and rods. The twigs and bark of most willows were highly respected Indian medicines and dentifrices. Bark and roots contain a bitter glucoside called *salicin,* which is a primal form of aspirin that was used to relieve headaches, fevers, arthritis, rheumatism, interal body aches and pains, and external swellings. Many naturalists and campers continue to regard willow bark, either chewed or brewed for tea, as the best trailside remedy for fevers, headaches, cramps, and colds - until conventional first aid is available.

WITCH HAZEL *(Hamamelis virginiana)* is a common indigenous shrub of the open woodlands, and considered an ancient Indian antiseptic. Leaves and twigs were widely used by many tribes as an astringent wash for wounds, bruises, and muscular aches. The shiny black seeds and woody pods were incorporated into some medicine ceremonies and ground into medicines. The Iroquois made a warming tea of witch hazel leaves steeped in spring water with maple syrup or honey.

Called tobacco wood, snapping hazel, and winterbloom in various regions, the spidery yellow blossoms of witch hazel appear in early winter, usually after the leaves have turned yellow and begun to fall. This is a harbinger of the harvest time and Indian Summer. Herbalists applied pounded bark poultices to skin tumors and inflammations, especially around the eyes. Indians chewed young twigs and bark to freshen the mouth, treat gum problems, and massage the gums.

Indians and colonists used the forked branches of witch hazel as divining or "witching" rods to locate water or special metals and lost objects. Witch hazel cutters continue to collect these renewable resources during the dead of winter for cottage industries that distill the bark for extract of witch hazel. This is one of the older time-honored antiseptics and liniments that continues to enjoy widespread use.

YAUPON HOLLY (*Ilex vomitoria*) is one of 11 native species of holly in North America. This attractive evergreen shrub, which can grow to tree size, ranges across our southern coastal plains and into the midwest, often growing in dense thickets along stream and ponds. It is also planted as a decorative shrub throughout the South.

For centuries, its leaves were collected and roasted, then brewed to produce the noted Indian "black drink," important in cleansing ceremonies to cement friendship and promote communication. Remains of inscribed shell cups used in the ceremonies accompanying the drinking of this brew have been found at the Temple Mound Culture site of Spiro in Oklahoma and other sites in the east, such as Etowah in Georgia. Creek and Cherokee people continue the traditional uses of the yaupon in their ceremonial and medicine practices today.

Non-alcoholic beverages are still derived from this plant, as its leaves contain an appreciable amount of caffeine, which stimulates the central nervous system. Yaupon was an especially popular tea during the Civil War, when conventional teas were often unavailable. A close relative is mate (*I. paraguariensis*) whose leaves are brewed into the most popular beverage in southern South America. Yaupon has at times been the source of cassina tea, a great favorite in the southern states and popular flavoring for soft drinks and ice creams.

These few plant profiles give a brief glimpse into the economic impact and cultural medicinal virtues of only a small fraction of America's native botanicals.

Natural health care is the most widely available complement to our wellness and healing today. We are living in an age of greater informed wisdom about many things. How we choose to use this knowledge shapes our tomorrows.

[In a similar form, this was first published in 1983 by the Smithsonian Institution Traveling Exhibition Service (SITES) in Washington, D.C. to accompany the exhibition, *Native Harvests: Plants in American Indian Life*, which I curated.]

OSWEGO TEA
Monarda didyma
(See pages 161–162.)

SAGEBRUSH
Artemisia tridentata
(See pages 162–163.)

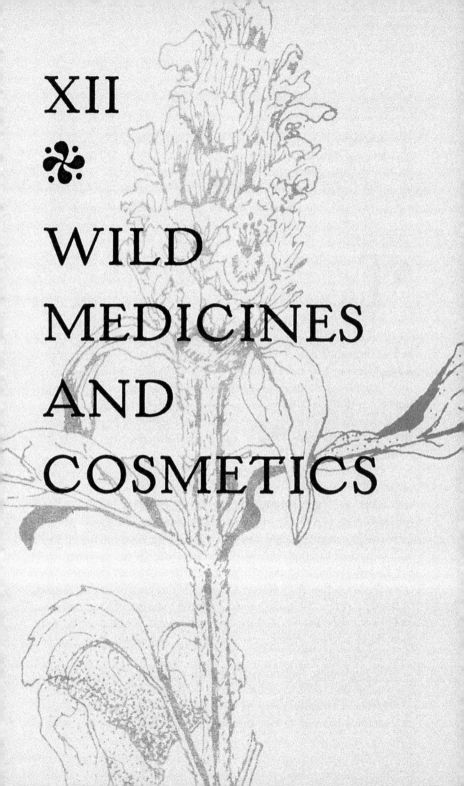

XII

WILD
MEDICINES
AND
COSMETICS

"For three nights I had the same dream. I was walking in the old Shantup burying ground along the banks of the river. There I saw a stand of three white birches near a flat rock."

> ... Burrill H. Fielding [1862-1952], Connecticut Mohegan

The Indians, our first scientists, discovered in the plant world the sources and the secrets of healing. Aboriginal knowledge and usage of native botanicals were remarkable, unique, and accurate. The Indians had an exceptional understanding of laxative, diuretic, emetic, birth-control, and fever-reducing drugs. Foxglove (*Digitalis purpurea*) was correctly used by the Indians for its cardiac-stimulant properties for centuries before William Withering discovered digitalis in England in 1785.

Primitive Indian diets, often frugal, were generally better balanced than those of the early settlers, and the Indians were afflicted less frequently with vitamin-deficiency diseases.

During the bitter-cold winter of 1535–1536, the three ships of Jacques Cartier were icebound in the St. Lawrence River near the present site of Montreal. Isolated and starving, the company of 110 men barely subsisted until mid-March, by which time scurvy had become so rampant that 25 men had died and the rest were so weakened that there was little hope for their recovery. Cartier's auspicious encounter with the Laurentian Iroquois chief Domagaia (who had cured himself of the same disease earlier that winter) brought the Iroquois people to the aid of the dying crew. Iroquois women gathered branches of local hemlock and black spruce trees, boiled the bark and needles, and fed the Frenchmen the decoction. Those treated internally and externally readily recovered their health.

Although these Indians were unaware of vitamin C, their curative knowledge and skills had provided an effective remedy for scurvy, which most Europeans believed was caused by "bad aire." Reading of this incident more than two hundred years after Cartier's experience,

HEMLOCK
Tsuga canadensis

James Lind, a British naval surgeon, launched the experiments that proved the dietary-deficiency basis of scurvy. Indian medicine accomplished much of the "pharmaceutical spadework" to broaden new frontiers in medical history. Continuing research into Indian drugs and treatments has been of enormous value.

The Virginia physicians and apothecaries during the early 1600s were often dependent upon many known Indian remedies. They searched the woods for the popular Indian medicines: hemp, tobacco, papoose root, bloodroot, dogwood, mandrake, ginseng, and wild ipecac.

The plant part most commonly used by the Indians was the root. Symbolic and revered, it represented many things to the early harvest-. ers of botanicals. Fresh roots and herbs were chewed and often powdered and boiled with animal fat to make salves. An observer writing in the *Aborigines of Virginia* (1608) noted that they made an ointment by crushing the roots of puccoon with bear grease and ashes. This mixture was rubbed on the skin to conserve the body's heat and also to keep lice, fleas, and vermin away. Obviously, the custom of greasing the body with vegetable or animal oils helped to protect the Indians from the cold. Along with this, plants of the mint family were commonly used by the Indians to prevent and relieve insect bites, and these herbs were often mixed with bear grease. According to many early accounts, the Indians were generally free of skin diseases and maintained smooth, healthy skin by frequently "washing" the skin with the oils of fishes and the fats of eagles, raccoons, bears, and so on — mixed with certain herbs to lend fragrance and added protection.

The native Americans were experts at gathering the wild plants of their environment. They would usually dig the *roots* of annuals in early spring, before the plant flowered. The roots of biennials and perennials were most often harvested in the autumn, after the season's growth had withered, leaving these roots rich in stored nutrients before winter. *Bark* was preferably gathered in winter or early spring, when it was easiest to remove. The *leaves* of most edible herbs were gathered before their blossoming time for maximum nutrients and tenderness.

The following treatments reflect specific usage by one or more tribes. *Those marked with an asterisk (*) can be poisonous unless used in moderation.*

AMERICAN GINSENG *(Panax quinquefolius)* is a perennial woodland herb which is becoming increasingly scarce due to over-harvesting. Amerindians used a decoction of the root to settle the stomach and to relieve nausea, vomiting, and the congestion of colds. Collect the roots *sparingly,* and only when found growing in abundance. This plant is on the endangered species list in many states.

AMERICAN GINSENG
Panax quinquefolius

*AMERICAN IPECAC *(Gillenia stipulata)* and BOWMAN'S ROOT *(G. trifoliata).* These perennial North American herbs are still known as "Indian-physic." Among many tribes the raw roots were eaten in moderation as a purgative.

AMERICAN MOUNTAIN ASH *(Pirus americana)* is an indigenous, smooth-barked small tree of the rose family. The bark's chemistry is very similar to that of wild cherry, and both were used medicinally by native tribes in tonics to reduce fevers. The attractive ash berries are antiscorbutic and, when ripe, high in malic acid.

AMERICAN WHITE HELLEBORE
Veratrum viride

*AMERICAN WHITE HELLEBORE *(Veratrum viride* and 4 spp.)* is a pubescent perennial wetland herb, some species of which are native to North America. *Highly poisonous*, the root was utilized as an aboriginal endurance drug. Many tribes used this botanical, in moderation, as a cardiac depressant, sedative, and internal treatment for arthritis. Certain alkaloids, acids, and mineral salts refined from the roots are used in medicine today.

AVENS, WATER *(Geum rivale)*. Boiled in a strong decoction, the roots, which contain tannin, were used by many tribes to relieve sore throats and coughs, as well as a healthful dark tea to strengthen the individual against disease rashes — that is, measles, chicken pox, and smallpox.

BLACK ALDER, Winterberry, Feverbush *(Ilex verticillata)*, was a noted medicinal to many tribes, who used the shrub's bark and fruit.

*BLOODROOT, or Red Puccoon *(Sanguinaria canadensis)*, was a favorite Indian rheumatism remedy. The red juice of the root contains a number of alkaloids and as a tea drink was used to cure ringworm. The juice was also rubbed on the skin, not only as a brilliant dye but as an insect repellent. *Caution: This plant can have poisonous effects on the system.*

BLOODROOT
Sanguinaria canadensis

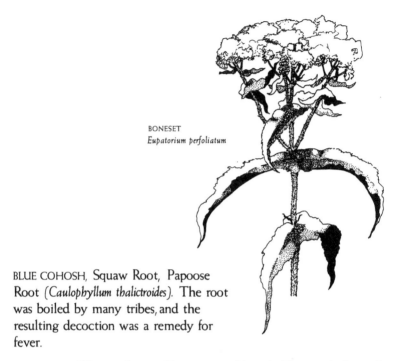

BONESET
Eupatorium perfoliatum

BLUE COHOSH, Squaw Root, Papoose
Root *(Caulophyllum thalictroides).* The root
was boiled by many tribes, and the
resulting decoction was a remedy for
fever.

BONESET or Thoroughwort *(Eupatorium perfoliatum).* Tea made from the
leaves and flowers was used by the Iroquois and Mohegans as a cold
remedy, to reduce fevers, and to relieve stomachaches and pain. This
wide-spread herb found in wet ground and thickets was usually harvested in August for use in numerous medicines.

BORAGE *(Borago officinalis).* Tea brewed from the leaves and flowers has a
natural saline content and helps to relieve fevers and cold discomforts.
An herb rich in calcium and potassium, it promotes healthy tissues. Indians used borage tea externally as well as internally.

BUGLEWEED or Water Horehound *(Lycopus virginicus)* is a common perennial herb indigenous to North America in low, damp, shady areas.
Medicinally it is a sedative (believed to be narcotic). A strong infusion
of the leaves and stems was drunk to lower the pulse and is beneficial in
the treatment of diabetes, chronic diarrhea, and dysentery.

*CATNIP *(Nepeta cataria).* This valuable, introduced herb was used extensively by the Mohegans as a medicinal tea to relieve cold symptoms and
soothe colic in infants, as it has a sedative effect. The leaves and whitish

flowers were harvested in August and September when in blossom and were dried before using.

CHAPARRAL, Creosote Bush, Blackbush *(Larrea tridentata)*. A strong-smelling, low shrub native to the sparsely vegetated alkaline soils of the desert and the plains of the southwestern United States, this rugged perennial was considered a veritable cure-all and was extensively used by many tribes. The dried leaves, twigs, and resinous gum were used in various preparations as an astringent, a diuretic, and a tonic for treating bruises, wounds, female disorders, kidney troubles, colds, and stomach disorders. Many Indians still sprinkle the powdered leaves inside their shoes to prevent rheumatism in their feet.

CLOVERS *(Trifolium* spp.*)* and SWEET CLOVERS *(Melilotus* spp.*)*. Early settlers and numerous Indian tribes used these sweet-scented annual/perennial herbs (many of which were naturalized in North America from abroad) in teas, additives to breads, flavorings for snuff and smoking mixtures, moth repellents, and so on. Medicinally they were a vital component in soothing salves to treat sores, ulcers and burns, and a strong infusion helped suspend coughing spasms.

CLUB-MOSSES *(Lycopodium* spp.*)*. The Blackfoot and Potawatomi tribes dusted the yellowish spores on wounds to stop bleeding. These are still used to absorb fluids from injured tissues as well as to prevent pills from sticking together in closed containers. (These same spores were also used at one time in theatrical explosives.)

COMFREY *(Symphytum officinale* and spp.*)* leaves and roots contain allantoin, a cell-proliferant, and have a long history of usage as a healing agent (both internally and externally) for broken bones and tissue damage. Introduced by the colonists to the Indians, it has known extensive use as an infusion to treat bruises, sores, insect bites, and burns. As a healthful tea it was drunk to relieve bronchial discomforts, coughs, colds, stomach disorders, and mouth sores. An infusion of comfrey leaves and roots is also soothing and beneficial in the bath water.

CORN *(Zea mays)* has impressive curative powers. It was used by the Incas and Aztecs to treat infections of the bladder and kidneys. CORN FUNGUS *(Ustilago maydis)* contains the alkaloid ustilagine (similar to ergot). Smut (predecessor of commercial penicillin) was principally used as a medicine to treat migraine headaches. Cornstarch and the smoke of burning corncobs were also used to relieve itching.

CULVER'S PHYSIC, or Culver's Root (*Veronicastrum virginicum*). A tall, graceful perennial North American herb. Many native peoples used the fresh root as a stomach tonic and laxative and to reduce fever.

DANDELION (*Taraxacum officinale*). After it was introduced to this country, the Ojibways, Mohegans, and other tribes used dandelion roots and leaves in medicinal tea decoctions for heartburn and digestive problems.

DOGWOOD (*Cornus* spp). "Hat-ta-wa-no-min-schi" is an old Indian medicine. The inner bark contains the glucoside cornin, and was boiled into a tea used as an astringent and to reduce fevers. The FLOWERING DOGWOOD (*Cornus florida*), or "Mon-ha-can-ni-min-schi" to the Delaware, was highly valued for its dense wood. The Indians also utilized its inner bark and twigs as a dentifrice, and as such these substances were both chewed and rubbed on the teeth and gums. The sturdy twigs were also carefully chewed in order to fashion natural paintbrushes. SILKY DOGWOOD (*Cornus sericea*) was known as "Milawapamule" to the Cree Indians of the Hudson Bay region. Scrapings of the wood and bark were mixed with herbs in the smoking mixture known as kinnikinnick; bark decoctions were used to treat coughs and fevers. Boiling the roots in water produced a good scarlet dye, and boiling with iron rust produced a fast black dye.

ELDERBERRY (*Sambucus canadensis*). The Iroquois boiled the inner bark and used it as a pain-killer; the dried, crushed leaves are an effective insect repellent; the flowers act as a stimulant and induce sweating.

EYEBRIGHT (*Euphrasia americana* and spp.) is a common low-growing annual herb, indigenous to open fields. Many cultures brewed a tea from the whole, fresh flowering plant that was used both externally and internally, primarily for ophthalmic disorders.

FEVERROOT, Horse Gentian, Wild Coffee (*Triosteum perfoliatum* and spp.). These coarse, leafy perennials indigenous to North America favor the open woodlands and limestone soils. The Cherokees brewed a decoction of the dark green leaves as a febrifuge. The dried roasted nutlets were (and are) an excellent coffee beverage. The Onondagas prepared poultices of the roots to treat swellings and to reduce inflammation and external pain.

GOLDENROD (*Solidago* spp.) blossoms were chewed by the Zunis to alleviate sore throats.

GROUND IVY, Gill-over-the-ground, Fieldbalm, Cat's-foot (*Nepeta hederacea*). An introduced member of the mint family, ground ivy was brewed and steeped as a cooling tea and external poultice.

HEAL-ALL, Selfheal, Carpenter-weed (*Prunella vulgaris*). Like its relative, ground ivy, this widely dispersed native member of the mint family was used as a cooling tea and poultice.

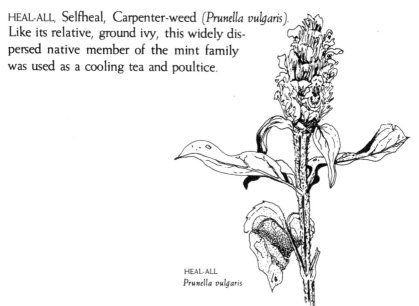

HEAL-ALL
Prunella vulgaris

HEMLOCK (*Tsuga canadensis*) has great nutritional value, and its tannin-rich bark was used in tanning animal hides. This native evergreen was used extensively by the Penobscot, Micmac, and Montagnais tribes as a tea to relieve colds, and a medicinal bath was prepared of the steeped branches. The Menominees and Forest Potawatomis also used hemlock tea to treat colds, to induce sweating, and to reduce fevers. Beds of hemlock branches refreshed their tired hunters and renewed their strength.

HOPS, or Common Hops (*Humulus lupulus*). This perennial, native of the Northern Hemisphere, was used medicinally as a tonic, febrifuge, and sedative. Since antiquity, hops have been used in brewing to preserve and to add a wholesome bitterness to the resulting liquid.

ICELAND MOSS lichen (*Cetraria islandica*) makes an excellent medicinal tea used to dissolve mucus congestion. Boil 1 teaspoon of the dried, powdered plant in 1 cup water for 30 minutes; strain and sweeten. Take one or two cupfuls daily.

INDIAN PIPE
Monotropa uniflora

INDIAN PIPE, Pinesap, Corpse Plant,
Convulsion-root *(Monotropa uniflora)*, is
indigenous to beech-dominant woodlands.
Found growing on dead or decaying
organic matter, this widespread
saprophyte flowers July through
September after soaking rains. The noted
Indian cure for inflammations of the eye
involved pulverizing the whole plant to
clear, glutinous fluid and mixing with
water. This was also used as a soothing
treatment for other irritations, even for
epilepsy.

*INDIAN TURNIP, or Jack-in-the-Pulpit *(Arisaema triphyllum)*. This familiar
woodland perennial wild flower was used by numerous tribes as a
headache treatment. The toxic root, containing the acrid poison calcium oxalate, was pounded with water into a pulp, then allowed to dry
several weeks (rendering it harmless). In this state it was used variously
as a palatable flour, as snuff, and as a medicinal tea.

INDIGO or Rattleweed *(Baptisia tinctoria)*. A slender, branching perennial
herb indigenous to the Northern Hemisphere, indigo has been used for
centuries as a dye and drug: many tribes used its roots and stems as an
"antiseptic" dressing for wounds and as a treatment for typhoid fever.

JEWELWEED or Touch-me-not *(Impatiens spp.)* is the common succulent
weed often found growing in or near poison ivy. Considered nature's
antidote, the clear plant juice of the jewelweed stems and leaves was a
widely used Indian remedy for external poison ivy rash and eczema. In
order to be effective it must be applied soon after contact.

JUNIPER *(Juniperus communis)*. Oil from the crushed berries was rubbed on
the skin as an insect repellent. The stems, leaves, and berries were also

brewed into a warming tea to drink or to use as an astringent. The berries and inner bark are excellent survival foods. Indians also burned the bark and branches of juniper and cedar and bathed in their healing smoke beside the warming fire. They also used the smoke to purify the air inside their dwellings.

LICORICE (*Glycyrrhiza glabra*). The leaves were brewed to a strong, warm tea, which was used as an external treatment for earache. Licorice root was used as a laxative and as a flavoring in medicines.

*LOBELIA or Indian Tobacco (*Lobelia inflata* and spp.). The leaves were dried and smoked (in moderation) as a popular asthma remedy. *Caution: This plant can be poisonous if used in quantity.*

*MAY APPLE, Mandrake, Wild Jalap (*Podophyllum peltatum*). *Poisonous* in large doses because it contains harmful alkaloids, may apple was used as an Indian suicide drug. In small quantities the root was used as a cathartic. It was also pulverized by the Penobscots as a treatment for warts and skin eruptions.

*MILKWEED (*Asclepias syriaca*). Latex was a specific Indian skin treatment for ringworm and warts.

*MULLEIN (*Verbascum thapsus*). Leaves and roots were dried and used in a variety of ways for respiratory problems. The Mohegans steeped the leaves in water and molasses to make a good cough remedy. Steeped longer, until very thick, the "candied" syrup can be dried into lozenges to treat mouth and throat sores. The Catawbas, Penobscots, Mohegans, and Forest Potowatomis used it in this manner. Many cultures smoked the dried mullein leaves to relieve the symptoms of asthma.

JEWELWEED
Impatiens biflora

MUSTARDS (*Brassica* spp.) are a large family of pungent, coarse, hairy herbs, naturalized on our continent from Europe and the Orient. They have escaped cultivation for long enough to be considered "common weeds." Indians used mustards as medicines, cosmetics, foods, and condiments. WILD BLACK MUSTARD (*Brassica nigra*) is the principal source of table mustard; its black seeds are used as food seasonings. The young leaves of WHITE MUSTARD (*Brassica hirta*) may be used in salads; its pale seeds are used for flavoring.

NANNYBERRY, Sheepberry, Wild Raisin (*Viburnum lentago*). The bark has many medicinal uses; gather it in spring as the shrub flowers; dry and store for later use. For an infusion to relieve cramps and abdominal distress, steep 1 ounce finely powdered bark in 1 pint boiling water until cool. Strain and take 1 teaspoonful three times a day, before each meal.

NETTLE or Stinging Nettle (*Urtica dioica* and spp.). The tops were brewed into a healthful tea to ease the discomforts of rheumatism. Steep 1 ounce of the fresh leaves in 1 pint boiling water for 10 minutes, then drink.

*PENNYROYAL, or Pudding-grass (*Hedeoma pulegioides*). The leaves and blossoms were steeped and used as a drink to relieve headaches by the Onondagas, the Apaches, and the Mescaleros.

PIPSISSEWA or Waxflower (*Chimaphila umbellata* and spp.). This member of the wintergreen family has been a popular Indian botanical for centuries. The whole plant was steeped in boiling water and the resulting liquid applied externally to treat blisters and internally to induce sweating and reduce fevers, as well as to ease backache and rheumatism.

STRIPED PIPSISSEWA
Chimaphila maculata

PLANTAIN
Plantago major

PLANTAIN or White Man's Foot (*Plantago major* and *P. lanceolata*) leaves were heated by the Shoshoni Indians and applied as a wet dressing to wounds. The root was chewed to relieve toothache and mouth sores. The whole plant was macerated and used as an antidote to reptile and insect bites. The seeds were used as a remedy for worms.

PLUM or Wild Plum (*Prunus americana*). The inner bark was scraped and boiled, and this decoction was then gargled and held in the mouth briefly to cure sores of the mouth and throat.

* POKEWEED or Pigeonberry (*Phytolacca americana*) was commonly utilized by the native Americans as a medicine, dye, ink, and spring potherb. Virginia tribes boiled the toxic berries in a tea to cure rheumatism. Concoctions of poke root were applied externally for various skin diseases and parasites. *Caution: This plant can be poisonous.*

SASSAFRAS (*Sassafras albidum*). The roots were boiled into a strong tea to treat fevers. The young sprouts were boiled to make an eyewash.

SENECA SNAKEROOT (*Polygala senega*). The old generic name of this indigenous shrub is derived from the Seneca Indians' noted use of this plant. Several Indian tribes used it to treat snake and animal bites, pneumonia, asthma, and rheumatism. An infusion of the leaves was also effective in the treatment of eye inflammations.

SASSAFRAS
Sassafras albidum

SKULLCAP *(Scutellaria lateriflora* and spp.). Common bitter perennial herbs of the mint family, though not aromatic, these ancient native botanicals were utilized by numerous Indian tribes as tonics for the nervous system. Their most unique recorded tribal usage was in treatments for tetanus and rabies.

SPRUCE, WHITE, or Cat Spruce *(Picea glauca).* Along with the RED SPRUCE *(P. rubens)* and BLACK or BOG SPRUCE *(P. mariana),* these stately native trees provide an impressive pharmacopeia of uses. Spruce beer is an original Indian formula to prevent vitamin deficiency, still used today. The twigs and cones of spruce are boiled in maple syrup and drunk hot, year-round. This delicious brew early became an important American folk medicine.

SQUASH and PUMPKIN *(Cucurbita* spp.) and GOURD *(Lagenaria* spp.). The dried seeds were chewed as worm expellents.

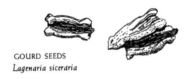

GOURD SEEDS
Lagenaria siceraria

STONEROOT or Horse Balm *(Collinsonia canadensis).* This large-leafed, strong-scented eastern North American perennial favors rich woodlands. Most eastern tribes used it as a medical panacea. A strong tea relieved headaches, cramps, indigestion, fevers, dropsy. It was also considered a stimulant and used to treat diseases of the respiratory tract, especially asthma; in addition, many tribes prepared poultices of the leaves and yellow blossoms to treat sores, wounds, bruises, and hemorrhoids.

SWEET FERN or Meadow Fern *(Comptonia peregrina)* is an indigenous, low shrub of the bayberry family *(Myricaceae)* and not a fern at all. Favoring open woodlands and clearings, and relatively sterile soil, this lacy-leafed shrub was sought for its very fragrant foliage. Its leaves and flowering tips were brewed into a nurturing tea, to treat diarrhea and other stomach disorders. The volatile oils from the crushed leaves act as insect repellents when rubbed on the skin. These fresh leaves are an especially effective poison-ivy antidote when applied to the skin immediately after contact.

*TANSY, Common Tansy, Gold Buttons (*Tanacetum vulgare*) of escaped European heritage, and *T. huronense*, a native herb indigenous to our Great Lakes regions, have centuries of annotated historical uses. Its resinous leaves and flowers were used externally to kill fleas and lice, and internally to treat worms. A warming tea was brewed to be used mainly in treating skin conditions. *Caution: Tansy taken internally can be fatal.*

TOBACCO (*Nicotiana* spp.). The leaves, when chewed, were a favorite Indian bee sting remedy and an insect repellent. The dried, powdered leaves are still an effective insect repellent. Tobacco smoking was used as a sedative and considered very relaxing to tired limbs.

VALERIAN (*Valeriana* spp.) is a hardy family of native (and introduced) perennial herbs. The odorous roots were often used as an antispasmodic and act as a strong sedative. The leaves were used in preparations for wounds. Because of this plant's high silica content and natural phosphorus, it makes a fine antiseptic.

WATERMELON (*Citrullus lanatus*). The dried seeds were used as a treatment for kidney and circulatory conditions.

WHITE OAK (*Quercus alba*). The inner bark was collected during the spring, when it was highest in tannic acid content; washed and brewed into a warming tea, it was used by many tribes to cure diarrhea and piles. The Mohegans used the bark as a cold remedy.

WHITE PINE (*Pinus strobus*) was extensively used by many Indians. New England tribes boiled the needles in water or maple syrup and drank this tea to prevent scurvy and to relieve coughs and colds. These needles contain five times more vitamin C than an equal amount of lemons, and they are also a rich source of vitamin A. Just chewing the freshly picked needles is very beneficial. The Objibway Indians used the seeds to flavor their cooking. The Iroquois Indians ate the sweet inner bark.

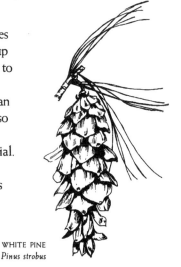

WHITE PINE
Pinus strobus

WHITE POPLAR or Silver Poplar *(Populus alba)*. The inner bark has properties similar to willow bark.

WILD BERGAMOT *(Monarda fistulosa)*. Extracted from the dried, boiled leaves, bergamot oil (which contains thymol) was used by numerous tribes to treat cold symptoms and bronchitis. This volatile oil is a stimulant and may be used to relieve stomach gases.

WILD GERANIUM
Geranium maculatum

WILD GERANIUM *(Geranium maculatum)*. The roots were gathered in the autumn, when their nutritive content was highest, then boiled with wild grape to make a liquid gargle for sores of the mouth and throat. This common native spring-blossoming wildflower was effectively used by a number of tribes. High in tannin, the dried, powdered roots were also used as a dressing to stop bleeding.

WILD LETTUCE *(Lactuca* spp)*. Its milky juices were used by the Menominees on poison-ivy rash; it was also used in medicines for its hypnotic, sedative, and diuretic properties.

WILD ONION *(Allium cernuum* and spp.)* The whole plant was used as an insect repellent and was rubbed all over the body.

WILD SARSAPARILLA *(Aralia nudicaulis* and spp.)*. The rootstock was dried and pulverized for medicinal teas, which were taken internally to treat colds and the effects of rheumatism, and applied externally for skin disorders. Infusion: Steep 1 teaspoon dried rootstock in 1 cup boiling water for 10 minutes. Drink 1 or 2 cupfuls daily.

WILLOW *(Salix* spp.*).* The inner bark contains the glucoside salicin, a primitive form of aspirin (which is acetylsalicylic acid). This prolific species was extensively used for many centuries by most North American tribes. The inner bark was used in Indian steam baths, to relieve rheumatic discomforts. Willow root and bark teas were brewed and drunk to relieve pain and to reduce fevers.

WINTERGREEN, Checkerberry, Teaberry *(Gaultheria procumbens).* The evergreen leaves and red berries, prepared in tea infusions, were used for centuries by the Indians as an astringent, diuretic, stimulant, febrifuge, and pain-killer. A poultice of wintergreen was also used to relieve rheumatic pains. Oil of wintergreen — methyl salicylate — is still used commercially to flavor other medicines.

WITCH HAZEL *(Hamamelis virginiana),* an indigenous shrub of the moist woodlands, is an ancient Indian antiseptic, widely used by many tribes as an astringent wash on wounds, bruises, and muscular aches. The shiny black seeds are edible, and the Iroquois made a warming tea of the sweetened boiled leaves.

*WORMWOOD or Prairie Sagewort *(Artemisia frigida).* An indigenous perennial herb with the fragrance of sage, wormwood was used as a source of camphor by many tribes. A tea of the boiled leaves was a noted treatment for bronchitis, sore throat, and colds.

*YARROW or Milfoil *(Achillea millefolium.)* The root was used by the Zuni Indians as a local anesthetic and antiseptic wash for wounds and ears. The chewed leaves were used to reduce swelling around wounds and to deaden toothache. Oil of yarrow (cineol) is a cooling, soothing treatment for burns; it was also used among many Indian tribes to prevent falling hair but was especially a noted contraceptive and abortive. The leaves steeped in water are a good styptic. Caution: Extended use can cause sensitivity.

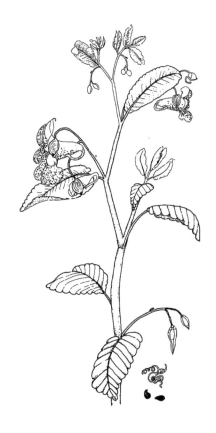

*JEWELWEED
Impatiens biflora
(See page 159.)

XIII

WILD
SMOKING
MIXTURES

"Moshup loved his great stone door-step. Frequently he would stand thereon and smoke his peudelah (his pipe). Once an offering had been made to him of all the tobacco grown on Martha's Vineyard, which was then called Nope by the Indians. With his peudelah filled with the last of this great gift he one day stood in the sunshine and smoked while he mused of his past . . . his big peudelah suddenly tilted sidewise; and, as the tide was high, the falling ashes therefrom were carried out and down to the east by the swift-running tide, until at last, caught by some drift on a shoal, they became fixed, and in time Nantucket — or "The Devil's Ash-Heap," as it is called by the older natives - grew little by little. . ."

> . . . 1904, Mary A. Cleggett Vanderhoop (1857-1935), Gay Head
> Wampanoag, from her Gay Head legend and folklore.

American Indians introduced the early settlers to smoking, which they used both medicinally and ceremonially. Pipes were most often used, although some tribes prepared and smoked cornhusk cigarettes.

The Indians' life-styles revolved around their cooking and habitation fires, and smoke was an important part of daily life. Specific types of twigs, wood, and pine cones were burned at certain times for their fragrances and for curing food. Soothing types of smoke were also used to bathe the body.

The Indians smoked a variety of dried wild herbs, blended with a very small amount of tobacco. Consequently, the nicotine content of their smoking materials was minor. By contrast, modern smoking materials use more flavorful tobacco, rolled in chemically treated papers to assist burning and to prevent flavor loss, and the nicotine content is considerable. It is valuable to note that the American Indians also used tobacco as a sacrificial offering, a medicine, and an effective insecticide (nicotine, $C_{10}H_{14}N_2$, is a poisonous alkaloid). Aside from the native tobacco, *Nicotiana rustica* and *N. tobacum*, the Indians smoked an impressive assortment of botanicals, many of which are still available at tobacconists today because of their beneficial qualities.

Those smoking substances marked with an asterisk (*) can be poisonous unless used in moderation.

ANGELICA
Angelica atropurpurea

ANGELICA or "La-go-nee-ham" (*Angelica atropurpurea*) has a fragrant odor and a warm, aromatic taste. Many tribes prized the dried leaves as a fine smoking commodity alone or mixed them with tobacco. This was also a favored ingredient in the medicine bag.

BEARBERRY, Kinnikinnick, Mealberry, Upland Cranberry (*Arctostyphylos uva-ursi*) is an evergreen member of the heath family. This trailing shrub has papery reddish bark and small paddle-shaped leaves. The Indian term for it originally meant a smoking mixture including sumac bark, native tobacco, spicebush, and bearberry. However, this low-growing plant became so popular as a smoke by itself that *kinnikinnick* came to refer to it specifically. The Chippewas mixed bearberry leaves with tobacco and red willow as a medicinal smoke to relieve headaches. The Potowatomis mixed bearberry with tobacco for a mild smoking blend. The early French settlers were especially fond of smoking bearberry leaves.

BRISTLY CROWFOOT (*Ranunculus pensylvanicus*) is indigenous to wetlands across America. The fruiting heads, seeds, and leaflets were harvested in autumn for smoking mixtures.

BUTTERWEED or Horse-weed (*Erigeron canadensis*) is a widespread native of the composite family. It was favored for its flowers and bristly leaves by numerous Indian tribes.

COLTSFOOT *(Tussilago farfara)*, European-introduced; and SWEET COLTS-FOOT *(Petasites palmata* and spp.), native. These perennial woolly boreal herbs of damp woodlands were sought for their broad leaves. Aside from seasonings, the dried leaves were enjoyed as a tobacco, providing relief for sore throats.

CORN *(Zea mays)*. Cornsilk, the fine, yellowish, silky threads of the stigmas from the female flowers of maize, was dried and rolled into cornhusk cigarettes by certain tribes.

DITTANY or "Mas-tin-jay" *(Cunila origanoides)* is a native perennial of the mint family. Its smooth, fragrant leaves were prized for smoking and chewing by numerous tribes.

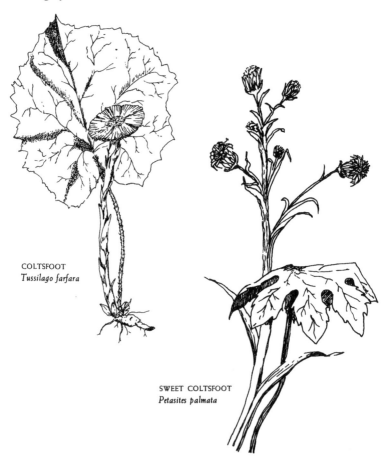

COLTSFOOT
Tussilago farfara

SWEET COLTSFOOT
Petasites palmata

FIELD MINT *(Mentha* spp.*)* was smoked alone or mixed with other herbs. The dried leaves are a flavorful and soothing tobacco.

GOLDENROD *(Solidago* spp.*)*. The fragrant flowers and leaves were enjoyed as a medicinal smoke by the Ojibwas, who also used this as a hunting smoke to attract deer.

LICORICE *(Glycyrrhiza glabra)* has good keeping qualities. Because of its flavor and medicinal properties it was frequently mixed with other herbal tobaccos.

LIFE EVERLASTING *(Gnaphalium polycephalum)* and PEARLY EVERLASTING *(Anaphalis margaritacea)* were valued Indian herbs. They were chewed to relieve hoarseness and irritations of the mouth and throat. Indian medicine men carried this fragrant herb, claiming that the leaves cleared and strengthened the voice and provoked the "urge to sing." It is a favorite pipe smoke, having a fragrance similar to hickory, and a good substitute for the tobacco-chewing habit. Indians also smoked this herb to relieve headaches.

PEARLY EVERLASTING
Anaphalis margaritacea

*LOBELIA or Indian Tobacco *(Lobelia inflata* and spp.*)*. Use with caution. This indigenous "wild tobacco" is a branching annual herb. The leaves of this plant were dried and used by many Indian tribes, principally as a stimulant and expectorant. It was a popular asthma remedy; however, taking too much of this plant induces coma and causes death. Lobelia contains the alkaloid lobeline, which, like nicotine, acts first as a stimulant and then as a depressant on the autonomic nerves. This alkaloid is used in a number of antismoking preparations because it induces nausea.

MEADOWSWEET *(Spiraea alba* and spp.*)*. This multi-useful perennial was favored by many tribes and as pipestem wood by the Chippewas.

MULLEIN
Verbascum thapsus

*MULLEIN (*Verbascum thapsus*) is a common biennial cosmopolitan herb whose leaves can be gathered and dried any time during the growing season. The American Indians smoked the dried leaves in their pipes for the relief of sore throats, asthma, coughs, congestion, and inflammation of the lungs. Many tribes made a sweetened infusion of the leaves and roots for use in relieving these same symptoms in children.

NEW ENGLAND ASTER (*Aster novae-angliae* and spp.) and other woodland and meadow asters. The roots and blossoms were dried and powdered to be used as smoking tobacco. The Ojibways favored these lovely plants as a hunting smoke to attract deer, and they used asters for food and medicinals.

PANICLED DOGWOOD (*Cornus racemosa* and spp.), RED OSIER DOGWOOD (*Cornus stolonifera* and spp.), and other indigenous shrubs of the dogwood family, were sought year-round, especially for their inner bark, which was dried, ground fine, and added to smoking mixtures.

PARTRIDGEBERRY or Squaw Vine (*Mitchella repens*), the low-growing woodland evergreen, was harvested principally by the Chippewas for smoking and was used also as a food and a medicinal.

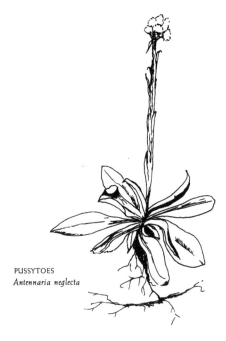

PUSSYTOES
Antennaria neglecta

PUSSYTOES (*Antennaria neglecta* and spp.) became known as Ladies' To-bacco. This small, widespread cosmopolitan weed was enjoyed as a fine smoking plant by many northeastern tribes. The diminutive gray-green plant has white to pink flowers in April and May. Both its blossoms and its leaves were dried and used.

SASSAFRAS(*Sassafras albidum* and spp.). Known to the Indians as "Shikih," this plant was well prized for its many uses. The Indians smoked the spicy, aromatic bark of the dried root like tobacco.

SMOOTH SUMAC (*Rhus glabra*) and STAGHORN SUMAC (*Rhus typhina* and spp.). The fuzzy red berries, harvested in the autumn, were cured by drying and were enjoyed alone as a healthful smoke or in mixtures of the dried sumac leaves and roots. Called "Kinikah" by the Plains In-dians, sumac was also smoked along with dried tobacco leaves.

According to the *Historical Dictionary of* 1813, sumac berries became so esteemed in Europe for smoking that they were preferred to the best cured Virginia tobacco.

SUNFLOWER (*Helianthus* spp.). The leaves were dried and used as a tobac-co substitute in cigars and pipes.

SWEET CLOVER *(Melilotus* spp.). The blossoms and leaves of about twenty species of wild clovers were dried and used to flavor tobacco smoking mixtures.

*TOBACCO *(Nicotiana* spp.) were sacred plants. The dried leaves were given as offerings before wild herbs were harvested or certain animals hunted. Also, the cured leaves were used in tribal council meetings and in religious ceremonies. Upward-drifting smoke was thought to carry messages to the Sky-World above, thus enabling the Indians to communicate with the Creator and ancestral spirits. Tobacco smoking was also considered calming to the spirit and relaxing for the body.

*WILD LETTUCE *(Lactuca virosa* and spp.) was dried and smoked to calm the nerves.

*WOOLLY YARROW *(Achillea lanulosa* and spp.). Yarrow was a favored native smoking commodity. This plant contains cineol, a dark blue volatile oil that is stimulating and cooling.

INDIAN TOBACCO
Lobelia inflata
(See pages 159, 189.)

XIV

❖

NATURAL CHEWING GUMS

*"They use to make great dance or frolicks. They made great dances or frolicks.
They made great preparations for these dances, of wampum, beads, jewels, dishes,
and clothing . . . Sometimes two or three families join in naming their children, so
make great preparations to make a great dance." (1624)*

. . . *Samson Occom (1723-1809), Mohegan Minister commenting on
customs of the nearby Montauk on Long Island.*

any plants and trees exude sap, latex, or resinous
material that contain essential nutrients as well as natural sugars. Indians
prized many different substances as "chewing gums," and Indian children made games out of seeking these out. Often, simply chewing on
several fresh pine needles until their sweet and sour essences were extracted was enough to satisfy thirst and relieve hunger pains. They were
also a source of vitamin C and a soothing treatment for mouth sores,
sore throats, and coughs. Other "chewing gums" were used to relieve
toothache, headache, and indigestion. Favored substances included the
following:

BALSAM FIR (*Abies balsamea*), as well as many other members of the pine
family, exudes a resinous pitch from the trunk and twigs when
wounded. This pitch is chewy and delicious raw, sticky to relatively
firm when aged. The Indians heightened its piny taste by heating the
pitch over a fire until it bubbled and crystallized.

BLACK BIRCH BARK (*Betula lenta*) was carefully peeled, and small pieces
were enjoyed raw or boiled for several minutes and then chewed. This
gum provides refreshing and beneficial juices. *Caution:* Peeling away
much of the outer bark will kill the tree.

CHICORY
Cichorium intybus

BLUE LETTUCE *(Lactuca pulchella)* was used by the Zunis, who cut the roots of the young plants and dried the exuded milky latex for chewing gum.

CHARCOAL from wood fires was used among most tribes to whiten and clean teeth, sweeten the breath, and relieve stomach gas. The natural tendency of charcoal is to absorb gases and purify substances.

CHICORY roots *(Cichorium intybus)* were chewed fresh by many tribes; they are fibrous, spongy, and nutritious.

CLEMATIS *(Clematis verticillaris* and spp.*)* was sought for its slightly woody stems and bitter-sweet plant juices.

DANDELION roots *(Taraxacum officinale)* were used much the same as fresh chicory roots, but their dried latex was especially prized as a chewing substance.

DOGWOOD twigs and bark *(Cornus* spp.*)* were used as a dentrifrice. The young twigs were peeled and the ends chewed to make paintbrushes, as well as to scrub and clean the teeth and gums.

HAWKWEED roots *(Hieracium canadense* and spp.*)* were chewed in summer to relieve thirst.

NARROW-LEAFED PLANTAIN
Plantago lanceolata

HOLLYHOCK (*Althaea rosea*) was favored for its peeled, fresh stems, which were chewed in small chunks.

INDIAN HEMP (*Apocynum cannabinum* and spp.) was sought most notably for cordage fibers, but its milky, sticky latex was chewed as gum by the Kiowas, Shoshones, and numerous other tribes.

LARKSPUR LETTUCE (*Lactuca ludoviciana*), as well as numerous other species of wild lettuce, was used like the Blue Lettuce.

LICORICE roots (*Glycyrrhiza glabra*) were esteemed as chewing substances in small pieces.

MARSHMALLOW (*Althaea officinalis*) was sought for centuries for its roots, which yielded the mucilaginous paste that was the original source of today's popular confection.

MILKWEED (*Asclepias syriaca* and spp.) exudes a milky, sticky latex which was chewed as gum by the Kiowas and Shoshones.

PLANTAIN roots (*Plantago major* and *P. lanceolata*) were chewed especially to relieve toothache and thirst.

PUSSYTOES (*Antennaria neglecta* and spp.). Its roots and silvery-gray leaves were chewed.

REED GRASS (*Phragmites communis*). Stalks were punctured, and the exuded pasty, sugary substance was hardened into gum. Indians collected this and compressed it into balls to be chewed as desired or toasted near the fire until brown, to be eaten like taffy.

SALSIFY or Oyster Plant *(Tragopogon porrifolius)*. The peeled stems and roots were chewed, in chunks, and the nutritious juices swallowed to relieve indigestion.

SPRUCE *(Picea rubens* and spp.*)*. The hardened exuded sap of these trees was aged 3 days, or more, before chewing.

SUGAR PINE *(Pinus lambertiana)* exudes a sugary, brown, gummy sap that is excellent for chewing.

SWEET GUM or RED GUM *(Liquidambar styraciflua)* is the source of the exuded resin gum copal, which is a pleasant chewing gum.

WHITE PINE *(Pinus strobus)* exudes a sticky amber sap that is very favorable for chewing.

Aside from the botanicals mentioned here, there are countless additional substances in nature that may be similarly used. Besides saps, resins, roots, and peeled stems of botanicals, the Indians also used many leaves and blossoms of herbs as seasonal chewing material. Principal among these was tobacco, which was chewed by many Indian peoples.

SALSIFY
Tragopogon porrifolius

XV

POISONOUS WILD PLANTS

"The wind blew and I was about to head for parts unknown, but I seemed glued to the spot. I said the Great Spirit has sent me a sign, so I stood and watched it. Finally I walked up to where I thought I had seen the ghost and put out my hand. I touched something that was cold, wet, and slimy. It felt like something from another world. I backed off and lit a match and there was my ghost. It was an old rotten stump covered with fungus growth; when the damp air settled on it, and the wind blew it, it glowed, changed colors and faded." (1936)

. . . *Lone Wolf, Narragansett historian and storyteller*

nly a small portion of the thousands of species of wild plants are dangerously poisonous. Certain other plants are toxic to the human system and can cause disturbing side effects but are not fatal if ingested. For safety's sake, keep the following guidelines in mind:

- Never use any plant that you cannot specifically identify as edible, especially berries, shoots, roots, and mushrooms. *Mistakes can be fatal!*
- Animals are *not* reliable indicators of edibility.
- Learn to recognize common poisonous plants and avoid them.
- Learn to identify plants that cause dermatitis and learn to recognize their natural antidotes. Jewelweed stems and leaves relieve the effects of poison ivy, while plantain leaves relieve the effects of stinging nettles.
- Teach children to avoid dangerous wild plants. Indeed, many common houseplants are poisonous.
- Be certain about which plant parts to harvest and their proper season. Some plants are delicious young but toxic at maturity; for example, wild asparagus, poke (shoots), milkweed (shoots and leaves), and so on. Other plants are edible when sufficiently cooked

POKEWEED
Phytolacca americana

but poisonous raw; for example, Jack-in-the-pulpit (roots), marsh marigold (leaves), young poke (spears), and unripe bittersweet (berries).

· Some plants are toxic if eaten in excess, because they are much higher in vitamins and minerals than our normal hybrid vegetables and therefore rougher on the average human system.

· Do not collect contaminated plants, especially ones growing by road margins (because of the buildup of toxic substances, primarily lead from exhaust fumes). Avoid plants growing in brackish or contaminated water. Be sure the plants you gather have not been sprayed recently with insecticides or growth retardants.

· *Never use anything you are unsure of.*

· *Sample your wild harvest sparingly.* Plant and body chemistries vary from individual to individual.

· Certain poisonous plants had significant technological uses to many Indian tribes. The highly poisonous Indian hemp or dogbane (*Apocynum* spp.) is easily confused in its early growth with the edible young common milkweed. Though the first two are definitely *inedible,* they were prized (at maturity) as fiber and cordage materials.

Many tribes utilized the turkey mullein (*Croton setigerus*), known as fish-weed, and the nuts of the red buckeye (*Aesculus pavia*). These botanical poisons were pulverized and spread on the surface of pools to paralyze fish. The dazed fish would float up to the surface and could be harvested easily and eaten without apparent harm to the human system. This type of local paralysis was usually temporary, and the fish could soon be revived in fresh water. Hundreds of pounds of fish could be caught easily by this method.

YARROW
Achillea millefolium

Yarrow (*Achillea millefolium*) is a wild herb whose flower clusters and lacy leaves may be used *in moderation*, but these plant parts contain a volatile oil that can react adversely in the human system. However, noted Indian usage of this plant was widespread. Chewing one or more (up to thirteen) feathery leaves and spitting them out after thorough chewing numbed the mouth. This was an adequate local anesthetic for toothache and tooth extraction.

It is essential to understand that plants and mushrooms have their own individuality. It is comparatively easy to assimilate the necessary knowledge to use plants properly, and it is vital to know which ones must be avoided.

The native Americans had an extensive knowledge of the poisonous and edible wild, and they utilized this information brilliantly. To a large extent this was also true of the Europeans who migrated to the North American continent, bringing with them their most important botanicals. The blending of these traditions continues to aid our understanding of the natural and cultivated worlds.

★AMERICAN HELLEBORE
Veratrum viride
(See page 156.)

XVI

NATIVE HEALING PATHWAYS AND SPIRITUALITY

"When we see an increase in the medicine plants, it is the Creator's way of showing and saying that we humans will have increasing need for them. We must figure-out the wisest uses."

... Claude Meford, Jr., Choctaw/Apache/American artist, basket weaver,
Native historian, Louisiana, 1983

Spiritual balance is a subtle factor in good health – the state of wellness. Whatever your spiritual motivation, your belief system affects your body in many ways. Spirituality is a powerful force in healing, once the balance of health has been tripped and altered. Traditionally, American Indians simply knew this.

From one tribe to another, as different as they were and are, they honored their traditional beliefs with daily prayers and frequent rites and rituals devised to keep the good life in balance. From birth through childhood, puberty, marriage and childbearing, through the body's increasing decades into old age, death, and the after life, Native traditional ceremonies blessed transitions along the continuing pathway of life. Some tribes saw this as "The Good Red Road" and others saw this as "The Pollen Path." The circle has always been seen as sacred and never ending.

The growing intrusion of other world religions imported to this continent became layered over Native traditions, often causing embraced Christian beliefs and rituals, which were colorfully incorporated within their Native rites, to add greater ceremony to some occasions. Within other tribes, missionaries worked tirelessly to stamp out all traces of Native traditional beliefs – never realizing that these ways were the underpinings of the people's whole life, health, and balance. This is not to say that everyone was well-off and perfectly balanced. Yet, the broad cultural fabric of life was very similar.

We have learned many things during the twentieth century, and just enough to realize that so much more still awaits our knowing. As we look back across the past five hundred years and into the ancient past of pre-Columbian America, we see that change has always been in progress. We are products of this change.

A closer integrity with Mother Earth will assure a better future for those of us who walk the healing pathways. The choice is always ours. We all wish to lead a healthy life. This is only possible to do on a healthy planet Earth. All of our consciencious work on mind/body/spirit/nature healing/balance/wellness will then come full circle.

> *We are the stars which sing*
> *We sing with our light.*
> *We are the birds of fire,*
> *We fly over the heaven,*
> *Our light is a star.*
>
> *We sing on the road of the spirits,*
> *The road of the Great Spirit.*
> *Among us are three hunters*
> *Who follow the bear.*
> *There never was a time*
> *When they were not hunting.*
>
> *We look upon the mountains,*
> *This is a song of the mountains.*

...Passamaquoddy Spirit Song, 1880

GLOSSARY

algae: Non-flowering plants, mostly aquatic, which undergo photosynthesis.

alkaloid: An organic substance having alkaline properties and containing nitrogen, such substances extracted from plants and used in certain drugs – for example, caffeine, morphine, cocaine, quinine. Some alkaloids are highly poisonous.

Amerindian: A contraction of American Indian.

annual: A plant that completes its life cycle in a single year.

antibiotic: Chemical substances, such as penicillin or strepomycin, which are produced by various fungi and microorganisms and capable of inhibiting or destroying bacteria. An antibiotic is used to treat infectious diseases.

antihypertensive: A drug that lowers blood pressure.

antiscorbutic: A botanical that contains significant amounts of vitamin C. A remedy for scurvy.

antiseptic: A substance that destroys the microorganisms that cause infection.

apocannoside: A cardiac glycoside; a substance that has a stimulating effect on the heart.

aromatic: A substance with a spicy scent and pungent, pleasing taste.

astringent: A substance that causes tissues to shrink or pucker, a styptic, for example, alum.

autonomic nerves: The system which innervates the blood vessels, heart, smooth muscles, and glands, and controls their involuntary functions.

biennial: A plant that completes its life cycle in two years, producing seeds in its second year.

botanical: Any wild or cultivated plant that has specific usefulness to man.

cambium: A layer of tissue between the inner bark and the wood of a tree, gorged with sap, sugars, and starches; a good, nutritious food source from some trees.

camphor: A substance used medicinally to soothe the irritation of infections and in the treatment of pain and itching.

cardiac: An agent that has an effect on the heart.

cardiac glycoside: A substance with a stimulating effect on the heart.

cardiotonic: Having a beneficial effect on the action of the heart.

cathartic: A strong purgative; a laxative, for example, the daylily or castor oil.

citric acid: A white, crystalline, sharply sour compound, $C_6H_8O_7$, contained in various fruits and also made synthetically.

concoction: A combination of ingredients, such as a mixture of herbs and botanical substances, which might have a strong, beneficial effect on the human system.

conifer: A cone-bearing plant producing naked seeds.

coumarin glycoside: A substance that prevents coagulation of blood.

cultigen: A domesticated plant species of unknown or obscure origin, distinct in its characteristics from known natural species:distinguished from indigenous.

cultivar: A specially cultivated horticultural or garden variety of plant, flower, etc.

cymarin: A cardiac glycoside which might have a stimulating effect on the heart.

deciduous: A plant that sheds its leaves annually.

decoction: A preparation made by boiling herbs in water for a specific period of time; usually hard materials (roots, barks, and seeds) require this type of preparation. Generally, boil 1 ounce botanical in 1 pint cold water in a covered container (preferably glass or enamel) for 30 minutes. Strain and cool.

dermatitis: Inflammation and irritation of the skin, for example, posion-ivy and stinging-nettle rashes.

digitalis: The genus of foxglove; the dried leaves or plant parts are used medicinally as a heart stimulant.

diuretic: An herb or medicine that causes an increase in the flow of urine.

emetic: A substance that causes vomiting, for example, ipecac.

emollient: A substance applied externally to soften and soothe the skin.

ethnobotany: A culture's use of its floral environment.

evergreen: A plant that remains green throughout the year.

expectorant: A remedy that loosens phlegm so that it may be easily brought up and expectorated.

extract: A substance refined through heat and evaporation to yield its essence, for example, maple sugar.

febrifuge: A remedy that reduces fever.

fiddlebead: The coiled or curled young shoot or frond of a fern.

floral: Adjective from flora. The aggregate of plants indigenous to a country or district: distinguished from fauna.

folic acid: An orange-yellow crystalline compound, $C_{19}H_{19}N_7O_6$, having vitamin-like properties and included in the vitamin B complex. It is found in green leaves, mushrooms, brewer's yeast, and some animal tissues and is used in the treatment of anemic conditions.

fomentation: A local application of cloths wrung out in hot water, with or without medicinals added.

frond: A fern leaf; the leaflike portion of seaweed.

fruit: Mature ovary of a flower containing one or more seeds; including berries, nuts, and grains.

fungi: A group of organisms lacking chlorophyll.

fungicide: A substance that destroys fungi.

glucoside: Any of an extensive group of compounds that, when treated with a dilute acid or decomposed by a ferment or enzyme, yield glucose.

glycoside: A naturally occurring substance consisting of sugars combined with nonsugars.

grain: Fruits peculiar to members of the grass family; they are small and dry and contain a single seed.

gruel: A thin, easily digested broth made by cooking cornmeal in water or milk.

herb: A plant that has special usefulness as a medicine, seasoning, or flavoring.

horticulture: The cultivation of a garden.

hybrid: Produced by interbreeding or cross-fertilization. An animal or plant of mixed parentage.

hygroscopic: A substance with the ability to absorb moisture from the surrounding environment, for example, honey.

infusion: A tea made usually of the softer plant parts (blossoms and leaves). Generally, pour 1 pint boiling water over 1 ounce botanical; cover and steep for 15 minutes; strain and use. Infusions are never boiled.

intertidal: The area of the continental shelf between the high- and low-tide marks.

laxative: A substance that causes the bowels to act.

macerate: To make soft or tender, usually by soaking.

malic acid: A deliquescent crystalline acid, $C_4H_6O_5$, with a pleasant taste. Contained in the juice of many fruits, especially apples.

mucilaginous: Slimy or mucilage-like; some mucilaginous plants, such as aloe and sassafras, have a soothing quality when applied externally.

mushroom: The fruiting body of a fleshy fungus.

narcotic: Any substance that produces a depressive effect on the central nervous system.

nut: A fruit with a hard, stony, or woody shell surrounding the seed.

perennial: A plant that lives from year to year and does not die after flowering.

petiole: The stalk to which the leaf is attached.

pistil: Female part of the flower.

potage: A soup or broth.

potherb: Any wild edible plant used as food or as a flavoring.

poultice: A surface preparation to remedy skin disorders. Fresh leaves are generally used; they are crushed and steeped in boiling water for a short time, then applied with moist heat to draw or soothe.

purgative: A physic; a substance that cleanses or purges.

restorative: A substance or compound capable of renewing health or strength; it is sometimes used to restore consciousness.

rhizome: A horizontal underground stem, enlarged by food storage, for example, gingerroot.

rootstock: A rhizome or subterranean stem.

salicin: A colorless, crystalline, water-soluble glucoside obtained principally from the bark of willows (the *Salix* genus), as well as other botanical substances.

saprophyte: A plant (usually lacking chlorophyll) that lies on dead organic matter, for example, the fungi.

sedative: A substance that calms the nerves.

shade-house: A large construction that is light and airy, but produces shade, under which shade-tolerant plants, such as ginseng, tobacco, woodland wildflowers, and tender, young hybrid plants are grown.

smudge: A smoldering, stifling smoke used to drive away insects.

spore print: Made by cutting off the pileus (cap) of a ripe mushroom and placing it with gills down on clean white paper; cover with an inverted glass or bowl and allow time for the spores to drop onto the paper (from two to eight hours).

stamen: The male, pollen-bearing part of a flower.

subtidal: Below the tide mark.

sweat lodge: A small, domed structure in which hot stones were placed and sprinkled with water to produce steam. As part of a purification process, people would sit on boughs of fragrant herbs near the steaming rocks.

tannin: Vegetable compound which is highly astringent.

thymol: A colorless, crystalline, solid distilled from oil of thyme. It has a pungent, aromatic taste and odor, and is used medicinally as an astringent and a fungicide.

tincture: An alcoholic solution of medicinal substances, usually 50 percent alcohol. Generally, mix 4 ounces water and 12 ounces spirits with 1 ounce powdered herb. Seal and let stand for 2 weeks; shake the container daily. Strain and bottle the clear liquid for use. Tinctures are made with plants whose active substances are not soluble in water.

tisane: An infusion of flowers.

tonic: A drug or medicine that improves the body tone; a substance that invigorates the system.

tuber: A swollen end of an underground stem that serves as a storage organ, for example, potatoes.

viscid: Covered with a glutinous, sticky layer.

weed: Any plant that grows where it is not wanted, espeically one that crowds out more desirable species in cultivated areas.

REFERENCE GUIDE
Books, Articles, Films, People

American Indian Culture

Axtell, James. *The Native American People of the East.* West Haven, Conn.: Pendulum Press, Inc., 1973.

Curtin, J. C., and Hewitt, J.N.B. "Seneca Fiction, Legends and Myths." *Bureau of American Ethnology, 32nd Annual Report.* Washington, D.C.: U.S. Government Printing Office, 1910.

Curtis, Natalie. *The Indians' Book.* New York: Harper & Bros., 1907.

Davis, Mary B., ed., *Native America in the Twentieth Century: An Encyclopedia,* New York: Garland Publishing, 1994.

DeForest, John W. *History of the Indians of Connecticut from the Earliest Known Period to 1850.* Hartford, Conn.: Wm. Jas. Hamersley & the Connecticut Historical Society, 1851.

The Early Americans (film). Indianapolis: Shell Film Library, 1975.

Fenton, William N., ed. *Parker on the Iroquois.* Syracuse, N.Y.: Syracuse Univ. Press, 1968.

Fowler, Carol. *Daisy Hooee Nampeyo.* Minneapolis: Dillon Press, Inc., 1977.

Harrington, M. R. *The Indians of New Jersey: Dickon Among the Lenapes.* New Brunswick, N.J.: Rutgers Univ. Press, 1963.

Hertzberg, Hazel W. *The Great Tree and the Longhouse.* New York: Macmillan Co., 1966.

Howell, Kenneth T. *From the Pootatuck Indians to the Diggings at Kirby Brook Site in Washington, Connecticut.* American Indian Archaeological Institute Library, Washington, Conn.

Kavasch, E. Barrie, ed., *Earthmaker's Lodge: Native American Folklore, Activities, and Foods*, Petersborough, NH: Cobblestone Publishing, 1994.

————, *Guide to Northeastern Wild Edibles*, Blaine, WA: Big Country Books, 1982.

————, *Introduction to Eastern Wildflowers*, Blaine, WA: Big Country Books, 1982.

Indians of the Eastern Seaboard. U.S. Dept of the Interior, Bureau of Indian Affairs. Washington, D. C. U.S. Government Printing Office, 1969.

Lamb, Trudie. Teacher and spokeswoman for American Indians for Development and for her People, the Schaghticokes.

Leland, Charles G. *The Algonquin Legends of New England or Myths and Folklore of the Micmac, Passamaquoddy and Penobscot Tribes*. Boston: Houghton Mifflin Co., 1884.

Logan, Adelphina. Teacher, artist, historian, lecturer, and leader for her people, the Onondagas.

MacNeish, Richard S. "The Origins of New World Civilization." *Scientific American*, Vol. 211, No. 5 (Nov. 1964), pp. 29-37.

————, "Ancient Mesoamerican Civilization." *Science*, Vol. 143, No. 3606 (Feb. 1964).

Marriott, A., and Rachlin, C. *American Indian Mythology*. New York: Thomas Y. Crowell Co., 1968.

Momaday, N. Scott. *The Way to Rainey Mountain*. Albuquerque, N.M.: Univ. of New Mexico Press. 1969.

More Than Bows and Arrows (film). Seattle, Wash.: Cinema Association, Inc., and the 13th Regional Corporation of Alaska Natives, 1978.

Rainey, Froelich G. "A Compilation of Historical Data Contributing to the Ethnography of Connecticut and Southern New England Indians." Ph.D. thesis, Yale Univ., 1933.

Richmond, David. Teacher, designer, and builder for his People, the Mohawks.

Russell, George, *American Indian Facts of Life: A Profile of Today's Tribes and Reservations*, Phoenix, AZ: Russell, 1997.

Sekatau, Eric, and Ella. Teachers, artists, and historians for their people, the Narragansetts.

Speck, Frank G. "Native Tribes and Dialects of Connecticut, A Mohegan-Pequot Diary." *Bureau of American Ethnology, 43rd Annual Report*. Washington, D.C.: U.S. Government Printing Office, 1925.

————, "Wawenock Myth Texts from Maine." *Bureau of American Ethnology, 43rd Annual Report*, Washington D.C.: U.S. Government Printing Office, 1925.

Strong, John A., *We Are Still Here! The Algonquian Peoples of Long Island Today*, Interlaken, New York: Empire State Books, 1996.

Swigart, Edmund K. *The Prehistory of the Indians of Western Connecticut*. Washington, Conn.: American Indian Archaeological Institute, 1974.

Waldman, Carl, *Encyclopedia of Native American Tribes*, New York: Facts On File Publications, 1988.

————, "The Foods of the Connecticut Indians." *Bulletin of the Archaeological Society of Connecticut, Inc.*, No. 37 (1972), pp. 27-47.

Washbum, Wilcomb. *The Indian in America*. New York: Harper & Row, 1975.

Woodhead, Henry, Ed., *The American Indians (A Series)*, Alexandria, VA.: Time-Life Books,1993.

Cookbooks

American Indian Cook Book, Alexandria, VA: Earth Art, Inc., 1974.

American Indian Society of Washington, D.C. Cook Book, Washington, D.C. 1975.

Beard, James. *New Fish Cookery*. Boston and Toronto: Little, Brown & Co., 1976.

Booth, Sally S. *Hung, Strung and Potted: A History of Eating Habits in Colonial America*. New York: C. N. Potter, Inc., 1971.

Carson, Dale, *New Native American Cooking*, New York: Random House, Inc., 1996.

_____, *Native New England Cooking*, Washington, CT: Institute For American Indian Studies, 1995.

Carson S., and Vick, A. W. *Hillbilly Cookin'*. Thom Hill, Tenn.: Clinch Mountain Lookout, Inc.,1972.

Cox, Beverly and Martin Jacobs, *Spirit of the Harvest: North American Indian Cooking*, New York: Stewart, Tabori & Chang, 1991.

Elverson, V. T., and McLanahan, M. A. *A Cooking Legacy*. New York: Walker & Co., 1975.

Frederick, J. G. *Long Island Seafood Cook Book*. New York: Dover Publications, 1971.

Herrmann Loomis, Susan, *Clambakes & Fish Fries*, New York: Workman Publishing, 1994.

Indian Cookin', compiled by Herb Walker, Amarillo, TX: Baxter Lane Company, 1977. [Practical & broadly Indian tribal dishes.]

Indian Cookin', compiled by Frances L. Whisler, USA: Nowega Press, 1973. [Principally Cherokee].

Indian Recipes From Cherokee Indians of Eastern Oklahoma, collected by Lulu Gibbons, Muskogee, OK: Hoffman Printing Co., 1967.

Kavasch, E. Barrie, *Enduring Harvests: Native American Foods and Festivals For Every Season*, Old Saybrook, CT: Globe Pequot Publishing, 1995.

_____, *American Indian Cooking: Traditional Native Ingredients Become Modern Dishes*. Bridgewater, CT., 1991.

_____, *Native Harvests: Recipes and Botanicals of the American Indians*, New York: Vintage/Random House, 1979.

Kavena, Juanita Tiger, *Hopi Cookery*, University of Arizona press, 1992.

Kimball, Yeffe, and Anderson, Jean. *The Art of American Indian Cooking*. Garden City, N.Y.: Doubleday & Co., Inc., 1965.

Kluger, Marilyn.*The Wild Flavor*. New York: Coward, McCann & Geoghegan, Inc., 1970.

Leslie, Miss Eliza. *New Receipts for Cooking*. Philadelphia: Peterson, 1854.

Manyan G. *The Country Seasons Cookbook*. New York: Crown Publishing Co., 1974.

Mirel, E. P. *Plum Crazy: A Book About Beach Plums*. New York: Crown Publishing Co., 1973.

Niethammer, Carolyn. *American Indian Food and Lore*. New York: Collier Books of Macmillan Co., 1974.

Pow Wow Chow: A Collection of Recipes from Families of the Five Civilized Tribes: Cherokee, Chickasaw, Choctaw, Creek, and Seminole, Muskogee, OK: Five Civilized Tribes Museum, 1984.

Rombauer, I. S., and Becker, M. R. *Joy of Cooking.* Indianapolis and New York: Bobbs-Merrill Co., 1931.

Russell, Helen Ross. *Foraging for Dinner.* New York: Nelson, 1975.

Samuels, Charleen, *Choctaw and Irish Foods, Facts, Friendships,* McAlester, OK: Walter's Cookbooks, 1982.

Stewart, Dr. A. M., and Kronoff, L. *Eating from the Wild.* New York: Ballantine Books, 1975.

Stobart, Tom. *Herbs, Spices and Flavorings.* New York: McGaw-Hill Book Co., 1970.

The Institute for Anquilliform Research and Mariculture. *The Eel Cookbook.* Bridgeport, Conn.: Univ. of Bridgeport Press, 1977.

Tinker, Alice, and Tinker, Sylvester. *Authenticated American Indian Recipes.* Pawhuska, Okla.: 1955.

To Make My Bread: Preparing Cherokee Foods, edited by Mary Ulmer & Samuel E. Beck, Cherokee, NC: Museum of the Cherokee, 1951.

Vigil, Priscilla. *Pueblo Indian Cookbook.* Sante Fe, N.M.: Museum of New Mexico Press, 1972.

Wallace, L. Haxworth. *Sea Food Cookery.* New York: M. Barrows & Co., Inc., 1944.

Wampanoag Cookery. Boston: The Children's Museum, 1974.

Whisler, Frances L. *Indian Cookin'.* Nowega Press, 1973.

Women's Alliance of the First Church of Deerfield, Mass. *The Pocumtuc Housewife: A Guide to Domestic Cookery.* Deerfield, Mass.: 1805.

Ethnobotany

Asch, David L., and Asch, Nancy B. "Chenopod as Cultigen: A Re-evaluation of Some Prehistoric Collections from Eastern North America." *Midcontinental Journal of Archaeology,* Vol. 2, No. 1 (1977), p. 3–37.

Balick, Michael J. and Paul Alan Cox, *Plants, People, and Culture: The Science of Ethnobotany,* New York: Scientific American Library, 1996.

Berglund, B., and Belsby, C. E. *Edible Wild Plants.* New York: Charles Scribner's Sons, 1977.

Coe, Sophie D., *America's First Cuisines,* Austin, TX: University of Texas Press, 1994.

Coon, Nelson. *The Dictionary of Useful Plants.* Emmaus, Pa.: Rodale Press, 1974.

_____, *Using Wayside Plants.* New York: Hearthside Press, 1960.

Densmore, Frances. *How the Indians Use Wild Plants for Food, Medicine and Crafts.* New York: Dover Publications, 1974.

Erichsen-Brown, Charlotte, *Medicinal and Other Uses of North American Plants,* New York: Dover Publications, 1979.

Fernald, M. L., and Kinsey, A. C. *Edible Wild Plants of Eastern North America,* rev. R. C. Rollins. New York: Harper & Row, 1958.

Hays, W., and Hays, R. V. *Foods the Indians Gave Us.* New York: Weathervane Books, 1973.

Hedrick, U. P. *Sturtevant's Edible Plants of the World*. New York: Dover Publications, 1972.

Lehner, Ernst, and Lehner, Johanna. *Folklore and Odysseys of Food and Medicinal Plants*. New York: Farrar, Straus & Giroux, 1973.

Mangelsdorf, Paul C. *Corn: Its Origin, Evolution and Improvement*. Cambridge, Mass.: The Belknap Press of Harvard Univ. Press, 1974.

McGee, Harold, *On Food and Cooking: The Science and Lore of the Kitchen*, New York: Charles Scribner's Sons, 1984.

Nathan, Joan. "An Indian Harvest Festival." Boston *Sunday Globe*, Nov. 28, 1976.

Saunders, Charles F. *Edible and Useful Wild Plants of the U.S. and Canada*. New York: Dover Publications, 1948.

Schultes, R. E., and Hill, A. F. *Plants & Human Affairs*, 2nd ed. Cambridge, Mass.: Botanical Museum of Harvard Univ., 1973.

Scully, Virginia. *A Treasury of American Indian Herbs*. New York: Crown Publishing Co., 1970.

Svoboda, Marie. *Plants That the American Indians Used*. Chicago Natural History Museum, 1964.

Weatherwax, Paul. *Indian Corn in Old America*. New York: Macmillan Co., 1954.

Yanovsky, Elias. *Food Plants of the North American Indians*. U.S. Dept. of Agriculture, Miscellaneous Publication 237. Washington, D.C.: U.S. Government Printing Office, 1936.

Yarnell, Richard A. *Aboriginal Relationship Between Culture and Plant Life in the Upper Great Lakes Region*, Anthropological Papers. Ann Arbor, Mich: Univ. of Michigan Press, 1964.

Yturbide, Teresa Castello, *Presencia de la Comida Prehispanica*, Mexico City: Mexico Banamex Fomento Cultural, R.C., 1986.

Guides and General Resources

Angier, Bradford. *Field Guide to Edible Wild Plants*. Harrisburg, P.: Stackpole Books, 1974.

————, *Feasting Free on Wild Edibles*. Harrisburg, Pa.: Stackpole Books, 1966.

Berglund, Berndt, and Bolsby, Clare E. *The Edible Wild*. Toronto: Pagurian Press, Ltd., 1971.

Brockman, F. C. *A Guide to Field Identification of Trees of North America*. Racine, Wisc.: Western Publishing Co., 1968

Foster, Steven and James A. Duke, *Peterson Field Guides to Medicinal Plants*, Boston: Houghton Mifflin, 1990.

Cobb, Boughton C. *A Field Guide to the Ferns*. Boston: Houghton Mifflin Co., 1956.

Crockett, James U. *Vegetables and Fruits*. New York: Time-Life Books, Inc., 1972.

Gibbons, Euell. *Stalking the Faraway Places*. New York: David McKay, 1973.

————, *Stalking the Healthful Herbs*. New York: David McKay, 1966.

————, *Stalking the Wild Asparagus*. New York: David McKay, 1962.

Hall, Alan. *The Wild Food Trail Guide*, New York: Holt, Rinehart & Winston, 1976.

Harris, Ben C. *Eat the Weeds*. New Canaan, Conn.: Keats Publishing Co., 1973.

_____, *The Complete Herbal*. Barre, Mass.: Barre Publishing Co., 1972.

Kavasch, E. Barrie, *A Student's Guide to Native American Genealogy*, Phoenix, AZ: Oryx Press/Rosen Publishing Group, 1996.

Leighton, Ann. *Early American Gardens*. Boston: Houghton Mifflin Co., 1970.

Lucas, Richard. *Common and Uncommon Uses of Herbs for Healthful Living*. New York: Arco Publishing Co., 1969.

Lust, John. *The Herb Book*. New York: Bantam Book, 1974.

McCleod, Dawn. *Herb Handbook*. North Hollywood, Calif.: Wilshire Publishing Co., 1968.

MacKenzie, Katherine. *Wild Flowers of the Northeast*. Plattsburg, N.Y.: Tundra Books, 1973.

Meyer, Joseph E. *The Herbalist*. New York: Crown Publishing Co., 1970. Facsimile reproduction of 1918 edition.

Niering, William A., *Audubon Field Guide to North American Wildflowers, Eastern Region*, New York: Knopf/Borzoi, 1979.

Peterson, Lee. *A Field Guide to the Edible Wild Plants of Eastern U.S.* Boston: Houghton Mifflin Co., 1978.

Peterson, Roger Tory, and McKenny, Margaret. *A Field Guide to Wildflowers*. Boston: Houghton Mifflin Co., 1968.

_____, and Fisher, James. *Wild America*. Boston: Houghton Mifflin Co., 1955.

Thomas, Lewis. *The Lives of a Cell: Notes of a Biology Watcher*. New York: Viking Press, 1974.

Medicines and Mushrooms

Aikman, Lonnelle. *Nature's Healing Arts*. Washington, D.C.: National Geographic Society, 1977.

Dr. Chase's Recipes; or Information for Everybody: An Invaluable Collection of About 800 Practical Recipes, A.W. Chase, M.D., Ann Arbor, MI: R.A. Beal, 1876.

Elbaum, Katherine. "A Cultural and Medical Evaluation of Child Mummy from Ancón, Peru: Mummy Autopsy." Thesis, Univ. of Chicago, 1975.

Emmart, Emily W., trans. *The Badianus Manuscript: An Aztec Herbal of 1552*. Baltimore: Johns Hopkins Press, 1940.

Haard, R., and Haard, K. *Poisonous and Hallucinogenic Mushrooms*. Seattle, Wash.: Cloudburst Press, 1975.

_____, *Foraging for Edible Wild Mushrooms*. Seattle, Wash.: Cloudburst Press, 1974.

Hand, W. M. *The House Surgeon and Physician*. Hartford, Conn.: S. Andrus & Son, 1847.

Harris, B. C. *Kitchen Medicines*. New York: Weathervane Books, 1968.

Hobbs, Christopher, *Medicinal Mushrooms: An Exploration of Tradition, Healing, & Culture*, Santa Cruz, CA: Botanica, 1986.

Hoffman, David, *The Herbal Handbook: A User's Guide to Medical Herbalism*, Rochester, VT: Healing Arts Press, 1987, 1988.

Kavasch, E. Barrie, *Guide to Eastern Mushrooms*, Blaine, WA: Big Country Books, 1982.

Krieger, L. C. *The Mushroom Handbook*. New York: Dover Publications, 1967.

Lehane, Brendan. *The Power of Plants*. New York: McGraw-Hill Book Co., 1977.

Lewis, Walter and Memory E.-Lewis, *Medical Botany*, New York: Wiley and Sons, 1977.

Lincoff, Gary H., *The Audubon Society Field Guide to North American Mushrooms*, New York: Knopf/Borzoi, 1981.

McKnight, Kent H. & Vera B., *Peterson Field Guides to Mushrooms*, Boston: Houghton Mifflin Co., 1987.

Miller, R. A., and Tatelman, D. *Magical Mushroom Handbook*. Seattle, Wash.: Homestead Book Co., 1977.

Millspaugh, Charles F. *American Medicinal Plants*. New York: Dover Publications, 1974. Facsimile reproduction of 1892 edition.

Ott, Jonathan. *Hallucinogenic Plants of North America*. Berkeley, Calif.: Wingbow Press, 1976.

Peschell, Keewaydinoquay, *Puhpohwee for the People: A Narrative Account of Some Uses of Fungi Among the Ahnishinaabeg*, Cambridge: Botanical Museum of Harvard University, 1978.

Schultes, Richard Evans. *Hallucinogenic Plants*. Racine, Wis.: Western Publishing Co., Inc., 1976.

Tantaquidgeon, Gladys. *Folk Medicine of the Delaware and Related Algonkian Indians*. Harrisburg, Pa.: The Pennsylvania Historical and Museum Commission, 1972.

_____, "Mohegan Medicinal Practices, Weatherlore and Superstition." *Bureau of American Ethnology*, 43rd *Annual Report*. Washington, D.C.: U.S. Government Printing Office, 1925.

Vogel, Virgil J. *American Indian Medicine*. Norman, Okla.: Univ. of Oklahoma Press, 1970.

Weiner, Michael A. *Earth Medicine—Earth Foods*. New York: Collier Books of Macmillan Co., 1972.

Principal Reference Resources

Axtell, James, *The Invasion Within: The Contest of Cultures in Colonial North America*, New York: Oxford Univ. Press, 1985.

Bailey, Liberty Hyde; Zoe, Ethel; and the staff of the L. H. Bailey Hortorium. *Hortus Third*. New York: Cornell Univ. and Macmillan Co., 1976.

Cronon, William, *Changes in the Land: Indians, Colonists, and the Ecology of New England*, New York: Hill and Wang, 1983.

Driver, Harold E. *Indians of North America*. Chicago: Univ. of Chicago Press,1969.

Fernald, Merritt L. *Gray's Manual of Botany*, 8th ed. New York: D. Van Nostrand Co., 1970.

Gleason, Henry A. *Britton and Brown Illustrated Flora of the Northeastern United States & Adjacent Canada*. New York: The New York Botanical Garden, 1952.

Handbook of North American Indians, William C. Sturtevant General Editor, Washington: Smithsonian Institution, 1990+ [numerous regional volumes]

Hedrick, U. P. *Sturtevants's Edible Plants of the World*. New York: Dover Publications, 1972.

Heiser, Charles B., *Seed to Civilization: The Story of Food*, San Francisco: W. H. Freeman and Co., 1973, 1981 [second edition]

Kavasch, E. Barrie and Karen Baar, *American Indian Healing Arts: Herbs, Rituals, and Remedies for Every Season of Life*, New York: Bantam Books, 1999.

Millspaugh, D. F. *American Medicinal Plants*. New York: Dover Publications, 1974. Facsimile reproduction of 1892 edition.

Moeller, Roger W. "Seasonality and Settlement Patterns of Late Woodland Floral and Faunal Patters in the Upper Delaware Valley." Ph. D. thesis, State Univ. of New York at Buffalo, 1975.

_____, and Reid, John.*Archaeological Bibliography for Eastern North America*, ed. R. W. Moeller. Washington, Conn.: Eastern States Archaeological Federation and American Indian Archaeological Institute, 1977.

Parker, Sterling P., and Parker, Ruth. Botany idenification, farm, and herbarium, Woodbury, Conn.

Salisbury, Neal, *Manitou and Providence: Indians, Europeans, and the Making of New England, 1500-1643*, New York: Oxford, 1982.

Seymour, F. S. *The Flora of New England*. Rutland, Vt.: C. E. Tuttle Co., 1969.

Watt, B. K., and Merrill, A. L. *Handbook of the Nutritional Contents of Foods*. New York: Dover Publications, 1975.

Weinstein, Laurie, ed., *Enduring Traditions: The Native Peoples of New England*, Westport, CT: Greenwood Press, 1994.

Spirituality

Achterberg, Jeanne, *Imagery in Healing: Shamanism and Modern Medicine*, Boston: New Science Library/Shambala, 1985. Comprehensive book bridging ancient healing practices to modern science by enlightened clinical professor reinforcing each wholistic gift.

Allen, Paula Gunn, *The Sacred Hoop: Recovering the Feminine in American Indian Traditions*, Boston: Beacon Press, 1986. Outstanding study by one of the more respected writers in Native contemporary prose.

_____, *Grandmothers of the Light: A Medicine Woman's Sourcebook*, Boston: Beacon Press, 1991. Shared "myths' that have guided female shamans toward an understanding of the sacred for centuries.

Atwood, Mary Dean, *Spirit Healing: Native American Magic and Medicine*, NY: Sterling Publishing, 1992. A self-help guide to the Native American spiritual path.

Awiakta, Marilou, *Selu: Seeking the Corn-Mother's Wisdom*, 1993; Golden, CO: Fulcrum; gifted insights of the cyclical rituals of life that touch us all, and especially the Cherokee People's traditions.

Bear Heart, with Molly Larkin, *The Wind is my Mother: "The Life and Teachings of a Native American Shaman,"* NY: Clarkson Potter/Crown Publ., 1996. Reflections, philosophies, and trainings in the life of this traditional Muskogee Creek Medicine Man/Healer and "road man" of the Native American Church.

Beck, Peggy V., Anna Lee Walters, Nia Francisco, *The Sacred Ways of Knowledge, Sources of Life,* Tsaile, AZ: Navajo Community College Press & Flagstaff, AZ: Northland Publishing, 1990, repr. Describes the "meaning, role, & function of sacred traditional practices & observances in the lives of The People, individually & collectively."

Brown, Joseph Epes, ed., *The Sacred Pipe: Black Elk's Account of the Seven Rites of the Oglala Sioux,* Norman: University of Oklahoma Press, repr. of 1953 ed. Noted descriptions of the rites given to Brown by the Keeper of the Pipe on the reservation in 1947-48.

Deloria, Jr., Vine, *God is Read: A Native View of Religion,* rev. ed., Golden, CO: North American Press, 1992 (1972). Classic work on Native religion and spirituality updated by this prominent Lakota author, scholar, lawyer.

Doore, Gary, compiled & ed., *Shaman's Path: Healing, Personal Growth, & Empowerment,* Boston: Shambala Publ., 1988. Leading authorities in these fields explore the subjects herein. An amazing compendium of resources!

Drysdale, Vera Louise, *The Gift of the Sacred Pipe,* Norman: University of Oklahoma Press, 1982. Beautifully illustrated account based upon Black Elk's details of the Seven Rites of the Oglala Sioux.

Gill, Sam, *Sacred Words: A Study of Navajo Religion and Prayer,* Westport, CT: Greenwood Press, 1981. Valuable reference text by a noted scholar.

Gold, Peter, *Navajo & Tibetan Sacred Wisdom: The Circle of the Spirit,* 1994; Rochester, VT: Inner Traditions Intn'l; an amazing exploration of numerous similarities & parallels.

Horse Capture, George, *The Seven Visions of Bull Lodge, As Told by his Daughter Garter Snake,* Ann Arbor, MI: Bear Claw Press, 1980. The story of the great visionary healer Bull Lodge (ca. 1802-1886) of the Gros Ventre or White Clay People of northeastern Montana.

Hultkrantz, Ake, *The Religions of the American Indians,* translated by Monica Setterwall, Berkeley: U of CA Press, 1979 (1967). Valuable overview with impressive meanings and sense of the great diversities of Native religions in the Western Hemisphere by this notable Swedish scholar.

Kalweit, Holger, *Shamans, Healers, and Medicine Men,* Boston: Shambala Publications, 1992, (1987). Ancient, earth-cherishing traditions working for personal, social, and environmental healing through millennia of shamanism, explored by a noted German ethnologist.

Kendall, Laurel, Barbara Mathe, Thomas Ross Miller, *Drawing Shadows to Stone: The Photography of the Jesup North Pacific Expedition, 1897-1902,* 1997; NY: AMNH. Exhibition catalog of a unique People during a unique time, fantastic!

Lame Deer, John Fire, and Richard Erdoes, *Lame Deer: Seeker of Visions: The Life of a Sioux Medicine Man,* NY: Simon & Schuster, 1972. Important collection of western Sioux thoughts and ideas from their chief medicine man.

McGaa, Ed "Eagle Man," *Mother Earth Spirituality: Native American Paths to Healing Ourselves and the World*, NY: HarperCollins, 1990. Popular New Age manifesto: addressing many current and forthcoming needs among all people, giving Native spiritual directions & solutions.

Miller, David H., *Ghost Dance*, Lincoln: University of Nebraska Press, 1985. Detailed examination of this major religious movement of the late 19th century among the western tribes.

Neihardt, John G., translated by, *Black Elk Speaks: Being the Life Story of a Holy Man of the Oglala Sioux*, NY: Pocket Books, 1972 (1932). Classic reference work and fine resource guide through this changing period in Sioux lifeways in the late 1800s.

Powell, Peter J., *Sweet Medicine: The Continuing Role of the Sacred Arrows, the Sun Dance, and The Sacred Buffalo Hat in Northern Cheyenne History*, Norman: University of Oklahoma Press, 1969. Impressive accounts of Cheyenne religion and traditions.

Pretty-shield, ed., Frank B. Linderman, *Pretty-Shield: Medicine Woman of the Crows*, Lincoln: University of Nebraska Press, 1972, repr. of *Red Mother* (1932), Fascinating autobiography of this respected Crow woman born near the Missouri River (c. 1858-1933?).

Qoyawayma, Polingaysi (Elizabeth Q. White), *No Turning Back: A Hopi Indian Woman's Struggle to Live in Two Worlds*, Albuquerque: University of New Mexico Press, 1964. Born at Old Oraibi, AZ (c. 1892-1990), this noted writer, teacher, potter, & musician served a long career in Indian education, winning a U.S. Distinguished Service Award.

The Way of the Spirit: Nature, Myth, & Magic in Native American Life, Time Life Books, 1997; full color, fabulous!

Tooker, Elisabeth, editor, *Native North American Spirituality of the Eastern Woodlands: Sacred Myths, Dreams, Visions, Speeches, Healing Formulas, Rituals and Ceremonials*, NY: Paulist Press, 1979. A most valuable, classic handbook by leading authorities!

Trimble, Stephen, *The People: Indians of the American Southwest, 1993*, Santa Fe: School of American Research; Great! Thorough exploration of the Native southwest tribal regions: spiritual, traditional, modern.

Handbook of American Indian Religious Freedom, edited by Christopher Vecsey, 1991; NY: The Crossroad Publishing Co.; important background & legal issues.

The Hopi Survival Kit, Thomas E. Mails, 1997; NY: Stewart, Tabori & Chang; traditional Hopi history & prophecies.

The Way of the Shaman, Michael Harner, 1980, 1990; Harper San Francisco; classic handbook & definitive study.

Shamanic Voices: A Survey of Visionary Narratives, Joan Halifax, 1979; NY: Arkana/Viking Penguin; amazing interviews.

The Shaman: Patterns of Religious Healing Among the Ojibway Indians, John A. Grim, 1983, 1987; Norman: U of Ok Press; many perspectives of shamanism, foundations of spirituality.

It is impossible to *catalog* all people, and yet it is the people, my richest and most varied of resources, who make this book live:

> my grandmother and my mother, who have instilled in me
>> the essence of nature, "to walk in harmony with all living things,"
> my children – and for the sake of children;
> the Native peoples from various tribal backgrounds who share in
>> our research and progress at The Institute;
> the librarians and libraries who have nurtured me;
> the many sincere and interested people who have shared with me
>> their special knowledge and talents,
>> the staff, trustees, and volunteers of IAIS,

> my gratitude!

BOTANICAL AND
MYCOLOGICAL INDEX

*Page numbers in italics
indicate illustrations*

GENERAL INDEX

About the Author

E. BARRIE KAVASCH is a master herbalist, ethnobotanist, ethnomycologist, and food historian of some Cherokee, Creek, and early Powhatan descent, with English, Scotch-Irish, and German heritage as well. She is a fourteenth-generation direct descendant of Pocahontas. Her work reflects a deep respect for multiethnic wisdom.

Her first edition of *Native Harvests* in 1977 was hailed by the *New York Times* as "The most intelligent and brilliantly researched book on the foods of American Indians." She has studied with many acclaimed Native Americans—some of whom contributed to this enlarged edition of the book. Her work has been featured in the *New York Times* and countless other publications.

Barrie is a botanical illustrator and camera naturalist with a forty-year career in publishing books and articles for adults and young adults in both the popular trade and school and library fields. Her ongoing success with *Native Harvests* led to *Enduring Harvests* (1995, Globe Pequot; 2002, iUniverse), plus the addition of select recipes in the award-winning anthology *EarthMaker's Lodge* (1995, Cobblestone), *American Indian Healing Arts* (1999, Bantam), and *The Medicine Wheel Garden* (2002, Bantam). She is a research associate at the Institute for American Indian Studies in Washington, Connecticut, where a previous edition of *Native Harvests* was published in 1998 to celebrate its twentieth birthday. She travels and lectures nationally and internationally, and has been guest lecturer on many college campuses and at numerous museums, environmental centers, and botanical gardens. The Herb Society of America gave her the Gertrude B. Foster Award for *Lifetime Excellence in Herbal Literature* in 2000.

Her range of writing is diverse in both fiction and nonfiction. Barrie authored a six-book series in the Library of Intergenerational Learning: Native Americans (1999, Rosen Publishing), of full-color reading books for children: *Apache Children and Elders Talk Together, Blackfoot Children and Elders Talk Together, Crow Children and Elders Talk Together, Lakota Sioux Children and Elders Talk Together, Seminole Children and Elders Talk Together,* and *Zuni Children and Elders Talk Together.* She is currently celebrating the success of her most recent book, *The Mound Builders of Ancient North America* (2004, iUniverse), and *Dream Catcher* (2004, R. C. Owens). Barrie's poetry has been widely published, especially her haiku. Her third book of poetry will be published in 2006, following the success of *Hands of Time* (2000, iUniverse) and *Ancestral Threads* (2003, iUniverse). Barrie is currently working on a series of young adult novels set in ancient mound-builders societies in prehistoric North America.

Barrie is a teaching Reiki Master with many years devoted to energy healing, creating sacred space, and shamanic counseling. She is the founder of the Medicine Wheel Wellness Center, a private teaching facility in Bridgewater, Connecticut. Learn more about her work at www.Kavasch.com.